Also by Jim Womack

The Future of the Automobile, with Alan Altshuler, Martin
Anderson, Daniel T. Jones, and Daniel Roos
The Machine that Changed the World, with Daniel T. Jones
and Daniel Roos
Lean Thinking, with Daniel T. Jones
Seeing the Whole Value Stream, with Daniel T. Jones
Lean Solutions, with Daniel T. Jones

Lean Enterprise Institute, Inc.
Cambridge, MA USA
lean.org

Version 2.0
October 2013

Lean Enterprise Institute

ISBN: 978-1-934109-38-0
Design by Thomas Skehan, Off-Piste Design
Library of Congress Control Number: 2010939596

Lean Enterprise Institute, Inc.
215 First Street, Suite 300
Cambridge, MA 02142
617-871-2900 • fax: 617-871-2999 • lean.org

For Dan, with profound gratitude for more than 30 years of gemba walking together.

A NOTE ON THE SECOND EDITION

When *Gemba Walks* was first published in the spring of 2011, I thought I was through. Ten years of walks. Ten years of monthly essays. Surely enough.

But I keep on walking. There is just so much to see. And I keep seeing things that I think are of interest to the Lean Community. In addition, the fall of 2013 is the twenty-fifth anniversary of the public launch of the term "lean" and I think this moment should be commemorated. So I have gathered my thoughts from the last two and a half years, written 12 new essays, and grouped them in a new section at the end of the original essays, "Gemba Walking in a New Decade." In addition, I have asked John Krafcik, my partner in the initial assembly plant surveys for MIT's International Motor Vehicle Program and the proposer of the term "lean," to coauthor a reflection on "lean" and its progress over a quarter century.

The original essays, introduction, and foreword by John Shook remain as they were in the First Edition. The volume does have a somewhat different appearance because the format has been changed in response to reader feedback that the original version was just a bit thick and heavy. However, the spirit of the material, old and new, continues as before.

Jim Womack
Barters Island, ME
October 2013

TABLE OF CONTENTS

TRANSFORMATION

DIFFUSION

THE GREAT RECESSION

FOREWORD

Lean conversation is peppered with Japanese terms. Consider the term "kaizen," which is now understood as the structured, relentless approach to continually improving every endeavor—even beyond lean circles. The use of the term "gemba" may be a little less widespread, but it's no less central to lean thinking.

Gemba (also spelled "genba" with an n) means "actual place" in Japanese. Lean thinkers use the term to mean real place or real thing, or place of value creation. Toyota and other Japanese companies often supplement gemba with its related term "genchi gembutsu" to emphasize the literal meaning—"genchi" like gemba means real place, and "gembutsu" means real thing. These terms emphasize *reality*, or empiricism. As the detectives in the old TV show *Dragnet* used to say, "Just the facts, ma'am."

And so the gemba is where you go to understand work and to lead. It's also where you go to learn. For the past 10 years Jim Womack has used his gemba walks as opportunities for both. In these pages, he shares with us anew what he has learned.

The first time I walked a gemba with Jim was on the plant floor of a Toyota supplier. Jim was already famous as the lead author of *The Machine That Changed the World*; I was the senior American manager at the Toyota Supplier Support Center. My Toyota colleagues and I were a bit nervous about showing our early efforts of implementing the Toyota Production System (TPS) at North American companies to "Dr. James P. Womack." We had no idea of what to expect from this famous academic researcher.

My boss was one of Toyota's top TPS experts, Mr. Hajime Ohba. We rented a small airplane for the week so we could make the most of our time, walking the gemba of as many worksites as possible. As we entered the first supplier, walking through the shipping area, Mr. Ohba and I were taken aback as Dr. Womack immediately observed a work action that spurred a probing question. The supplier was producing components for several Toyota factories. They were preparing to ship the exact same component to two different destinations. Dr. Womack immediately noticed something curious. Furrowing his brow while confirming that the component in question was indeed exactly the same in each container, Dr. Womack asked why parts headed to Ontario were packed in small returnable containers, yet the same components to be shipped to California were in a large corrugated box. This was not the type of observation we expected of an academic visitor in 1993.

Container size and configuration was the kind of simple (and seemingly trivial) matter that usually eluded scrutiny, but that could in reality cause unintended and highly unwanted consequences. It was exactly the kind of detail that we were encouraging our suppliers to focus on. In fact, at this supplier in particular, the different container configurations had recently been highlighted as a problem. And, in this case, the supplier was not the cause of the problem. It was the customer —Toyota!

Different requirements from different worksites caused the supplier to pack off the production line in varying quantities (causing unnecessary variations in production runs), to prepare and hold varying packaging materials (costing money and floor space), and ultimately resulted in fluctuations in shipping and, therefore, production requirements. The trivial matter wasn't as trivial as it seemed.

We had not been on the floor two minutes when Dr. Womack raised this question. Most visitors would have been focused on the product, the technology, the scale of the operation, etc. Ohba-san looked at me and smiled, as if to say, "This might be fun."

That was years before Jim started writing his eletters, before even the birth of the Lean Enterprise Institute (LEI). The lean landscape has changed drastically over the past 10 years, change reflected in Jim's essays. From an emphasis on the various lean tools for simple waste elimination in manufacturing firms, attention has steadily shifted to a focus on the underlying management principles, systems, and practices that generate sustainable success in any type of organization. Also, the impact of lean continues to grow, moving from industry to industry, country to country, led by a growing number of practitioners and academics and other lean thinkers. Entirely new questions are being asked today of lean, as a result of the practice of the Lean Community, most of whom have been transformed by Jim's work.

Receiving praise for all he has accomplished in inspiring the lean movement that has turned immeasurable amounts of waste into value, Jim always responds with the same protest: "I've never invented anything. I just take walks, comment on what I see, and give courage to people to try."

"*I just take walks, comment on what I see, and give courage to people to try.*" Hmm, sounds familiar. Toyota's Chairman Fujio Cho says lean leaders do three things: "Go see, ask why, show respect."

Yes, Jim takes many walks, as he describes in these pages. And in doing so he offers observations on phenomena that the rest of us simply can't or don't see. He has a remarkable ability to frame issues in new ways, asking why things are as they are, causing us to think differently than we ever did before. Saul Bellow called this kind of observation "intense noticing." Ethnographers teach it as a professional tool. Lean practitioners learn it as a core proficiency.

But simply seeing—and communicating—lean practice is but one way that Jim has inspired others. Jim gives *encouragement* in the real sense of the term: *courage* to try new things. Or to try old things in different ways. I don't know if there's a stronger embodiment of showing respect than offering others the courage to try.

Without Jim's encouragement, I certainly would not be here at LEI. I probably would not have had the courage to leave Toyota many years ago to discover new ways of exploring the many things I had learned or been exposed to at Toyota.

But I am just one of countless individuals Jim has inspired over the past two decades. And with this collection of 10 years of gemba-walk observations, be prepared to be inspired anew.

John Shook
Chairman and CEO
Lean Enterprise Institute
Cambridge, MA, USA
February 2011

GEMBA WALKS

INTRODUCTION

Gemba. What a wonderful word. The place—any place in any organization—where humans create value. But how do we understand the gemba? And, more important, how do we make it a better place—one where we can create more value with less waste, variation, and overburden (also known, respectively, as muda, mura, and muri)?

I've been thinking about these questions for many years, and learned long ago that the first step is to take a walk to understand the current condition. In the Lean Community we commonly say, "Go see, ask why, show respect." I've always known this intuitively, even before I had a standard method, and even when I labored in the university world where it seemed natural to learn by gathering data at arm's length and then evaluating it in an office through the lens of theory. Now I work in an opposite manner by verifying reality on the gemba and using this understanding to create hypotheses for testing about how things can work better.

I learned long ago that the most productive way to walk is to follow a single product family or product design or customer-facing process from start to finish. As I do this I look at each step with the eye of the customer and from the perspective of those actually creating the value, asking how more can be achieved with less.

Over the past 30 years I have tried to take as many walks along as many "value streams" as I could. Nearly 10 years ago, in the aftermath of September 11, I felt the members of the Lean Community should be in closer contact, and so I started writing down and sharing my thoughts and observations from these walks. They took the form of my monthly eletters that have been sent in recent years to more than 150,000 readers around the world. These have sometimes been based on a single walk, but are often the merged insights of many.

In handing off the baton of leadership at LEI to John Shook in the fall of 2010, I wanted to bundle up the findings of these gemba walks. I have organized these eletters by the most important themes and now present them to the Lean Community in one volume.

In reading through my letters, I found one critical topic—lean management—where I had not written all I wanted to say. So I have composed two new essays [for the first edition], "The Work of Management" and "Modern Management vs. Lean Management," and placed them at the end of the section on Management. I also found myself reflecting on where the lean movement has been and on what I need to focus on in my future walks. My thoughts are presented in a final essay, previously unpublished, titled "Hopeful Hansei."

I have tried to treat my letters as historical artifacts, produced at a specific time and informed by a visit to a certain place. Thus I have largely resisted the temptation—felt by every author—to improve them. However, I have removed some material that is no longer relevant and corrected a few errors of fact. More important, I discovered in reading over the letters that on a number of points I wasn't as clear in explaining my ideas as I should have been and once thought I was. Now, after reflection and a bit of kaizen—the C and A steps in Dr. Deming's plan-do-check-act improvement process—I hope I am.

This said, it's important to make you aware that these letters were never written to some grand plan. They were driven by problems I was hearing from the Lean Community at a given moment or by what I was encountering on the gemba, often accidentally while looking for something else. Thus there is some repetition of themes. And some important issues—notably standardized work and lean accounting—get very little attention.

In addition, the essays are no longer presented in the chronological sequence of their composition. I have instead grouped them by categories that I have devised after rereading the entire collection. While I think this is helpful to the reader, many essays—including the first one on "Purpose, Process, People"—could easily be placed within several categories because they address more than one topic. To deal with the difficulty this may present for readers with a specific issue or question in mind, an index of the themes, topics, terms, individuals, and organizations covered in the essays appears at the end of this book.

I do think these eletters—which I will refer to in this book as essays to denote their modest modification from the originals—stand the test of time. But most need to be placed in context: Why this topic at this time to address this issue? What is the connection of this essay to the others? I have provided a context with commentaries prior to or after each essay. In these brief passages I reflect on why a given topic is important or offer additional insights I have gained subsequent to my walk and writing of the original essay.

A book recounting gemba walks could never have been written without a gemba to walk. Lacking any of my own, excepting LEI, I have had to ask for help from many members of the Lean Community. And you have been invariably helpful in granting me what used to be known—a long time ago when I was in high school—as a "hall pass," a permit to roam freely in your organizations and often to ask awkward questions. I will always be grateful for the help I have received from so many, and I hope I have been true to my promise to reveal nothing uncomplimentary about any efforts of yours that are identified by name in my essays. (Of course, I found many things to criticize anonymously and many more things to remark on privately during or after my visits, I hope for a good end.)

I could never have had such productive visits without others to walk with me, both in person and in an intellectual dialogue. Foremost among these is Dan Jones, my frequent coauthor, sometime cowalker, and constant cothinker about all things lean for more than 30 years. Many of my walks and the resulting essays tackled a certain topic, took a specific form, or arrived at certain conclusions after collaborative lean thinking with Dan. And a few summarize our joint work in the books we have written. I have been truly blessed to have such a friend for more than half of my walk through life.

I was lucky again nearly 20 years ago when I encountered John Shook. There are many walks I would not have taken without John's urging, perhaps most memorably my walk through Ford's empty Model T factory in Highland Park, MI (*see back cover*). And on many other walks

I would not have noticed the truly important thing without John's sensei guidance. In addition, several of the essays are involved centrally with John's contribution to the promotion of value-stream mapping and A3 thinking.

We are still walking together as John takes on the leadership role at LEI, and I join Dan in the role of senior advisor. I trust that we will keep on gemba walking together for years to come.

Finally, anyone who knows me knows that I've needed lots of help just finding the starting point to take my walks. For many years the team at LEI has struggled daily to keep me pointed in the right direction. I thank them all, but I'm especially grateful to the following:

Helen Zak and Rachel Regan helped me determine which gemba to visit, especially when many members of the Lean Community suggested their gemba, and my time was limited. They also read and organized for my review the many comments I received.

Jean Krulic figured out how to get there, got the plane tickets, found a hotel, and provided comprehensive directions. She was also my refuge when things went wrong en route, as they often did. (Air travel is not a capable process!)

Jon Carpenter figured out the expenses and tactfully refrained from asking (as was his right as LEI's CFO) whether the benefits were always greater than my costs.

Tom Ehrenfeld edited my monthly eletters for the nearly 10 years I wrote them, and he provided invaluable advice in putting this volume together. It's hard to put up with an editor who constantly tells you that you can do better, but I have tried to grin and bear Tom's advice, with major benefits for my readers.

Chet Marchwinski, in his role as LEI communications director, and Josh Rapoza, LEI director of web operations, prepared the eletters for sending and tried to catch any errors.

George Taninecz, as project manager, guided this volume from start to finish with a schedule that kept staring at me sternly as I kept thinking of other, easier things to do instead.

Thomas Skehan, as with practically all LEI publications, gave this volume its look and feel. The high visual and tactile quality of our publications at LEI over the 13 years I ran the organization owes everything to Thomas and nothing to me.

Jane Bulnes-Fowles played the final, critical role at LEI of efficiently and effectively coordinating production planning and the distribution and launch of the book.

I hope you will enjoy these essays. They have been a great joy to me because the walks upon which they are based have been my primary means of learning. I hope you have, or will develop, a similar method that provides similar satisfaction and insight. And I hope that as long as you have an interest in creating value you will continue to go see on the gemba, through periodic walks, and that you will ask why while showing respect. I'll be continuing my walks in my new role as senior advisor at LEI, so I hope I will see you there.

Jim Womack
Senior Advisor
Lean Enterprise Institute
Cambridge, MA, USA
February 2011

PURPOSE

My purpose in taking a walk is simple: to see and to understand how more value can be created with less waste. But what is the purpose of the value stream along which I'm walking? That is, just what "value" should it provide for its customer? This is a critical question for the lean thinker because diving in to "fix" a process (a value stream) so it can provide more of the wrong "value" can only be an exercise in frustration. Yet I find that many lean practitioners seem hardly aware of the issue.

The three essays in this section are unlike those in the rest of this volume because I tackle the issue of a value stream's purpose before taking the first step of a walk. Indeed, in these essays I never put on my walking shoes. Instead, I try to explain why lean thinkers must begin with a clear understanding of purpose—the value that needs to be created—before they can fruitfully take a walk.

Once purpose is understood, it's easy to proceed to the more familiar questions of how to create the best process for achieving that purpose and how to creatively engage people in implementing, operating, and improving this process. But purpose comes first, which makes this section the proper place to start this compendium.

Purpose, Process, People

I often hear from members of the Lean Community wanting to know how to evaluate the lean efforts of their organization. "How do we know how lean we are?" "What metrics should we use to measure our progress?" "Are we 'world-class' in terms of lean?" (Whatever 'world-class' is!) Because I've been getting calls of this type for years, and they seem to keep coming, let me share my answer.

I always start by asking about *customer purpose*: What do your customers want that you are not currently able to supply? Lower price, which is currently impossible because your costs are too high? Better quality? More rapid response to changing orders? Better support once the product is delivered? More robust and flexible product designs? Or, perhaps, a completely new definition of value, to solve problems in their lives even better?

And what about your *organizational purpose*? I assume that at a minimum it is to survive. So what does your organization need to survive and even to prosper? Higher margins? The ability to exploit new opportunities rapidly in order to grow? A new way to solve customer problems so you can redefine and expand markets?

Purpose always has these two aspects: what you need to do better to satisfy your customers, and what you need to do better to survive and prosper as an organization. Fortunately, addressing the former issue often solves the latter, but as you start you must know precisely what the gap is between what your customer wants and what you are currently able to deliver.

For example, when I visited Jefferson Pilot's (now Lincoln Financial Group's) policy-writing operation for life insurance several years ago, managers were able to tell me immediately about their purpose. This was to reduce the time needed to write a policy from 30 days to as little as one. This improvement benefited both the insured and the agents selling policies, who only get their commission once the policy is delivered to the customer. More to the point for the company, superior service would cause independent agents to select Jefferson Pilot as the preferred insurance to sell, and would permit JP to grow sales rapidly without cutting prices in an otherwise stagnant market.

Yet I'm often amazed that there seems to be little or no connection between current lean projects and any clearly identified organizational purpose. Setup reduction is pursued because it's the right, lean thing to do. Pull systems are installed because push is bad and pull is good. Twenty-four kaizen events will be run this quarter because this is 50% more than were run last quarter, creating a true "stretch goal." Meanwhile customers are no happier and the organization is doing no better financially. So start with purpose, defined both for you and your customer. Then ask about the gap between where you are and where you need to be.

Customers, of course, only care about their specific product, not about the average of all your products. So it's important to do this analysis by product families for specific products, summarizing the gaps in customer needs that your lean efforts must address.

With a simple statement of organizational purpose in hand, it's time to assess the *process* providing the value the customer is seeking. A "process," as I use this term, is simply a value stream—all of the actions required to go from start to finish in responding to a customer, plus the information controlling these actions. Remember that all value is the end result of some process and that processes can only produce what they are designed to produce—never something better and often something worse.

Value-stream maps of the current state are the most useful tool for evaluating the state of any process. They should show all of the steps in the process, and determine whether each step is valuable, capable, available, adequate, and flexible. They should also show whether value flows smoothly from one step to the next at the pull of the customer after appropriate leveling of demand.

But please note that the map must be interpreted in terms of organizational purpose. Not every step can be eliminated or fixed soon, and many steps may be fine for present conditions even if they aren't completely lean. So work on the steps and issues that are relevant to the customer and the success of your organization.

I know from personal experience how easy it is to get confused and pursue what might be called the voice of the lean professional rather than organizational purpose. When I was involved in a small bicycle company some years ago (see "The Value of Mistakes" on page 189), we welded and assembled eight bikes a day, shipped once a day, and reordered parts once a day. (This was a revolutionary advance from the previous state of the company.) But I was determined to be *perfectly* lean. I urged that we build bikes in the exact sequence that orders were received, often changing over from one model to the next in a sequence of ABABCBAB.

This was deeply satisfying. But we only shipped and ordered once a day! The sequence AAABBBBC would have served our customers and our suppliers equally well and saved us five changeovers daily that required human effort we badly needed for other purposes.

I had a similar experience when I visited a company where setup time on a massive machine had been reduced from eight hours to five minutes. A big kaizen burst had been written on the current-state map next to this high setup time step. A dramatic reduction seemed like a worthy goal to the improvement team. However, when I asked a few questions, it developed that the machine only worked on a single part number and would never work on more than a single part number! Setup reduction on this machine—to reduce changeover times between part numbers—was completely irrelevant to any organizational purpose, no matter how lean a five-minute setup sounded in theory. The lean team justified their course of action by pointing out how technically challenging the setup reduction had been and how much everyone had learned for application in future projects. But that's exactly what I had thought at the bike company where every penny counted to support the current needs of the business. I'm now older and wiser.

Brilliant processes addressing organizational purpose don't just happen. They are created by teams led by some responsible person. And they are operated on a continuing basis by larger teams, in which everyone touches the process and value-stream managers lead the work. So the next question to ask is about *people*: Does every important process in your organization have someone responsible for continually evaluating that value stream in terms of purpose? Is everyone touching the value stream actively engaged in operating it correctly and continually improving it to better address your purposes?

My formula for evaluating your lean efforts is therefore very simple: Examine your purpose, then your process, and then your people. Note that this is completely different from the multiple metrics that members of the Lean Community often seek: How many kaizen events have been done? How much has lead time been reduced? How much inventory has been eliminated? And how do all of these compare with competitors or some absolute standard?

Good performance on any or all of these "lean" metrics may be a worthy goal, but to turn them into abstract measures of leanness without reference to organizational purpose is a big mistake. At best they are performance measures for the lean improvement function. What's really needed instead is purpose measures for every value stream. These measures must be developed and widely shared by a responsible value-stream manager and understood and supported by the entire value-stream team.

June 12, 2006

I have long felt that a great weakness of the lean movement is that we tend to take customer value as a given, asking how we can provide more value as we currently define it, at lower cost with higher quality and more rapid response to changing demand. This is fine as far as it goes. But what if the customer wants something fundamentally different from what our organizations are now providing?

For example, suppose your organization manufactures cars, and you propose to apply lean methods to do so at lower cost with fewer defects, delivering exactly the options customers want with a short lead time. But what if customers actually want to solve their mobility problem by working with a provider who puts the right vehicle (with the right options at an attractive price and no defects) in the driveway, while also taking care of maintenance, repairs, inspections, insurance, financing, recycling, and new vehicles as needed? These customers do not want a car for its own sake. Rather the car is part of the means to a complex end. This is a very different customer purpose, one that can lead to happier customers if creatively addressed and to a more successful, growing organization. But understanding and then providing precisely what customers really want requires a different statement of provider purpose if it is to be achieved. And it often requires collaboration with many organizations that currently don't speak to each other.

After years of thinking about this issue, I went to work with my longtime coauthor Dan Jones to rethink value and purpose. The essay that follows, based on our book *Lean Solutions*, is a summary of this very different thought process.[1]

1. James P. Womack and Daniel T. Jones, *Lean Solutions* (New York: Free Press, 2005).

Lean Consumption

I see every value-creating organization as a collection of primary processes (involving many steps that must be performed properly in the proper sequence at the proper time): A product and process development process, from a concept addressing a customer need to a finished/tooled/ laid-out value stream. A fulfillment process, running from order through production to delivery. A customer support process, from sales and delivery through a product's useful life.

To these must be added a host of support processes to make the primary processes possible: A supplier management process to obtain needed parts. A human resource process to get the right people with the right skills in place at the right time to operate the primary processes. An improvement process to make the primary and support processes steadily better. And so on.

In fact, everything we do in our work lives should be creating value in some process. Or else why are we doing it? And much mental energy in the Lean Community is devoted to thinking of ways to eliminate process steps that don't create value.

This is great, but it's still not the whole story. For years Dan Jones and I have been carefully recording our experiences as consumers. We have known intuitively that consumption also is a *process*, performed by the consumer to solve one of life's problems. For example, most of us have a personal computing problem that we solve by searching for a personal computer, ordering it, installing it, integrating it with our other electronic equipment and software, maintaining it, repairing it, upgrading it, and then recycling it. This is another way to describe a consumption process with seven big steps: search, obtain, install, integrate, maintain, repair, recycle. And each big step consists of lots of little steps.

The problem is that the typical *consumption process* doesn't work very well. We often can't find what we want, when we want, where we want. And the process of installing, integrating, maintaining, repairing, and recycling is often frustrating and time-consuming as we deal with strangers who seem to have no interest in our difficulties. The root cause is that the *provision process* created by those supplying us doesn't match up with our *consumption process*. And this creates great opportunities for lean thinkers in every organization.

To help our thinking, Dan and I propose some simple principles for lean consumption that every organization providing services or goods should consider:

- *Solve the customer's problem completely, by insuring that everything works the first time.* No customer wants to call a help line, so turn your help lines into kaizen opportunities to identify and eliminate the root cause of customer calls.

- *Don't waste the consumer's time.* For example, challenge the need for queues of any sort. You will discover that queues always waste both the customer's time and the provider's money.

- *Provide exactly what the customer wants.* The level of out-of-stocks of the right items and overstocks of the wrong items is remarkably high in almost every aspect of business. These consumer frustrations are almost completely avoidable with lean replenishment systems utilizing pull principles.

- *Provide value where the customer wants.* Most providers want the customer to come to them. For example, the best pricing is often available in a Walmart-style, big-box retail format that customers must drive miles to access. Yet most customers want just the opposite, with attractively priced goods conveniently available nearby. The application of lean principles can provide most value where it is wanted at lower cost.

- *Provide value when the customer wants.* Most current-day sales and production systems encourage customers to place orders at the last moment with no warning. This makes level loading of production systems impossible. Yet most of us actually plan ahead, particularly for big-ticket items like computers, cars, and white goods. Some simple lean principles can turn strangers into partners who plan ahead with their providers, dramatically reducing costs for customers and providers.

- *Reduce the number of problems customers need to solve.* Most of us would like to deal with only a few providers to solve our big problems—computing and communication, mobility, healthcare, financial management, shelter, personal logistics (better known as "shopping"). Yet with the web we have been going in the opposite direction from industry. Firms following lean principles are asking a much smaller number of suppliers to solve much larger problems, even as consumers are asking ever- larger numbers of strangers to solve tiny problems on a one-off basis, wasting time and creating frustration. Lean principles show a way to do much better.

Dan and I realize that the very term "lean consumption" sounds strange. But we hope you will rotate it around in your head. We think that lean consumption in combination with lean provision is the next big leap for the Lean Community.

March 7, 2005

Additional reading and listening:

James P. Womack and Daniel T. Jones, "Lean Consumption," *Harvard Business Review*, March 2005.

James P. Womack and Daniel T. Jones, *Lean Solutions* (New York: Free Press, 2005). Available as hardcover book and audio recording.

Repurpose before You Restructure

I considered the issue of organizational purpose to be particularly important in the recent economic crisis, yet I rarely found this topic discussed in the media. In this final essay in this section, I offer a few thoughts on "repurposing" organizations before embarking on structural changes or process improvements, taking both General Motors and Toyota as examples.

One of my favorite questions when meeting with senior leaders of enterprises is, "What is your organization's purpose?" The typical and immediate response is, "To make money and grow." "But," I respond, "this answer has nothing to do with your customers, who provide the money your organization needs to profit and grow." I then restate my question, "What does your organization do to solve your customers' problems better than your competitors so that customers old and new will pay good money for your products and buy more over time?"

In recent years a fashionable alternative to "make money and grow sales" was that organizational purpose was to steadily grow shareholder value. But now the king of shareholder value, General Electric's retired chairman Jack Welch, has acknowledged—thank goodness—that this is a result, not a strategy for achieving this result.[2]

Now that investors as well as customers are on strike during the great financial crisis, the whole management world is being forced to rethink purpose from the standpoint of the customer.

Confusion about purpose is particularly painful to watch in the collapse of General Motors because this organization was so brilliant for so long in clearly defining its purpose. On June 9, 1921, GM's great leader Alfred Sloan presented a simple memorandum to the Executive

2. Francesco Guerrera, "Welch Denounces Corporate Obsessions," *Financial Times,* March 13, 2009.

Committee on the topic of "Product Policy" that defined General Motors' purpose for generations to come. Sloan stated that General Motors would provide a carefully configured range of products for "every purse and purpose," from used Chevrolets at the lower end of the market (with dealer financing for these traded-in vehicles) to a "fully loaded" Cadillac at the top end.

This simple memo rationalized GM's chaotic product lineup so its vehicles would not overlap in the market. Instead, they would each have a clearly defined place in a status hierarchy and would always be more refined, a bit "classier" with a slightly higher price, than competitor products in each market segment.

This memo about market policy was much more than the now familiar market segmentation with a value proposition for each segment. Sloan created something qualitatively different by redefining GM's central purpose as creating an aspirational escalator for every customer through the life cycle. This went from the used Chevrolet as the first purchase to the fancy Cadillac as the last (often concluding with a Cadillac hearse on the way to the cemetery!). And it worked brilliantly. General Motors was probably never as efficient in production as Ford, and it was rarely a technology leader. But it provided a clear product pathway on the customer's life journey. Customers embraced this purpose and opened their wallets to pay higher prices for more refined products within each market segment. Within a decade of Sloan's memo, GM had become the largest and most successful corporation in the history of the world.

Moving forward, it is saddening to observe GM's efforts to deal with its crisis. With the exception of the plug hybrid Volt (an unproven technology for an unproven market to be produced at tiny volume in the early years), the focus is entirely on "restructuring" and shrinking. That is, it's about what General Motors isn't. It isn't Saab or Hummer or Saturn (or Pontiac). It won't have nearly as large a dealer network. It isn't a manufacturer with a significant North American footprint outside of Michigan and Ohio. Etc.

The natural instinct of senior managers in any crisis is to restructure and downsize. But the question is always, "Restructure and downsize toward what?" No customer cares about a company's structure. No customer cares about downsizing. Customers only care about a company solving their problems along life's path.

So here's my advice to new leaders of GM: Before you restructure, restate GM's purpose. Today no one knows. Do it in a simple memo. Indeed, do it in a single-page A3 format. Sloan needed only a few pages in 1921, so practice continuous improvement to get down to one! And remember that no amount of restructuring without a clear and compelling purpose will save this stricken giant (or any other failing enterprise).

Let me note in concluding that there seems to be confusion about purpose at Toyota as well. Until the mid-1990s the clear purpose of Toyota was to be the best organization in the world at cost-effectively providing refined, durable "value" products in all market segments. This meant fewer defects and superior durability through extended use. The assumption was that growth would naturally follow, and it did.

But then the purpose seems to have shifted to becoming the biggest auto company as rapidly as possible by adding capacity everywhere, a purpose that no customer cares about. At the same time competitors, led by Hyundai, have closed the gap on Toyota's original purpose and everyone is doing hybrids where Toyota initially took the lead. An A3 on repurposing Toyota is surely what new president Akio Toyoda needs as well.

April 9, 2009

PROCESS

If "gemba" is a wonderful word, "process" is its equally wonderful complement. By a process I mean all of the steps, mostly human actions, required to put a given amount of value in the hands of a customer. Learning to see a process requires considerable effort, particularly when a process creating one type of value (whether a good or a service or some combination) is intermingled with many others as it flows through an organization.

A key objective of the lean movement is to teach everyone to untangle intermingled processes in order to see clearly the specific process that they manage or touch as it flows from start to finish. Then, with a clear understanding of the current state of this process, they must improve its performance so that everyone is better off—customer, employee, supplier, investor. Doing this requires a method, which is the subject of the essays that follow.

These essays start with the act of determining the current state of a process and creating an action plan for improving it. They progress in sequence through the measures that will be needed to create a lean value stream.

Taking a Value-Stream Walk at Firm A

I was out walking through a company this past week that had asked what I thought of their lean efforts to date. I paid a visit to find out, and while flying home it occurred to me that you might find my method and checklist of some use in your own improvement activities. So let me share it with you.

As often happens, when I arrived at the firm the senior managers wanted to start in a conference room with a lengthy overview of who they are and what they are doing to improve, focusing on their current lean "program." After a few minutes I suggested—as politely as I could but very firmly—that we should delay our discussion until we had all taken a brief walk together.

I then suggested that we pick one product family and follow its value stream from the customer's order back to materials in receiving. Once we had selected a sample product family and started walking, I asked 10 very simple questions:

1. What are the business issues with this product? Inadequate return on investment? Poor quality? Inability to meet customer ship dates? Inflexibility in the face of volatile markets? If a firm doesn't know what its business issues are, how is it going to know what to improve? [This, of course, is simply a restatement of the purpose questions I posed in the previous section.]

2. Who is responsible for the value stream for this product? If no one is responsible for anything, and everyone is responsible for everything, how can the firm improve?

3. How are orders from the customer received?

4. Where is the pacemaker process, triggered by these customer orders?

5. How capable, available, adequate, and waste-free are assembly activities?

6. How capable, available, adequate, and waste-free are the fabrication activities feeding assembly?

7. How are orders transmitted up the value stream from the pacemaker process?

8. How are materials supplied to the assembly and fabrication processes?

9. How are materials obtained from upstream suppliers?

10. How are employees trained in lean procedures and motivated to apply them?

After a 30-minute walk to answer the 10 questions, I knew everything that I needed to be able to tell the senior managers just where they stood regarding their progress toward a truly lean production system. While we had looked at only one value stream, I knew from long experience that the issues we had found would be present in every other value stream. (Another walk would be required, however, to answer the parallel questions of how lean their product and process development and customer support processes were. That would involve following a sample product design from concept to launch and then into use by the customer.)

The Answers at Firm A

I thought you might find the answers to these questions interesting for the real (but disguised) company I recently visited. They make what may seem a rather abstract list quite concrete. However, it is important to note that this is a discrete parts manufacturer in the automotive industry, with high volume and relatively low variety. If this had been a financial-services firm or a healthcare provider, the precise questions would have varied slightly. The aspects of value creation the questions address would not.

1. *What are the business issues with this product family?* Due to continuing price pressure from the two customers for the product, Firm A was losing money even though it was meeting a high quality standard and shipping on time. It followed that costs needed to be reduced quickly.

2. *Who is responsible for the value stream for this product?* This question was easy, too: No one. The product (and the order) simply made its way through many departments and areas—sales, production control, assembly, fabrication, purchasing—as best it could with no individual assigned responsibility for managing and improving the total flow of value. At the same time, a corporate improvement group—the "Lean Team"—was making several interventions in the product family's value stream at isolated points to improve wasteful practices.

3. *How are orders from the customer received?* Firm A was receiving a monthly forecast and a weekly schedule from its two customers for this product family. Shipping releases were controlled by physical kanban brought by milk-run drivers sent by the customers.

On the face of it, the use of simple kanban for shipping releases seemed "lean." But when we looked at the actual situation, we discovered that kanban wasn't kanban and lean wasn't lean. One customer sent kanban every two hours, paying careful attention to leveling demand so that short-term production variations in the customer plant did not affect operations in the supplier plant. The other customer sent its kanban erratically within wide pickup windows. A brief glance at the pattern of kanban arriving showed that this customer was actually amplifying the production variations in its own plant in its orders to its supplier.

The supplier responded to these differing customer approaches in a way that was easy to see: The shipping lane for the first customer was very short, containing only the goods being assembled for the next shipment. The shipping lane for the second customer was quite lengthy (even though average demand was the same) and contained much more than was likely to be needed for the next shipment. This permitted Firm A to deal with the variations in order flow while achieving 100% on-time shipments.

4. *Where is the pacemaker process?* Another simple answer: There was no pacemaker. Instead, Firm A used a master schedule developed each weekend from the customers' weekly schedules, and sent these schedules to each of the fabrication and assembly areas along the value stream. This was inevitably supplemented during the week by area managers resequencing orders to deal with changes in demand and with production problems along the value stream. This was not at all lean. There was no takt image (a visual measure of the rate of customer demand) and no ability to know within a few minutes whether operations were supporting the customer.

5. *How capable, available, adequate, and waste-free are assembly activities?* A recent kaizen at Firm A had created an assembly cell combining a number of assembly and subassembly activities formerly conducted in different areas of the facility. The processing steps had been placed in close proximity in a U-shaped area, and the area manager for assembly stated that Firm A had now achieved continuous-flow assembly.

However, only a moment's observation showed that work was poorly balanced in the cell, with little evidence of truly standardized work, and that small piles of inventory were building up between each step. In addition, the production analysis board next to the cell showed clearly that output was varying markedly from hour to hour. The explanations in the margin of the board showed that the processing machinery was both capable and reliable but that materials shortages often stopped the cell. My eyes told me immediately that the cell should be able to run steadily at its planned output, based on takt time, with about half the operator effort. This should have a major effect on costs.

6. *How capable, available, adequate, and waste-free are fabrication activities?* A recent kaizen led by Firm A's lean team had also created two fabrication cells for the product, with the first cell directly feeding the second cell so that they were effectively linked as one cell.

However, a moment's observation and a look at the production analysis board for both cells showed major problems with capability and availability. Indeed, the cells together seemed to be stopping—either due to producing defective parts or the inability to cycle at all—about

20 minutes out of each hour. As a consequence, a large amount of overtime was being run, and considerable buffers of work-in-process were kept after the first cell and at the downstream end of the second cell. Clearly there was a need for the lean team to focus immediately on both quality and maintenance if costs were to be reduced.

7. *How are orders transmitted up the value stream from the pacemaker process?* Observation of the area managers in assembly and fabrication showed that a key element of their jobs was to continually adjust the schedule to deal with demand shifts downstream and process problems upstream. What was needed instead was a simple supermarket system between each step with a simple pull system to trigger work by the upstream process only as parts were needed by the downstream process. Doing this would reduce the total amount of inventories needed and free up management attention for further improvements in the value stream.

8. *How are materials supplied to the final assembly and fabrication processes?* The production control and logistics manager proudly showed off the new water spider system (using a tugger pulling carts of parts on a standard route at a standard interval) to supply materials to the fabrication and assembly areas from a receiving supermarket. The water spider circulated through the plant once an hour to deliver needed materials to each production area and to collect finished goods for transport to the shipping area.

What could be leaner? Actually, everything. The water spider was not involved in distributing production instructions, and had only a vague idea of what each production area would need. The improvement team's solution had been to put an ample supply of practically every part number on the lengthy tugger train so that whatever part was needed could be supplied. A moving warehouse!

In addition, there was considerable confusion in the storage locations for each part number and no plan for every part (PFEP) showing exactly how it would be reordered, packed, shipped, received, placed in the supermarket, and distributed. While some parts expediting might have been eliminated by the new materials-delivery system, it was achieving only a fraction of its potential benefits.

9. *How are materials obtained from upstream suppliers?* Supplier shipments were triggered by Firm A's master schedule, which was itself being adjusted from hour to hour. As a result, the area manager in receiving was continuously working with area managers on the floor and with purchasing to change orders to suppliers and keep production running. This manager seemed to be very proficient at this task, but why was it necessary? Couldn't suppliers instead be put on a pull system with appropriate leveling so that any short-term variations in the plant's performance would not be inflicted on the suppliers? And couldn't supplies be collected by frequent milk runs in small amounts rather than by the current direct shipments from the supplier to the plant every few days in large amounts?

10. *How are employees trained and engaged in lean procedures?* This was perhaps the most shocking aspect of Firm A's operations. Most of the production associates were actually employees of a manpower firm working on short-term contracts. This held wages down and discouraged recent efforts by several unions to organize the plant. But this approach also meant that standardized work was hard to maintain, multiskilling was difficult to implement, and that no production associate could reasonably be expected to contribute to kaizen activities. From observing the efforts of production associates, I concluded that the savings in cost per labor hour were very likely more than offset by poor productivity during each hour worked.

These questions cover only production, and I would like to have taken a similar walk through product and process development and along the customer support stream beyond the factory. However, the point for current purposes is that a walk taking only 30 minutes was sufficient to assess just how "lean" Firm A is in its factory and to come up with a prioritized list of steps the firm should take soon.

An Action Plan for Firm A

As for "lean" at this firm, my simple conclusion was "just barely on your way and without a clear plan." My proposed action plan was as follows:

1. Clearly identify all your value streams, and clearly state the business issues confronting each. For the specific value stream we observed, set a cost-reduction target that will produce an adequate return.

2. Appoint a value-stream manager for each product family to both manage and improve the value-creating process, addressing the business as well as operational issues.

3. Work with customers to smooth demand and eliminate amplification. (And, at a minimum, use finished goods as a buffer to smooth the flow of production upstream from the shipping point at the end of the plant.)

4. Send production instructions up the value stream by means of pull loops, with leveling from the pacemaker process at the final assembly cell.

5. Make the assembly and fabrication cells into real cells by tackling capability, availability, and workforce-utilization issues.

6. Establish a paced withdrawal system for materials received from suppliers, with short intervals (perhaps 20 minutes) and a rigorous PFEP.

7. Work with suppliers to smoothly transmit demand and to get frequent deliveries on a precise schedule in small amounts.

This list is only the beginning for Firm A, of course. But it is a real beginning, leading toward a truly lean enterprise instead of another program involving isolated interventions with doubtful results.

March 12, 2003

Creating Basic Stability

This and the next two essays describe the sequence of measures needed to implement the actions in the improvement plan. These start with achieving basic stability in each step in the process.

On recent walks through several companies, I've had an important realization. I had been assuming that in most companies the process steps in a typical value stream are sufficiently stable that it's practical to introduce flow, pull, and leveled production right away. By "stable" I mean that each process step is *capable*. That is, it is able to produce a good part or outcome every time it operates. And I also mean that each process step is *available*. By this I mean that the step is able to operate every time it is needed. Capability and availability in combination provide what I call *basic stability*.

I've long known that at Toyota a new assembly process would launch with operational availability of about 97% with practically no defects or rework and would strive to reach 100% through kaizen. And in even the most complex transfer lines, like engine-block machining, Toyota achieves and maintains operational availability of 85% or more with practically no defects or rework in the process. That's a good definition of basic stability.

But on my recent walks I've been surprised to discover that operational availability in cellular assembly (which is much less demanding than long, car-assembly tracks) is often no more than 90%, even when there are no delays due to lack of materials. And there are significant amounts of defects and considerable rework at the end of the cell or end of the plant. In complex machining, operational availability is often below 60%, and sometimes as low as 40%, with many defects discovered and considerable rework, both within the process and at the end. And these are household-name, global companies that claim to be well down the path to lean production!

With stability this low, trying to introduce continuous flow by linking steps and connecting areas of flow with pull systems is certain to be an exercise in frustration. The only way these systems can work at all is to maintain large buffers of work-in-process between each step—inventories that hinder further improvement by hiding problems. So I've been forced to conclude that a lot of us need to focus on creating basic stability before we try to flow and pull.

(Let me hasten to add that this problem extends far beyond factory equipment. I recently made an appointment for a medical test and had to postpone it twice because the complex equipment wouldn't work. And does anyone know how to maintain jetways at airports? I find on my travels that jetway problems delay the arrival and deboarding on about one flight in 20. And how can one of those simple moving sidewalks in airports ever break down? But I seem to stumble onto at least one unmoving walkway on every trip. And why can't anyone keep our LEI email server running? Poor operational availability is pervasive—and avoidable—in every aspect of our lives.)

Inadequate stability traces to six types of problems:

1. Downtime, when a process won't run at all (also termed major breakdowns or major stoppages).

2. Changeover time to convert from one product to the next.

3. Minor stoppages of just a few seconds.

4. Cycle time fluctuation, when a process takes longer than planned.

5. Scrap, meaning some production is lost.

6. Rework, in which parts must be run through the process again, reducing the time available for new parts.

All of these are bad and all should be reduced. But be careful to avoid simple calculations of equipment utilization that confuse availability with uptime. The former is always good: equipment must be able to run when you need it. The latter can be good or bad: high utilization (uptime) to overproduce items that are not needed is one of the worst forms of waste. Reducing time lost to changeovers by producing bigger batches rather than by reducing setup times is a big mistake as well. And reworking products at the end of the line in order to keep the line moving a high fraction of the time is an equally bad practice.

The most important point is that these problems don't go away with a bit of random kaizen. And they certainly don't go away if firms are only practicing breakdown maintenance without identifying trends and determining root causes. They also appear quickly in new equipment (sometimes bought because the old equipment would not run consistently to meet demand) unless the equipment is carefully designed from a maintainability standpoint and then systematically maintained.

The challenge is to create a rigorous maintenance process that involves everyone, gathers the appropriate data, discovers the root causes, and installs fixes so known problems don't recur, and new problems are anticipated (for example, from predictable wear during the equipment's life cycle).

With these measures in place, the lean goals of flow, pull, and leveled production are vastly easier to achieve. Even better, as basic stability is created, many firms will discover that they don't have capacity constraints. Indeed, they may find that they have too much capacity rather than too little.

May 25, 2004

Note: Much of the material in this essay was based on conversations with Art Smalley, whose career at Toyota focused on equipment maintenance. If I were writing this essay today, I would discuss all four of the Ms needed to create basic stability: machine plus man, method, and materials. I had been studying Total Productive Maintenance at the time this essay was written and restricted my focus to machinery. I rectify this shortcoming with respect to the supply of materials in the next essay.

The Power of a Precise Process

If basic stability is achieved in each step in the process, it is time to create stability in the activities supporting the value stream. The specific example discussed here is materials supply.

When I first started to study the Toyota Production System many years ago, I was struck by something very simple: its utter precision. There was a place for every tool and part, and there was standardized work for every task. There was a standard amount of inventory at every point where inventory was necessary and a standard way to send signals for everything production associates needed, from more parts to help with a problem. Equally striking, there was a clear knowledge of the current state of each operation and a vision of a better state to be achieved quickly through kaizen. Nothing seemed to happen by chance, and continuous improvement was easier because the base condition was visible to everyone.

But if the heart of this system is precision, and if more and more managers say they embrace this system, why has there been so little movement toward precise processes? The biggest problem is that most managers still don't appreciate the need to get every step in every process precisely specified and conducted correctly every time. And even if they do, this seems too hard to achieve all at once. So managers tackle precision at specific points in the process in hopes that kaizen on each point will gradually lead the complete process from chaos to order.

The problem, in my experience, is that they will never get there. Take the case of material handling. In most facilities I visit, the material handling system is a mess. If there is a central schedule (often in the form of a materials-requirements planning system), it calls for materials to be delivered to points of use in precise amounts at precise times from receiving, a storage area, or an upstream activity. But the schedule is continually changing and many of the centralized instructions don't reflect on-the-gemba realities. Or, if there is a pull system in place, it is run very loosely, with the same part number stored in many locations, vagueness about standard inventories, and confusion about who makes deliveries and when.

In either case the material handling is largely reactive and ad hoc, focused on expediting parts to the point of use as shortfalls suddenly emerge. As a result, when I ask on my walks why an area scheduled to produce at the moment of my visit is not producing, the most common explanation is "lack of materials" or "wrong materials."

But please note that even if the management believes in the need for a precise material handling process, it's not possible to get there incrementally with point kaizen fixing individual process steps. Nor is it possible to get there with flow kaizen for a single product family's value stream, of the sort we have popularized through the LEI workbook *Learning to See*.[3] What's needed instead is *system* kaizen in which the material-handling system for an entire facility, supplying every value stream, is redesigned to create a bulletproof delivery process that is utterly precise and stable.

Such a system must include a plan for every part (PFEP) that documents all relevant information about each part number in the facility, including its storage location and points of use. It must also include precisely designed supermarkets, both for purchased parts and for work-in-process, that assign each part number a single storage location and minimum and maximum inventory quantities. In addition, a lean material-handling process requires precise delivery routes with standardized work to get every part from its storage location to its point of use exactly when needed. Finally, a lean material-handling process requires a pull system that is absolutely precise in triggering deliveries of parts to the point of use. Only when we put all four steps in place can we have a truly precise process and a stable base upon which to improve.

Oct. 1, 2003

3. Mike Rother and John Shook, *Learning to See* (Cambridge, MA: Lean Enterprise Institute, 1999).

Additional reading:

Steven Spear and Kent Bowen, "Decoding the DNA of the Toyota Production System," *Harvard Business Review*, September/October 1999.

Rick Harris, Chris Harris, and Earl Wilson, *Making Materials Flow*, (Cambridge, MA: Lean Enterprise Institute, 2003).

Lean materials supply is impossible without precise knowledge of what materials to supply and what product to make next. This brings us to the issue of information management in a lean enterprise.

Lean Information Management

Recently on a walk through a manufacturing operation, I found myself wondering about the principles of lean information management. In particular, I wondered about production control and fulfillment.

The facility in question was typical in having a central brain—a computerized MRP—telling each operation what to do next. It's what I call a cognitive system, in which all feedback goes into a central processor using complex algorithms that think through the optimal next step for everyone.

But as also is typical, the instructions being sent by the central brain often seemed nonsensical to the managers and operators on the plant floor. When the system told them to make some item for which they lacked parts, they simply overrode the system and made some item for which they did have the parts. Needless to say, this further confused the central brain and, at the time of my visit, it appeared to me that there was an official scheduling system from the MRP and a real scheduling system conducted manually by managers on the shop floor. The results were not impressive.

What could be done instead? Here are six simple principles of lean information management:

1. *Simplify every process to minimize your need for information management.* For example, the simple act of moving activities from departments to a continuous-flow layout —in which an item goes automatically from one step to the next—eliminates all of the information needed to tell each department and step what to do next. Compressing your value streams by relocating sequential process steps from across the world to across the aisle also eliminates the need for a world of information.

2. *Make every step in your processes capable and available.* Breakdowns, turnbacks, and materials shortages generate the need for managers to manage more information. Instead of automating this task, try

to eliminate the need for it. (On another recent walk, I was given a full explanation of the information management systems in a logistics company. The management proudly explained that their system permits them to determine exactly where they had lost a package, in fact thousands every night. My question was, "Why do you keep losing packages? If you had a truly capable process you wouldn't need this expensive safety net. Even worse, the existence of the safety net removes the pressure to make your process capable. Think of your IT system as a different type of 'just-in-case' inventory.")

3. *Schedule each value stream from only one point.* Taking this simple step will make information management easier throughout your operation.

4. *Use a reflexive production control upstream from the scheduling point.* Lean thinkers call this pull concept "reflexive" because it is like your reflexes. When the downstream process uses material, an automatic order is placed to replenish the same amount from the next upstream process. There is no need to consult a central brain.

5. *Send information in small batches.* Amazingly, many MRPs are still run on the weekend to produce a weekly schedule. And many sales and order management systems still work with weekly or even 10-day batches, even if their organizations are moving toward overnight runs to produce a daily schedule. What managers really need to know is what to do in the next 15 minutes based on what happened in the last 15 minutes. Piling up information in a large inventory is as bad—maybe worse—than piling up large inventories of products.

6. *Make your information management transparent and intuitive.* Perhaps the saddest thing to see is good managers working furiously to override IT systems with opaque algorithms, making the situation even worse through their frantic efforts. Simple information management methods like kanban cards and web-based electronic kanban, plus simple heijunka algorithms, seem too simple to many managers. Yet they are intuitive. And anomalies quickly become obvious. So why spend enormous sums to keep yourself in the dark?

I'm not naïve about getting the world to embrace lean information management. We're not quite yet at the end of thinking that more information is always better and that if we just had all possible information, perfect algorithms, and lightning-fast central processors, life would be easy.

Despite 50 years of evidence that this isn't true, we are now embarking on a new experiment with radio-frequency identification (RFID) in which every item in every process can be tracked individually. The managers of a gigantic retailer that I recently visited—whose stores average four inventory turns per year, with no fixed storage positions for any item, multiple storage points for every item, and a high level of out-of-stocks—told me that an RFID tag on every carton will eliminate current "treasure hunts" and insure a high level of customer service.

My question was, "Why do you need so much inventory with so many storage locations? If you have only one storage location for each item—on the shelf where the customer puts the item in the cart—and replenish every item every night from a central distribution facility serving many stores, the information you already gather from bar codes at customer checkout will tell you everything you need to know."

My prediction is that as the amount of available RFID information overwhelms our ability as managers to figure out what to do with it (even as our fundamental value-creating processes deteriorate), many managers will finally realize that simple is best. In the meantime, lean thinkers can save themselves enormous sums and frustration by avoiding the latest IT wave and implement instead the six simple principles of lean information management.

Nov. 5, 2004

The Wonder of Level Pull

If a process has achieved basic stability supported by lean materials supply and information management, it is time to pull all of the pieces together.

Many years ago in Toyota City I first witnessed the twin concepts of level production and the smooth pull of needed items throughout a complex production operation. My education occurred at a supplier of components to Toyota assembly plants that had created a small and precisely determined inventory of finished components near the shipping dock. (And I had thought Toyota suppliers in Japan had no inventories!) This supplier used finished goods inventory to decouple itself from any day-to-day and hour-to-hour gyrations in Toyota's demand as expressed through frequent deliveries of kanban. (And I had thought that there were no fluctuations in Toyota's demand!)

My guide explained that the supplier had carefully calculated Toyota's average demand for components, by total volume and by mix within this total, and was running a level production schedule at the pacemaker process (which was component final assembly). Placing a precisely calculated amount of inventory at the downstream end of the facility effectively created a sea wall that protected all of the upstream production operations from disruption by sudden waves or troughs in demand. This permitted internal inventories at every point in the process to be very small, leading to low total inventories in the plant.

My guide also pointed out that information management was "reflexive" in the sense that each step in the process simply signaled its immediate need to the next upstream step in the process. There was no need to send information to a "central brain" in the form of a computerized MRP system that could then tell every process step what to do and when.

The analogy he used has always stuck with me: "When you put your finger on a hot stove, do you send information to your brain that this is a stove, and that it is on, and that your finger is starting to smoke, so maybe you ought to remove your finger? Or do you let your reflexes pull your finger away without bothering your brain? So why are you using a brain to manage demand information in your factory when your reflexes can do a better job by simply pulling needed materials from the next upstream process?"

Because the operation was so precise, total inventories were so small, and the logic of the concept was so compelling, I imagined that it would be only a short time before every production facility across the world converted to level pull. I was wrong! As time has passed I've realized that many aspects of lean thinking are easy to implement. But this has not been one of them.

Thus I was enormously pleased last week when I visited a plant in a tiny Mexican town far south of the border and saw a level pull system in operation that would be right at home in Toyota City.

This facility had:

- Analyzed actual customer demand, based on orders over the past several months, so it could stop using weekly forecasts and daily ship orders to schedule the plant.

- Calculated an exact finished-goods inventory amount for each product, consisting of cycle, buffer, and safety stocks.

- Leveled the final production schedule by both volume and mix.

- Identified a pacemaker process (component final assembly) as the single point to schedule each product family value stream.

- Delivered material to final assembly while taking away finished goods by means of a fixed-time conveyance route responding to kanban signals.

- Established markets in front of upstream processes with small amounts of inventory.

- Utilized signal kanban to trigger production in upstream batch processes (such as molding and stamping).

- Implemented kanban signals and a second conveyance route to deliver materials, tools, and instructions to upstream processes.

- Created a purchased-parts market with a plan for every part (PFEP), with precisely calculated inventories of every purchased item and with kanban signals for reordering.

As I drove away I realized that if these techniques can work in this remote location and if they are now spreading this far, there must be a widespread willingness today to make the level pull transformation I anticipated many years ago.

March 3, 2004

Additional reading:

Art Smalley, *Creating Level Pull* (Cambridge, MA: Lean Enterprise Institute, 2004).

I was being optimistic when I wrote this essay in 2004. Today I still routinely see organizations making random improvements to processes that lack the stability, rigorous supporting processes, and clear information flow that are necessary for lasting success. The problem is not with the techniques. These work. The problem lies somewhere in the mindsets and behaviors of managers and employees. This brings us to the third step in the purpose-process-people sequence. People are the subject of the next set of essays.

PEOPLE

People must be engaged in understanding and improving the processes that create the value desired by the customer if organizational and customer purposes are to be achieved. But how can we as leaders and managers engage them? This section of essays explores this key question on several dimensions. I begin with a simple observation that we are all involved in processes in everything we do in life, whether as producers or consumers. And we often react badly—that is, we become negatively engaged—when we encounter defective processes with no apparent means to improve them. The question is how we can focus on improving the broken process rather than simply blaming each other.

Bad People or a Bad Process?

Recently, I encountered an amazing scene at London's Heathrow Airport. While checking in for my flight on a Monday morning, I found myself in a nightmare line stretching around the corner from the check-in counter and far down the hall.

After standing in the line for about 45 minutes, I finally advanced to the corner just in time to see passengers ahead of me taking out their frustration. There were six check-in counters but only one agent was on duty to perform check-ins. So several passengers jumped over the counter and started handing out the empty agent chairs to the passengers standing in line so they could sit down while waiting. The single agent on duty immediately stopped checking in passengers to prevent this irregular action. A tug-of-war ensued over one of the chairs and, after losing the battle, the agent retreated to his desk to call the police. To complete the scene, imagine loud shouting in many languages as a group of heavily armed security guards approached.

I know a "terminal" mess when I see one and broke ranks at that point to search for the "I'm going to miss my plane" alternative check-in path that seems to exist in all airports these days. (Think of this as simply another form of rework.) When I found it—in a far corner of the terminal—and talked with the agents, I discovered that scenes of this sort happen every Monday morning and Friday evening—the periods of highest travel volume—when "some passengers just go crazy." In their minds it was a clear case of "bad passengers."

As I reflected on this experience, I realized that we encounter situations of this sort in life all of the time. Every day we are involved in a series of processes—getting our computers and software to work, taking our cars in for repair, going to the doctor, getting our work done at an office or in a production facility—whose steps must be performed properly in the proper sequence to get the results we seek. For example, at the airport, staff scheduling and flight departures must be carefully synchronized with the pattern of passenger demand to create a smooth check-in process. Otherwise some variant of the scene I witnessed is pretty much inevitable.

What I find fascinating is that when good people (that's you and me) are put in a bad process, we often become "bad" like the process—mean-spirited, foul-mouthed, and even violent. Ask everyone involved what the problem is, and they are very likely to blame everyone else—in this case, the crazy passengers, the petty bureaucrat check-in agent, the authoritarian security force, the tight-fisted airline—rather than step back and think about the process itself and how it could be improved.

The widespread existence of bad processes in every area of life is actually a great opportunity for lean thinkers. We should be leading the way in showing how to rethink every process producing "bad" people along with poor results. I'm truly excited by the prospect for the Lean Community to move ahead rapidly down this path, going far beyond our starting point in the factory to introduce rigorous process thinking across society.

In the meantime, I hope you will encounter good processes full of good people. Failing that, I hope you will step back (probably while waiting in a queue), seize the opportunity to sharpen your lean thinking, and envision ways to improve any bad processes along your path.

July 28, 2004

If bad processes create bad employees (and crazy customers, too), it turns out that a bad process for process improvement can create more fault-finding and bad employees of a different sort. The next essay explores why this happens far more frequently than many lean thinkers seem to realize, and proposes a way to resolve the problem.

Making Everyone Whole

I've had a big smile on my face for much of the last month. That's because I've had the opportunity to visit progressive organizations on three continents to look at their efforts to create lean value streams. Walking through any process, good or bad, can put a smile on my face for one of two reasons. If the process is awful, it's easy to see how it could be better. And, if it has already been significantly improved from its original condition, I'm both pleased by the progress and aware that the next layer of waste is now visible and ready for elimination.

However, I also found myself frowning recently as I walked along some value streams. This happened when I heard improvement teams complaining about the difficulty of gaining and sustaining the engagement and cooperation of every person and every part of the organization touching the process being improved.

For example, on a walk through an information processing activity in a large service company, the team was complaining about the resistance of the company's information technology department to substantially modify the company-standard software in order to support the improved process. In another case, a team was bemoaning the resistance of experienced financial service workers to share the details of how they work their way around the problems in the existing process. In both cases I found the teams defaulting to the most comfortable explanation for the lack of engagement: bad people.

When this happens I try to take off my technical-analysis hat and put on my human-empathy hat. I ask, "How do the team's requests feel to the individuals or departments being asked to do something different?"

As I do this I remember the Italian economist Vilfredo Pareto (1848–1923), who gave us the 80/20 rule. (Pareto's first statement of this rule was based on his research indicating that throughout history 80% of the wealth in societies was controlled by 20% of the population. Joseph Juran later (1941) extended the 80/20 rule to quality problems where he found that 80% of a problem is typically caused by 20% of the possible causes. And today the 80/20 rules seems to find application in practically every activity.)

Pareto had a second insight of direct relevance to what I saw on my walks. This was his concept of economic optimality, which states that any proposed action in society (for example, a new law) should be judged in a positive light when no one is worse off and some individuals and organizations are better off. Public policy analysts (of which I was one early in my career) later realized that this concept applied particularly well in evaluating policy changes by governments. "Pareto Optimal" outcomes, as they came to be called, were desirable on grounds of equity because no one was worse off and at least some citizens were better off. And achieving them by transferring some of the winners' gains to compensate losers (creating Pareto Optimality if it was not otherwise present) also made such policies much more feasible politically because potential losers were much less likely to resist change.

Applying this idea to the value-stream improvements I was observing, I asked if the IT department and the experienced employees would be better off with the changed process. And the answer, after a bit of discussion, was clearly "no." The IT department would seriously overrun its annual budget in responding promptly to the team's request while falling behind on other projects. The experienced employees would very likely be replaced by younger, lower-paid employees able to operate the new process without the need for all the veterans' workarounds.

The root cause of the problem was not, therefore, bad people. In fact, those affected were reacting quite rationally to protect their interests because they would be hurt by the changes. Instead the problem was a lack of discussion and negotiation between the heads of IT, HR, and the improvement teams about how winners could compensate losers to make everyone whole.

As the outside observer, I found it particularly striking that Pareto Optimality could easily be achieved in these value streams by reallocating the substantial savings gained from improving both processes. The total saving would be much more than adequate to compensate IT for the additional hours and cost incurred in modifying the software quickly. And the substantial savings from the revised financial process were ample for giving the experienced employees, most of whom were near retirement, a generous severance package or transferring them at similar compensation to other jobs opened up by the organization's high turnover. Yet the implicit, unexamined thinking of the improvement teams was that all of the savings (plus the positive customer response to the improved processes) would be captured by the departments at the end of the processes and that everyone else should just get used to this new reality.

Understanding how change affects every participant in a value stream takes an extra effort, and I often find that improvement teams shudder at the prospect of negotiations with leaders of all affected parts of the organization. But my experience over many years is that making visible efforts to make everyone whole—by striving for Pareto Optimality whenever possible—is the best way to make and sustain big improvements in core processes. So please give this concept a try in your organization the next time you find "bad people" standing in the way of valuable improvements in your value streams.

Nov. 5, 2009

Fewer Heroes, More Farmers

The two previous essays concentrated on the effects of bad processes and flawed process improvement on good people. But what about the behavior of managers and leaders? Why do they find it so hard to put in place the "good" processes that would stop the creation of bad customers and bad employees? In this essay I argue that a large part of the problem is what we think leaders and managers should do. Indeed, I explain that we confuse the role of a manager with the role of a leader—to our detriment.

I recently met with the chief executive of a very large American corporation organized by business units, each self-contained with its own product development, production, purchasing, and sales functions. I asked what a CEO does in this situation, and got a simple answer: "I search for heroic leaders to galvanize my business units. I give them metrics to meet quickly. When they meet them, they are richly rewarded. When they don't, I find new leaders."

I noted that his firm, like many others I've examined, has a high level of turnover in its business unit heads. So I asked a simple question: "Why does your company need so many heroes? Why don't your businesses consistently perform at a high level so that no new leaders are needed? And why do even your apparently successful leaders keep moving on?"

The answer was that business is tough, leadership is the critical scarce resource, and that a lot of turnover indicates a dynamic management culture. But I couldn't agree. As I look at this and many other businesses I encounter on my walks, I see three problems apparently unnoticed by the heroic leader at the top rolling out the latest revitalization program.

These are (1) confusion about the business purpose of the organization's core processes; (2) poorly performing product and process development, fulfillment, supplier management, and customer support processes that tend to get worse instead of better; and (3) dispirited people operating these broken processes at every level of the enterprise. Needless to say, there are also mini-heroes at every level devising workarounds for the defective processes.

What's needed instead? More farmers!

Let me explain by means of a second example. Recently I received a copy of the leading motor industry magazine with its annual listing of the 50 most influential (read "heroic") leaders in the global motor industry: Bill Ford at Ford, Carlos Ghosn at Renault/Nissan, Rick Wagoner at GM, etc.

What I found striking was that the list contained no "leaders" from Toyota, except for one American in a U.S. marketing job. Yet Toyota has been one of the world's most successful car companies for decades. How could one of the most successful companies have practically no heroes? Because its managers still think like the farmers around its headquarters in the remote Aichi region of Japan where the company was created.

The job of the hero is to tackle a situation in which everything is out of control and quickly impose some semblance of order. And sometimes heroes are necessary. Taiichi Ohno, Shotaro Kamiya, Kenya Nakamura, and Kiichiro Toyoda certainly took heroic actions at Toyota in moments of crisis as the company's core processes were being defined after World War II.

But heroes shouldn't be necessary once an organization is transformed. Instead every important process should be steadily tended by a "farmer" (a value-stream manager) who continually asks three simple questions: Is the business purpose of the process correctly defined? Is action steadily being taken to create value, flow, and pull in every step of the process while taking out waste? Are all of the people touching the process actively engaged in making it better? This is the gemba mentality of the farmer who year after year plows a straight furrow, mends the fence, and obsesses about the weather, even as the heroic pioneer or hunter who originally cleared the land moves on.

Why do we have so many heroes, so few farmers, and such poor results in most of our organizations? Because we're blind to the simple fact that business heroes usually fail to transform businesses. They create short-term improvement, at least on the official metrics. But these gains either aren't real or they can't be sustained because no farmers are put in place to tend the fields. Wisely, these heros move on before this becomes apparent. Meanwhile, we are equally blind to the critical contribution of the farmers who should be our heroes. These are the folks who provide the steady-paced continuity at the core of every lean enterprise.

I hope that as you think about your job you will become a lean farmer who takes responsibility for the processes you touch and that you will work every day to plow the straight furrow, mend the fence, and obsess about the weather. These are the real value-creating aspects of management. When present they insure that no heroes will be needed in the future.

May 12, 2006

This essay was written long before Toyota's recent difficulties. But it is highly relevant. Surely the task for Akio Toyoda, in his role as president, is to reinvigorate the farmer culture that made Toyota great through its attention at the gemba to the details of every value-creating process. Several recent presidents of Toyota sounded very much like heroic visionaries. And the result of their tenure was a focus on dramatic results (e.g., rapid growth in market share and return on sales) rather than process improvements needed to achieve and sustain these results. Too many heroes, too few farmers.

The Problem with Creative Work and Creative Management

A refrain I often hear is that lean managers (farmers) can't be creative. That is, they aren't free to do new and dramatic things without bureaucratic interference. And the heroic leader lurking somewhere in all of us wants above all to be creative. In addition there is the widespread belief that only heroic, individual action can break through the straightjacket of organizational inertia. How lean thinkers should approach this important topic is the subject of this essay.

Years ago I heard a presentation from someone at Toyota explaining how to introduce the Toyota Production System. "Start by analyzing the work to be done." This meant listing all the actions required to create the value in a given process and then dividing these actions into three categories:

- *Value-creating work*: activities adding directly to the value of the product as determined by the customer. (Manufacturing examples are painting the product or adding parts during assembly.) A simple test is to ask whether customers would mind if this work was not done but their product still performed properly. If they would mind, it is value-creating. For example, almost all customers expect their products to be painted with all the parts assembled, so these steps are value-creating.

- *Incidental work*: activities that are currently necessary to create a product for a customer but which have no value to the customer. Examples include handling materials, clamping fixtures to hold the work, and returning kanban cards. No customer ever bought a product or offered to pay more because the kanban were all returned to the scheduling point!

- *Waste*: activities that create no value and can be completely eliminated. Examples include rework, storing items between work steps, and searching for missing materials. No customer anywhere wants to pay for these activities, and there is no need for them to be performed if lean principles are fully applied.

Categorizing the existing steps is a great way to start lean thinking, and it's pretty easy in a factory environment while drawing a value-stream map. But when lean thinkers move beyond the factory, as many are today, it's easy to get confused about the nature of work. In particular, in any office environment and in healthcare, maintenance, overhaul, retail, and other operational environments not involving factories, many employees and managers tell me that they are doing "creative work." They state that the outcome of each step is unpredictable, that steps may need to change with each new product, and that work can't be clearly planned. Therefore they can't easily list the steps they will need to take to produce a given result. And, from their perspective, most of the steps they are currently taking are value-creating, not incidental work or waste.

However, as I observe their work I usually see something very different. A few situations really do require creative modifications in the middle of the process—for example, the patient who has a heart attack during a routine appendectomy. But most nonfactory work is actually transactional. That is, the same steps need to be performed the same way every time to get a good result. And most activities fit into clear product families that are performed over and over: the standard appendectomy, the monthly closing of the books, the D check (heavy maintenance) on a 747.

The reason the work appears to be "creative" is because product families are not clearly identified, the steps are not clearly defined, and many of the support processes needed to successfully perform each step are lacking. For example, the needed instruments or drugs for the next step in a medical procedure are missing so the doctor, nurse, or technician goes treasure hunting to find them. What appears to the employees as mostly value-creating work with a bit of incidental work appears to me as a small amount of value-creating work, a bit of incidental work, and an enormous amount of waste.

But this is not all the waste I see. Looking one level back from the point of primary work, I see armies of managers running madly to unkink holdups in the process. Many of their workarounds are indeed "creative." But does the customer really want to pay for management interventions (that is, for rework) in processes that would not require any intervention if properly designed? Surely these are all examples of creativity we can do without, and it's a shame that so few employees and managers notice that in many cases creativity and rework are the same thing.

Please do not misunderstand: There is truly creative work to be done every day. For example, finding an ingenious new way to design a product. But this is a very small fraction of total work and most of what bears the label "creative work" is actually pure waste.

By contrast, the truly creative act that all of us should perform as employees and managers is to fundamentally rethink the processes we operate and manage so that product families are identified, steps are precisely specified and standardized, and waste is eliminated while incidental work is minimized. But even here we need to use the standard process of value-stream mapping with A3 analysis. This is the real role for creativity at work.

May 10, 2005

Respect for People

Let's suppose that you and I want to tap the creative, process-improving energies of the people touching every process in our organizations. That is, we want to truly engage every member of our organization in continuous improvement. How can we do that? This is a deeply human matter requiring us to rethink what it really means to show respect for people.

For years I've visited companies where "respect for people" is stated to be a core element of the corporate philosophy. So I've asked managers in many of these companies a simple question. "How do you show respect?" I usually heard that employees should be treated fairly, given clear goals, trusted to achieve them in the best way, and held accountable for results. For example, "We hire smart people, we give them great latitude in how they do their work because we trust them, and we hold them to objective measures of performance. That's respect for people."

In recent years Toyota made respect for people one of the pillars of the Toyota Way (the other being continuous improvement). So I decided I should ask the best Toyota-trained managers I know how they show respect for people. The answer I heard is a good bit different from what I heard at many other companies. It goes as follows:

The manager begins by asking an employee he or she supervises what the problem is with the way work is currently being done. Next the manager challenges the employee's answer and enters into a dialogue about what the real problem is. (It's rarely the problem showing on the surface.)

Then the manager asks what is causing this problem and enters into another dialogue about its root causes. (True dialogue requires the employee to gather evidence on the gemba for joint evaluation.)

Then the manager asks what should be done about the problem and asks the employee why he or she has proposed one countermeasure instead of another. (This generally requires considering a range of countermeasures and collecting more evidence.)

Then the manager asks how they—manager and employee—will know if the countermeasure has achieved a positive result, and again engages in dialogue on the best indicator.

Finally, after agreement is reached on the most appropriate measure of success, the employee sets out to implement the countermeasure.

For many of us that doesn't sound much like respect for people. The manager after all doesn't just say, "I trust you to solve the problem because I respect you. Do it your way and get on with it." And the manager isn't a morale booster, always saying "Great job!" even when the problem hasn't been fully solved. Instead the manager challenges the employee every step of the way, asking for more thought, more facts, and more discussion when the employee just wants to implement his or her favored solution.

Over time I've come to realize that engaging in this problem-solving process is actually the highest form of respect. The manager is saying to the employee that the manager can't solve the problem alone, because the manager isn't close enough to the problem to know the facts. The manager truly respects the employee's knowledge and his or her dedication to finding the best answer. But the employee can't solve the problem alone either, because he or she is often too close to the issue to see its context, and may refrain from asking tough questions about his or her own work. Only by showing mutual respect—each for the other and for each other's role—is it possible to solve problems, make work more satisfying, and move organizational performance to an ever-higher level.

Recently I walked through two distribution centers in the same city providing the same type of service for their customers. As I walked I found a wonderfully clear example of the difference that mutual respect for people makes.

In the first facility managers were focused on controlling the workforce through individual metrics. Employees were told to get a given amount of work done but given considerable latitude on just how to do it. They were judged at the end of the day, week, month, and quarter on whether they achieved the desired results, using data collected by a computerized tracking system. Front-line managers were busily engaged in working around current problems but none was systematically engaged in actually solving these problems at the root cause in collaboration with the employees. This was a task for higher-level managers and staff experts as time permitted, usually without the involvement of the production associates.

In the second facility, the management had worked with employees to create standardized work for every task and had introduced visual control with status boards so everyone could see how everyone else was proceeding with their work. Because the condition of the entire process was instantly visible to everyone, employees could help each other with any problems that emerged. And because the work process was very stable due to strict adherence to standardized work, line managers could devote most of their energy to problem-solving and improvement by engaging production associates in dialogues to get to root causes and implement sustainable countermeasures. Indeed, every associate spent *four hours every week* on improvement activities.

What is the result? Both facilities are in the same city, have employees with the same educational level, and pay roughly the same wage. Yet annual turnover of associates in the first facility is 70% (which seems to be typical in distribution centers) and there is significant management turnover as well. Meanwhile, in the second facility, associate turnover is 1% and practically no managers leave.

When I asked managers and associates in the second center why, the answer was simple: "The work here is always challenging because we are always solving problems using a method we all understand. And we all respect each other's contribution."

The differences continue: In my rough estimate, labor productivity in the second facility is about twice that of the first even with less automation. This is partly because the first facility is constantly hiring and training new employees while the second distribution center spends practically no time on this task. In addition, all employees in the second facility are experienced and working at the top of their learning curve. Large amounts of confusion about what to do next and larger amounts of rework are eliminated.

Finally, in the second facility, quality as experienced by customers is higher even though there is less internal rework. And the total amount of inventory on hand to provide the next-day service that both facilities promise their customers is much lower in the second distribution center.

I trust you can guess which facility is a Toyota parts distribution center and which facility belongs to a distribution firm stuck (like most) in the age of mass production with command-and-control management methods but little discussion with employees of how they can best do their jobs.

I also trust that all of us want to show respect for people. The challenge for those of us in the Lean Community is to embrace and explain the true nature of mutual respect for people—managers and associates—so all organizations can move toward a new and better way of solving their problems. This is the true path to tapping and harnessing employee creativity as well.

Dec. 20, 2007

With a lean perspective on purpose, process, and people in mind, what remains is to put them together in a creative combination. This daunting task is the role for the lean manager and for lean management, the topic of the next section.

MANAGEMENT

In recent years I have found myself increasingly thinking and writing about management, by which I mean the routine activity of aligning people and processes with customer purpose. And I have paid special attention to the profound difference between *modern management,* as taught in business schools or learned through observation of traditional bosses in traditional enterprises, and *lean management,* as learned through experience on the gemba under the continuing guidance of a more senior lean manager.

Management is a vast topic with many dimensions, and I have tackled it from a number of angles: The correct use of lean tools by lean managers. The challenge of execution through strategy deployment. The endless potential of A3 thinking. The difference between authority (which everyone seems to understand) and responsibility (which hardly anyone understands). The confusion I often see about the different roles of line management and staffs in supporting a lean enterprise.

Each essay in this section on management provides a different perspective, and I hope that together they bring the topic into clear focus. I also hope they give some insight into how lean managers think and behave. I begin with a big picture look at the difference between simply applying lean tools and truly practicing lean management.

From Lean Tools to Lean Management

I've been thinking about the challenge of lean transformation since I started studying Honda and Toyota as part of the MIT global automotive project in 1979. That's a long time, and during this period I've watched lean thinking progress through a series of stages.

In the early years much of the focus was on sorting out what was specific to a culture. Could anyone outside of Japan. embrace lean thinking? Could anyone outside of Toyota, Honda, and Mazda (which had itself copied Toyota after its crisis in 1973) and their supplier groups? In addition, there was much confusion about the elements of a lean business system. Was it just in the factory? Or did it apply to every aspect of an organization, including product and process development, supplier management, customer support, and general management? In *The Machine That Changed the World* in 1990, Dan Jones, Dan Roos, and I made the case that lean thinking can be applied by any company anywhere in the world, but that the full power of the system is only realized when it is applied to all elements of the enterprise.[4]

As this view became accepted, the focus turned to how organizations everywhere could transform themselves from mass producers into lean exemplars. Given the magnitude of the task and its many dimensions, it's understandable that lean tools came to the foreground: 5S, setup reduction, the Five Whys, target costing, simultaneous and concurrent engineering, value-stream maps, kanban, kaizen. Indeed, I think of the period from 1990 to the mid-2000s as the Tool Age of the lean movement.

The attraction of tools is that they can be employed at many points within an organization, often by staff improvement teams or external consultants. Even better, they can be applied in isolation without tackling the difficult task of changing the organization and its fundamental approach to management. I often say that managers will try anything easy that doesn't work before they will try anything hard that does, and this may be a fair summary of what happened in the Tool Age.

---

4. James P. Womack, Daniel T. Jones, and Daniel Roos, *The Machine That Changed the World* (New York: Rawson & Associates, 1990).

Over 15 years we all learned about a lot of lean tools. We also learned how to apply them and we had some success. But we hardly created a multitude of lean enterprises. By contrast, the previously dominant, mass-production approach to management—as perfected by Alfred Sloan at General Motors in the 1920s, building on Ford's earlier breakthrough in flow production—was widely and successfully copied within a short period of demonstrating its superiority.

Fortunately, the lean movement is finally tackling the fundamental issues of lean management. I've recently had a number of conversations in a number of countries—the United States, Germany, China—with senior managers who realize that they need to think more about lean management before thinking further about lean tools.

What do I mean by "lean management"? Let me start with some general observations about organization and management:

- All value created in any organization is the result of a lengthy sequence of steps—a value stream. These steps must be conducted properly in the proper sequence at the proper time.

- Getting the right value to the customer at the right time with the right cost to the organization is the key to survival and prosperity.

- The flow of value toward the customer is horizontal, across the organization.

- All enterprises are organized vertically by department (engineering, purchasing, production, sales, etc.). They always will be because this is the best way to create and store knowledge and the most practical way to channel careers. What's more, value almost always flows to the end customer through many independent organizations, each organized vertically and each acting vertically as an entity to support its own interests.

- Someone needs to see, manage, and improve the entire process of horizontal value creation on behalf of the customer, from concept to launch, from order through production to delivery, and from delivery through the product's use cycle.

- In most organizations no one is actually responsible for the horizontal flow of value by product family, despite what senior managers may think. The product's value stream is an organizational orphan.

- In most organizations managers at every level are being graded on whether they make their department-specific numbers. These are the metrics—usually financial—set by high-level managers as they attempt to fully utilize assets and "control" the organization. Each independent organization touching the product—supplier, manufacturer, distributor, retailer, etc.—has its own metrics.

- Improvements to value streams are managed by staff experts (or consultants) who usually don't see the whole flow of value, the most pressing needs of the customer, and the most urgent business needs of the organization. They use the tools they feel most comfortable with to solve the problems that seem easiest.

How can "lean management" help us do better? Here are three simple elements of lean management worthy of experimentation:

1. Make sure every value stream has someone responsible—a value-stream manager—for overseeing the whole flow of value and continually improving every aspect of the process in light of the needs of the customer and the business.

The question for this value-stream manager to ask is, "How can I make customers happy, while making money, by engaging the full energies of our people (including our suppliers upstream and distributors downstream) to improve this value stream?"

Note that the value-stream manager doesn't need a large staff or authority over employees touching the value stream. Instead, the value-stream manager needs to negotiate with the department heads about the needs of the product and resolve any differences by appealing to the most senior managers.

Similarly, no employee should have more than one boss. A good system of value-stream management gives every lower-level employee a boss in his or her department who has talked with the value-stream manager to determine what that department needs to do to support the value stream. This avoids complex matrices in which employees have two (or more) bosses.

2. Instead of developing complex metrics, ask value-stream managers how they will improve the value-creating process they are overseeing.

If managers focus on their process, the performance metrics will come out right; but if managers focus on their numbers, the process is likely never to improve. And note that most metrics are nothing more than end-of-the-line quality inspection: at the end of the quarter or the end of the year, everyone looks to see what happened, at a point long after the mistakes have been made.

3. Teach all managers to ask questions about their value streams (rather than giving answers and orders from higher levels). Turn these questions into experiments using the scientific method by means of plan-do-check-act (PDCA).

Only management by science through constant experimentation to answer questions can produce sustainable improvements in value streams. A3 (as discussed in the essay "It Takes 2 (or More) to A3" on page 65) is a wonderful tool toward this end.

Please understand: Lean tools are great. We all need to master and deploy them, and our efforts over 15 years to do so are not wasted. But just as a carpenter needs a vision of what to build in order to get the full benefit of a hammer, we need a clear vision of our organizational objectives and better management methods—indeed, lean management—before we pick up our tools.

Nov. 11, 2006

What I've Learned about Planning and Execution

It is fine to talk about the concept of lean management, but what should lean managers actually do every day? One essential task is to deploy new initiatives that address customer and organizational purpose. How to do this successfully is the topic of this essay.

By the time I founded the Lean Enterprise Institute in 1997, I had been thinking for years about how organizations prioritize and plan. And I had carefully read the strategy deployment (hoshin kanri) literature emerging from Japan since the 1970s. So I thought it would be easy to develop and implement both a long-range and a one-year plan.

I asked my friend Pat Lancaster (then the chairman of Lantech and the subject of Chapter Six of my and Dan Jones's book *Lean Thinking*)[5] to come to Boston to help us as a facilitator. Our whole team set out with great energy and, two days later, after much frank discussion, we had our plan. We had agreed on our organizational direction (our North Star), selected our major priorities for the next few years, set targets, and defined specific initiatives to achieve them. We had won the war against chaos and indecision!

But there was a problem: We soon discovered that we had no practical means to implement the plan. Specifically, we had no effective way to assign responsibility for our initiatives, which cut across the organization. We had no workable way to measure our progress. And we had no means of determining why we were often not getting the results we expected from our initiatives and what to do about shortfalls. In short, we had conducted a great two-day exercise with the help of a brilliant facilitator and we had produced a great plan. But it produced no benefit for our organization. Quietly, we soon abandoned the whole approach and substituted a simple annual budgeting process.

5. James P. Womack and Daniel T. Jones, *Lean Thinking* (New York: Simon & Schuster, 2003).

Fortunately, this simple process was sufficient for LEI to flourish as a small organization over the next decade. However, I kept reflecting on why we were so good at picking the right things to do (and creating our annual budget) but were much less adept at getting the right things done. In the language of plan-do-check-act (PDCA), introduced by W. Edwards Deming, we were great at P but struggled with DCA.

In the past year we've grown dramatically, and LEI has become a much more complex organization. Suddenly, our simple budgeting process was no longer adequate and I was forced to revisit the issue of prioritization and planning. At the same time, in our research activities I was watching many organizations struggle as they tried—as we had—to introduce complex planning systems derived from the standard Japanese-derived texts on hoshin kanri.

I was delighted therefore when Toyota alumnus Pascal Dennis approached me with the suggestion that strategy deployment can be made much simpler and more effective. During the past year, as I've reviewed Pascal's work and tried to apply it in managing LEI, I've gained some real insights into how to do strategy deployment properly. Let me share them briefly:

- The P (plan) part really is simple. But it's critically important that as you start you reach agreement on where your organization really stands—its current state. This means developing simple, visual measures of current performance that everyone can see and agree on. Otherwise the plan is based on illusion.

- The D (do) part will succeed if the plan tells a simple, persuasive story and each element of the plan is easily understandable by everyone. Toyota's A3 method for describing on a single sheet of paper the issue each plan element is addressing—and the way the organization will solve it—has startling power once everyone learns how to read A3s. (I've been amazed at what A3 analysis has done for our value-stream management at LEI and what it has done for my ability to communicate to everyone the direction LEI is taking.)

- The C (check) part of the plan is critical and is almost universally ignored. Yet there is no point in deploying a plan unless there is a standardized method for measuring the results and senior-management commitment to follow through.

- The A (act/adjust) step is equally important but requires effective problem-solving to understand why the plan is not achieving its intended results (as shown in the C step). Even organizations that check their progress are usually very weak at adjusting. Yet almost no plan produces exactly the results expected. Adjustment is inevitable and continual.

- Every element in the plan needs a deployment manager who can look across the functions, see the whole, and take responsibility for a good result. This is like the chief engineer at Toyota. And the good news is that designating a deployment manager for each plan element requires no adjustment to the organization chart. Deployment is simply an additional task for designated senior managers, one that becomes much easier as experience is gained over several years.

- Some organizations can deploy plan elements for each product family value stream, as we have at LEI. However, many organizations—far more than I had realized until recently—have shared processes (e.g., equipment maintenance, materials supply, supplier management) that lack basic stability. They may be better off starting with organizationwide themes like quality, delivery, and cost in order to create stability before they switch to a value-stream approach.

- Perhaps most important: It's all about people. I've recently reflected on Toyota's quality concept of jidoka, often described as "autonomation with a human touch." This means that employees are actively engaged at every level in insuring that process technology—no matter how sophisticated—works properly with properly trained and supported employees to produce a good result every time. It has occurred to me that strategy deployment as it ought to be practiced is similar. It's not an exercise in cold logic, done once and forgotten. Rather it is "hoshin kanri with a human touch" in which everyone in the organization becomes a scientist participating in continual experiments with every plan element by means of PDCA.

Dec. 14, 2006

Additional reading:

Pascal Dennis, *Getting the Right Things Done* (Cambridge, MA: Lean Enterprise Institute, 2006).

It Takes 2 (or More) to A3

Subsequent to the publication of Pascal Dennis' book on strategy deployment, I became aware that the biggest management challenge is to successfully implement the few important initiatives needed to fundamentally change the performance of an organization. This, of course, is one of the uses of A3, and we were soon at work at LEI on a book explaining how to utilize A3. This was not just as a tool, but as a core method of lean management.

We've just launched John Shook's new book, *Managing to Learn*,[6] and I'm tremendously excited. I think it is the most important work we have published at LEI. This is because John clearly explains why A3 thinking is the core of the lean management system and shows how the repeated act of creating A3s also creates lean managers.

But I'm worried as well as excited. Eleven years ago when we launched John and Mike Rother's *Learning to See*, I expected readers would use the wonderful tool of value-stream mapping (VSM) to engage in a dialogue with everyone touching value streams. I hoped that they would start with the business problem, map the current state as a team activity, and envision a future state able to address the problem while engaging everyone's best efforts.

What often happened instead was that value-stream maps were assigned to staff members in improvement offices. They drew maps of the current and future states, frequently without clear definition of the business problem and with only passing interaction with those touching the value stream. They then assumed that line management would embrace the proposed future state and make it a reality. Frequently nothing happened. Or if anything did happen, it couldn't be sustained. In this way, misused VSMs became corporate wallpaper.

---

6. John Shook, *Managing to Learn* (Cambridge, MA: Lean Enterprise Institute, 2008).

So as we all embrace A3—and I detect a tremendous swell of interest across the Lean Community—let's be careful not to make the same mistake. Instead let's make A3 the foundation of lean management.

To do this we have to realize that no one can create a useful A3 in isolation. It takes at least two individuals and often many more. Developing an A3 is an organizational drama in which someone identifies a condition or problem needing attention. When this person is at a higher level, he or she assumes the role of mentor, assigning responsibility for creating the A3 to someone at a lower level—the owner— who is closer to the gemba where value is actually created.

However, the owner of the A3—at whatever level of the organization—cannot address the condition or solve the problem alone. He or she must go to the gemba and talk directly with everyone touching the problem, aware that most problems in an organization are the result of a poorly defined or poorly managed process shared by different areas, departments, and functions (often including customers and suppliers).

As the owner proceeds with the A3 analysis, an intense dialogue ensues between the mentor and the owner, one that soon includes everyone touching the troublesome process. This dialogue gradually clarifies the problem, its root cause, the range of potential counter-measures, the best apparent countermeasure, the steps that need to be taken (the "who, what, when, where") to implement the best countermeasure, the appropriate check on the results, and the necessary reflection on next steps (which often lead to another A3).

The real magic here is that the owner takes responsibility for addressing a problem—often running horizontally across the organi-zation—through intense dialogue with individuals in areas of the business where he or she has no authority. During the A3 process, the owner actually manufactures the authority for putting the countermeasure in place. However, this type of authority is not a matter of control delineated on an organization chart. People in different areas with different bosses energetically participate in implementing the countermeasure because they have actively participated in the dialogue that developed what they believe is the best counter-measure for an important problem.

The additional benefit of the complete A3 cycle is that it develops the owner to become a higher-level manager. This is why John uses the dynamic terms "mentor" and "owner" in *Managing to Learn* rather than the static terms "boss" and "direct report." At the same time, mastering the skill of A3 prepares those touching the process at lower levels in an organization to someday become lean managers. This occurs when they are assigned responsibility for their own A3s. Or, even better, it occurs when they spontaneously take the initiative to identify opportunities for improvement by developing A3s for evaluation by their mentors.

As we launch *Managing to Learn*, I wish every member of the Lean Community rapid success in mastering the critical skills of A3 management. But please, don't try to A3 all alone!

Oct. 7, 2008

Additional reading:

John Shook, *Managing to Learn* (Cambridge, MA: Lean Enterprise Institute, 2008).

The Problem of Sustainability

Deployment is hard, although a lot easier once all the managers in an organization master A3. But many readers have told me over the years that sustaining the gains, once initial breakthroughs are made, is harder still. In response I have found myself thinking about the problem of sustainability.

I recently got a call from an old friend who led one of the first lean implementation efforts in healthcare in the mid-1990s. He has moved on to other challenges, and we hadn't had a chance to catch up in recent years. So I asked him what happened to the lean initiative in the healthcare organization where he had been a senior manager.

The answer was what I feared. "We created a lean improvement team and conducted a comprehensive campaign to kaizen the organization's key value streams. And we had dramatic results. Faster patient flows. Better patient outcomes. Lower costs. But we couldn't sustain the gains. The improvement efforts weren't connected to the way the organization was managed, and the value streams started to regress to the mean as soon as the improvement team left. After I left the organization, the whole program came to an end. What a shame."

My friend is far from alone. In our annual LEI web survey of the Lean Community, a leading problem that lean thinkers note about their improvement efforts is "backsliding to old ways of working" after initial progress. And the most frequently cited issue is "middle management resistance" to change. In short, the lean movement has a sustainability issue we need to address.

What is at the heart of our sustainability problem? More important, what can we do about it?

I believe that the root cause of regression in most organizations today is confusion about priorities at different levels of the organization, compounded by the failure to make anyone responsible for the continuing performance of important value streams as they flow horizontally across the enterprise.

To prevent regression, someone—a value-stream manager—needs to periodically clarify priorities for each value stream and identify the performance gap between what the customer needs and what the value stream is providing. The manager taking responsibility then needs to engage everyone touching the value stream in carefully capturing the current condition (the "current state") of the value stream that is causing the gap. The next step is to envision a better value stream and determine who will need to do what by when to bring it into being.

Finally, the value-stream manager needs to determine what will constitute evidence that the performance gap has been closed and collect the data to demonstrate this. This exercise is Dr. Deming's plan-do-check-act (PDCA) cycle conducted repetitively by the responsible person, ideally employing A3 analysis.

I'm not proposing a dramatic change in the organization chart to reassign authority. Indeed, I've hardly ever seen an organization improved by a "reorganization." And I'm not suggesting the creation of a matrix organization where everyone has a vertical and a horizontal boss. Rather, someone with another job in the organization needs to take on the management role of periodically (and quickly) auditing the horizontal flow of value and bringing to the attention of everyone touching the stream how the organization is performing along that stream.

Note that periodic audits of processes within small areas (for example, a continuous-flow work cell or a materials-replenishment process) are a well-established aspect of lean practices that I call "standard management." So auditing across departments and functions to examine value streams from end to end is a scaling up of current best practice, not something wholly new.

Auditing every value stream will expose problems with the flow of value and contradictions in organizational objectives. Indeed, it will expose many problems and many contradictions. And that is precisely the point. Most value streams currently have substantial performance gaps, but the magnitude of the gap and the precise causes are hard for anyone to see. (Hence the confusion and resistance of many middle managers. They are doing well on one, vertical set of objectives—asset utilization in their department, for example—when lean methods require another, horizontal set.) And fixing the root causes of poor performance will require someone—and quite possibly everyone—touching the stream to change their behavior.

It follows that the responsible manager needs to engage in a dialogue with the leaders of the functions and, if necessary, with top-level management to gain agreement on who must do what by when to achieve a sustainable leap in performance that will benefit the customer and the whole organization. (One of the "whats" is rethinking the metrics against which the change-resisting middle managers are being judged.) The responsible person then must periodically revisit the value stream, not just to prevent regression but to continually move it to a higher level of performance.

A special problem as we tackle this issue is that we can't simply copy current-day Toyota. In the past, Toyota went through many iterations of how to solve the problem of value-stream management across the organization. But today its mature organization relies on hoshin kanri at the macro level and a cadre of line managers auditing their areas at the micro level. Because there is no confusion about objectives from top to bottom and because managers have been taught from the very beginning of their careers how to see the flow of value under their management, no formally appointed value-stream managers are needed.

Other organizations—yours and mine, for example!—are different, and what we need now are experiments with value-stream management. Whatever the final answer, everyone in the Lean Community has a big stake in our solving the sustainability problem. Otherwise, the current surge of interest in lean may become just another episode in the long history of unsustainable improvement campaigns.

May 30, 2007

From Staffs Conducting Programs to Line Managers Solving Problems

As I have thought further about sustainability, I have come to understand that a big part of the problem is who is doing the deployment and who is doing the sustaining. I have found in far too many organizations that improvement and process maintenance are outsourced by line management to staffs or consultants. And I have become convinced that this is an impossible mission. What's needed instead is to rethink what line managers really do.

Recently I visited a number of organizations well along in their lean transformations. I asked the leaders of these initiatives about their methods, their experiences to date, and their trajectories. Then I took a walk along several of their value streams to observe performance and to talk with line managers about their perspectives on the lean leap. Here's a typical story:

Organization A has an ambitious "lean six-sigma" program for the whole enterprise. As seems to be increasingly common, it is a consolidation of initially separate lean and six-sigma programs into one unified activity, with participants reporting to a vice president for process improvement and quality at headquarters.

The program is being conducted by a large staff team assisted by a few external consultants. Much progress has been made in reconciling the approaches of lean and six sigma by adapting DMAIC (define-measure-analyze-improve-control) as the organization's PDCA (plan-do-check-act) problem-solving method. (I'm often asked whether DMAIC or PDCA is the "correct" method to use, and I always say, "Pick one, adapt it as necessary to your needs, make sure everyone understands it, and get going. The right method is the one that produces consistently good results in your organization, and you will be able to judge that for yourself over time.")

The team has offered introductory training in lean thinking and process capability for a wide range of employees and has conducted black-belt and lean certifications for a substantial number of line managers. It has done this while leading a large number of rapid-improvement activities (labeled "kaizen") that engage both line managers and the front-line employees touching value streams. It also conducts six-sigma analyses of quality issues over an extended period, collecting and analyzing large amounts of data.

The individual improvements have often been very impressive, particularly as measured in financial terms using six-sigma methodology. But as I talked with line managers I discovered that the improvements are not connected end-to-end as key processes cross areas, departments, and functions in the organization. Perhaps as a consequence, the business results for the organization are much less than the sum of individual achievements would suggest. This led to an observation I hear frequently: "How do we save so much money and improve quality so much on individual process steps, yet little seems to be dropping to the bottom line and customers seem no happier?"

Even these isolated improvements are not easily sustained once the improvement team's focus shifts to the next project. The line managers are sympathetic to the concepts they have learned but note that they are still fighting fires due to issues upstream and downstream from the areas they manage. This leaves them little time to install standardized work to sustain what has been achieved and no time for planning the next leap. In addition, none of the corporate metrics upon which they are being judged have been changed, so it's easy to get poor performance on a metric despite a worthwhile improvement in a process. Finally, many managers noted that they will soon be rotated out of their job—as part of the organization's high-speed management advancement—without a good means of handing over what they have learned about the process to whoever takes charge next.

When I visited Organization A, the lean six-sigma team was reflecting on its achievements over several years and asked my view on where the program should be going in the next five years. I believe they were expecting me to say that they needed to speed up the pace of improvement, with more training, more improvement events, and, quite possibly, a larger staff. My answer was quite different:

"You need to transition during the next five years from a point-improvement program driven by a staff team to a new way of thinking and acting by line managers. The line managers' key work must be to continually solve problems end-to-end in primary and support processes for which they are given responsibility. Put simply: You need to transition from a staff conducting a program to line managers routinely solving problems important to the organization, often with the technical assistance of your lean team."

I assured them that a change in focus would not reduce the importance of the lean team. Rather it would create demand for tackling process issues that are more technically interesting, as line managers take the lead on easier problems. And it should also create a role for the lean team in advising on design of the production process for each new product. This is a critical weakness of the current organization, which routinely launches products with poorly conceived production processes, leading to the immediate need for kaizen. (It turns out that there is even a Japanese word for this practice—"touzen"—which is used to describe kaizen which should not have been necessary.)

Unfortunately, I couldn't be so reassuring on what I see as the lean team's biggest challenge: They need to make the case to senior management that Organization A's management methods need to be fully rethought. Every important value stream needs to have a fully responsible manager who stays on the job long enough to really understand the process. And the corporate measures of management performance need to be carefully rethought so managers are consistently rewarded for doing the right thing for the extended process over an extended period.

It may seem difficult for a staff team to make this case to senior management. But I wonder who can if those members of the organization with the greatest knowledge of process thinking and with the best understanding of what is happening today can't. So I urged them to try and promised to help to the extent I can through my writing and speaking.

Before I sign off, please understand that I'm not criticizing lean "programs," which Dan Jones and I helped popularize in *Lean Thinking*. They are often essential to get people's attention, move organizations off dead center, and rapidly introduce new ideas while clearly demonstrating their potential. But they are never sufficient. What every organization must do at some point is make the conversion from lean programs led by staffs to deployment and problem solving by line managers. And the faster and more completely an organization makes this transition the more successful it is likely to be.

July 17, 2008

Even when the concept of lean management is fully grasped, it turns out that unfortunate things can occur when would-be lean managers try to mechanically apply lean management tools, notably strategy deployment and A3. These tools are wonderful companions. But to successfully transition from managing by vertically oriented results (modern management) to managing by horizontal processes (lean management), managers need to embrace a distinctive way of thinking as well.

The Mind of the Lean Manager

Several years ago I started to talk about the need to move beyond lean tools—including the very powerful concept of value-stream mapping—to lean management. At the same time we at LEI began to publish a set of volumes on lean management techniques. These consist of strategy deployment to set priorities from the top of the organization, A3 analysis to deploy new initiatives and solve problems in the middle of the organization, and standardized work with standardized management and kaizen to create stability and sustainability at the bottom of the organization where value is actually created.

Recently I've been walking through a range of organizations to see how these lean management techniques are being used. Let me cite several illustrative cases:

In one organization I found a remarkably elaborate strategy-deployment matrix posted throughout the headquarters and in the plants. It was the familiar X-shaped diagram with important business objectives on the left side, the initiatives needed to achieve the objectives along the top, the specific results to be achieved in the current year on the right side, and measures of success on the bottom. In addition, there was an array to the right side showing who in which part of the organization was taking responsibility for each initiative and which parts of the organization were affected by each initiative.

But I found very little success in achieving the goals. Instead, the organizational focus at the end of the budget year (which came at the time of my visit) was on explaining why progress had not been what had been anticipated and who was at fault.

In a second organization I found that the COO had decreed that all problems were henceforth to be tackled using A3 analysis employing a standard eight-box format. At the review meeting I attended, all the managers showed up with a filled-out A3 to prove they were on top of their jobs. (This was despite the fact that the issues to tackle with the A3s had only been assigned the previous week. There surely had been no time to visit the gemba, talk with those touching the problem, and look for root causes, much less to find the best countermeasure.) And, because this organization was transitioning from a decades-long tradition of preparing lengthy reports on every problem (with pages of documen-tation), the text on the A3s was minuscule in order to crowd in all of the details that would have been included in a traditional report. When these were projected as PowerPoint slides at the meeting, it turned out that no one in the room could actually read them. But every manager had done his job.

In a third organization I found all of the elements of standardized work—work standards, work combination tables, kaizen opportunity lists—clearly posted in work areas, but no standardized work and no standardized front-line management. A few minutes' observation revealed that the work was not actually being done in the way the work standards required, that kaizen activities were not based on clear problem definition, and that the front-line managers were only vaguely aware of the current condition of the processes they were managing. Yet the management took pains to show me how much progress they had made with this splendid technique of standardization as shown by their new visual management system.

As I walked through these and other organizations I was sobered to realize that these new lean management techniques had become more tools—in this case, lean management tools. They were being followed as organizational ritual without thinking about their actual purpose. As so often happens in organizational life, means had become ends.

I was not surprised. Tools—for process analysis and for management —are wonderful things. They are absolutely necessary. And managers love them because they seem to provide shortcuts to doing a better job. But they can't achieve their potential results, and often can't achieve any results, without managers with a lean state of mind to wield them.

What do I mean by a lean state of mind?

First, the lean manager eagerly embraces the role of problem solver. This means going to see the actual situation, asking about the performance issue, seeking the root cause, and showing respect for lower-level managers and for colleagues at the same organizational level by asking hard questions until good answers emerge. It's this critical, probing state of mind that permits lean tools to be put to good use. The lean manager applies the right tool for the specific problem and does this in context on the gemba rather than in the abstract in some conference room. Empty ritual is replaced with a rigorous thought process that engages employees and pulls forward their best abilities.

Second, the lean manager realizes that no manager at a higher level can or should solve a problem at a lower level. (And one of the worst abuses of lean tools lies in trying to do just this.) Instead, the higher-level manager can assign responsibility to a manager at a lower level to tackle the problem through a continuing dialogue, both vertically with the higher-level manager and horizontally with everyone actually touching the process causing the problem. The lean law of organizational life is that problems can only be solved where they live, in conversation with the people who live with them and whose current actions are contributing to the problem. But this requires support, encouragement, and, yes, relentless pressure from the higher-level lean manager.

Third, the lean manager believes that all problem solving is about experimentation by means of plan-do-check-act. No one can know the answer before experiments are conducted, and the many experiments that fail will yield valuable learning that can be applied to the next round of experiments.

Finally, the lean manager knows that no problem is ever solved forever. Indeed, the introduction of a promising countermeasure is sure to create new problems at some other point in the organization. This is not bad. It is good provided that the critical, probing mind of the lean manager keeps on the case in pursuit of perfection.

In short, the traditional manager is usually passive, going through rituals and applying standard remedies to unique problems. By contrast, inside the mind of the lean manager lies a restless desire to continually rethink the organization's problems, probe their root causes, and lead experiments to test the best currently known countermeasures. When this lean mindset is coupled with the proper lean tools, amazing things are continually possible.

July 30, 2009

Homicide by Example?

In reading over the previous essay I find myself in agreement with everything I wrote. But a recent visit to the gemba has made me aware of one additional aspect of lean management thinking. Going to the gemba is a wonderful thing for every manager to do frequently, but it turns out that a can-do spirit to tackle every problem right now can carry an unexpected message if not tempered by respect for people, who always come first.

My LEI colleague Dave LaHote is fond of saying that managers—and especially senior managers—overestimate their effectiveness, particularly as they seek to improve their organizations through formal initiatives. And they under-estimate the impact (often negative) of their daily personal actions on employees. Recently I witnessed a striking example while visiting a metal-casting plant in a developing country owned by a multinational corporation headquartered in a highly developed country. (I hope you will understand why I'm careful not to identify places I visit unless I can offer praise. I try to show respect for my hosts when they allow me to be a guest at their gemba, and I truly want them to do better. Public shame and blame can never be an effective means to that end.)

The plant was in an inherently dangerous industry. So I was surprised and pleased to see a visual display at the entrance to the shop floor showing the causes of reportable injuries in the past month. It was very detailed and up-to-date. The senior plant managers accompanying me stated that it truly focused everyone's mind on safety and was part of a comprehensive safety-awareness program mandated by headquarters to reduce injuries.

But then I did some math. The chart showed that, in the last month, 12% of the plant's workers had lost days from work due to injuries! And the chart also indicated that this was a typical month. Simple arithmetic showed that the average worker could expect to be injured, to the extent of losing time from work, once every eight months! There seemed to be a yawning gap between the goals of the safety initiative and the results, and I wondered why as I continued my walk through the facility.

As it happened, the plant was experiencing a serious quality issue with its massive engine castings for heavy-duty vehicles. As a result, a senior manager from headquarters had just arrived. Our paths crossed at the shaking table designed to knock the remaining sand out of the castings as they tumbled down a chute from the molding operation. Just as I walked up, the senior manager was explaining that, to solve a problem, it was important to trace it to the source, which might be the shaking table. And suddenly this very large man mustered surprising strength and agility, and swung himself by an overhead bar up onto the shaking table while it operated, as massive castings tumbled down the chute and bounded across the table toward him.

At first I thought this was a crazy risking of this senior manager's own life. But then, as I turned to see the looks on the workers' faces as they stood watching him, I realized that it was more likely that he was risking their lives in the future. The official message of the company's senior management was that injuries were a top priority for management, to be reduced through a comprehensive safety program. But the actions of one senior manager—well intentioned in the sense that managers certainly should go to the source of problems rather than talk about them in a conference room—sent an opposite and much more powerful message: "If you want to get ahead around here you need to dive in and take action without regard to risks." Will this become, I wondered, a case of homicide by example?

This was a single and blatant instance, of course, and especially upsetting for me because I had just driven through the remote shantytown where the front-line workers lived, with little chance for good wages beyond this one plant. But I realized that I see less salient and dangerous examples all the time in my travels.

For example, recently I have seen many instances of managers trying to turn over a new leaf by embracing strategy deployment, A3 analysis, and standardized work (including for line managers) as part of comprehensive lean programs. And the workforce usually responds very positively. But then something goes wrong in the operation or the newly minted "lean" manager just gets tired after a long day. And the modern manager that lurks in us all springs forth to give top-down direction, to prescribe a solution before there is any agreement on the problem, or to resort to workarounds without documentation that undercut all efforts to impose standards. (I could relate more than a few examples from our own organization involving its leader—me—but will spare myself the pain. Suffice to say that I am often guilty as charged.)

Fortunately, I sometimes see counterexamples as well. A few weeks ago I spent a day with a CEO I will call Bob as he struggled to stick with his efforts to manage and improve his company's core processes by using A3 analysis. He was going against an entire work life of giving orders from his office and managing by results, and his A3s really weren't very good. He struggled in particular with getting to the root cause. And I noted that the other elements of his company's lean initiative were pretty rough as well, especially efforts to achieve basic stability in core processes.

But I was struck by Bob's doggedness, even at the end of a long day when many things had gone wrong and he was tempted to revert to old ways. And I saw the remarkable positive effect he was having on his direct reports, who were getting out of their offices and asking questions they had never asked before, while struggling with their far-from-perfect A3s. What I was seeing was the powerful impact of positive personal example in a situation where the formal elements of the company's lean initiative did not yet appear to be sophisticated or effective. I knew that a year or two from now, Bob's organization would be far down the path toward a lean enterprise while the casting plant would still have a glossy safety program with nothing to show for it.

So I urge everyone, and I certainly include myself, to do a bit of hansei (critical self-reflection) at frequent intervals. Ask a simple question: Is the message that I and the other leaders of my organization are sending through formal rules, programs, initiatives, and new management tools like A3, the same as the message we are sending daily through our personal example? And if not, what can we do to make our walk consistent with our talk?

July 13, 2010

As it happened, the casting plant I visited suffered an explosion shortly after my visit that injured many more workers. Apparently the elaborate safety program was still failing to improve safety despite the heroic stance of management. But at least the carnage was clearly displayed on the chart at the entrance to the plant floor!

As we approach the end of this section on management, two important issues remain. One is a clearer focus on what managers actually do that creates value. The other is a comparision of the modern management systems most of us grew up with in contrast with the lean management we will need as we move forward.

Although I've been thinking about these issues for years, I found in rereading the essays I wrote over the past decade that I never actually tackled these topics head-on. So I have prepared two new essays for this volume, the first concerned with what managers do to create value.

The Work of Management

When looking at a value stream, lean thinkers have the useful habit of asking, "What is the work to be done?" That is, which of the many activities occurring actually create value for the customer? And which steps are waste that can be eliminated? But I find that we rarely look at the process of management in organizations in the same way, asking of managers, "What is the management work to be done?" That is, what are the value-creating activities of the managers who oversee the value streams? It is only by being clear about which activities create value that we can eliminate the wasted efforts of managers.

What is the work of management? What value do managers actually create? My answer, informed by insights from John Shook, is that managers create value—that is, they do useful work—through four types of actions:

- *Gaining agreement on the few important things the organization needs to do.* This means focusing on how the organization can dramatically improve its ability to create more value, and the right type of value, with less time, effort, investment, errors, etc. Gaining agreement is predominantly the work of senior managers, using the lean management tool of strategy deployment. (But please note that the top managers don't decide in isolation about the few important things. Rather, they gain true agreement through catch-ball dialogue with different levels of the organization about problems and opportunities.)

- *Deploying the few important initiatives selected by strategy deployment, solving problems as they arise, and evaluating proposals from lower levels of the organization.* This is predominantly the work of middle managers, using the lean management tool of A3 analysis that puts plan-do-check-act cycles into an organizational and customer context.

- *Stabilizing the organization.* This means making every step in every process capable, available, adequate, and flexible so the value stream can flow smoothly from end to end and improvements can be sustained. This is predominantly the work of front-line managers, using the lean management tools of standardized work with standardized management and kaizen.

- *Creating the next generation of lean managers.* This is the work— perhaps the most important work—of every manager at every level, using the lean management tool of A3 analysis. New lean managers can only be created in intense dialogue between mentors and problem owners through many cycles of gemba learning.

If this is the work of management, how does my list compare with what managers actually do every day? In my experience, there is hardly any overlap. Most managers I observe spend most of their time with incidental work—box-checking, meetings that reach no actionable conclusions, report writing, personnel reviews that don't develop personnel, etc. And in the time left over they do rework. By the latter I mean the firefighting to get things back on course as processes malfunction. Most managers seem to believe that this is their "real" work and their highest value to their organization.

I see the gap between the true work of management and the things managers actually do as the muda of management, a vast reservoir of wasted effort and lost opportunities that we all need to address. Removing this muda is one of the greatest challenges facing our movement in the years immediately ahead.

November 2010
(original essay for the first edition)

Modern Management vs. Lean Management

Managers can only do their work in the context of a management system. This consists of all the roles and responsibilities of managers as they are connected to an organization structure that defines authority. In this essay, also written for this book, I contrast two remarkably different systems for conducting the work of management.

After a lot of walking through many organizations in recent years, I have concluded that the greatest impediment to the successful introduction of lean thinking is the modern management system that was pioneered early in the 20th century by General Motors and adopted by most organizations. This is the type of management that most of us have learned, either in school or on the job. There is, of course, a contrasting management system, pioneered by Toyota shortly after World War II, which facilitates the introduction of lean thinking.

Because this issue is so central to the success of the Lean Community, I thought it would be useful to provide a simple comparison of the two systems. In the figure shown at right on page 85, I have listed modern management practices on the left and compared them with the practices of lean management on the right.

This list needs some elaboration, so let me go through these points one at a time. In each case I will describe a modern management practice first and then compare it with an alternative lean management practice. As I do this I think you will find it useful—and entertaining as well—to determine what type of management system is in place at your organization.

Authority vs. Responsibility

Modern managers seek authority to take action by referring to the organization chart. The manager who thinks this way is essentially saying to the boss, "Don't give me the responsibility for any requested action without giving me authority over the people and assets involved."

Modern Management vs. Lean Management

Modern Management	vs.	Lean Management
Authority	vs.	Responsibility
Results	vs.	Process
Give answers	vs.	Ask questions
Plans	vs.	Experiments
Formal education	vs.	Gemba learning
Staffs improve processes	vs.	Line managers and teams improve processes
Decisions made remotely with data	vs.	Decisions made on the gemba with facts
Standardization by staffs	vs.	Standardization by line managers and teams
Go fast to go slow	vs.	Go slow to go fast
Vertical focus	vs.	Horizontal focus

Surely all of us have said this at least once—and probably often—in our careers in modern management organizations. Note the implication that tackling important problems going across departments and functions requires reorganization. Not surprisingly, I have found that endless reorganization is one of the telltales of modern management practice.

Lean managers seek responsibility to address important issues by leading as if they have no authority. Leading without the benefit of authority is actually critical in any organization because even in authority-based organizations managers rarely have control over everything touching a process. However, leading without authority is not seen as legitimate in traditional organizations and inevitably leads to conflict.

The uncoupling of responsibility from authority is perhaps the most important idea I have learned from John Shook, who learned it during his years as a manager at Toyota. The method that lean managers use to lead without authority is A3 analysis. As they work through the problem, the root cause, and the best countermeasures, in dialogue with everyone touching a process, they "manufacture authority" for making sustainable improvements.

Results vs. Process

Modern managers manage by results, to make their efforts look effective at the end of some reporting period (when the problems have already occurred). Unfortunately, there has never been a metric invented that can't be gamed in some way to make the results look better than they really are. As a car dealer once told me about the customer-satisfaction metric used by the car company supplying his vehicles, "It's a lot easier to fix the score than fix the store, so that's what I do, and I've been very successful."

Lean managers manage by process by knowing at all times the condition of their process (which produces the results) so problems can be solved and improvements implemented before rather than after the fact. This is based on the knowledge that a good process will produce good results.

Of course, in order to succeed the lean manager must deeply understand the process in question. This is the big impediment to managing by process in most modern management organizations, where traditional managers often seem to have only the vaguest notion of how processes work and are currently performing. I'll have more to say below on the practice of understanding processes.

Give answers vs. Ask questions

Modern managers give answers to their direct reports about the nature of a problem and its solution.

Lean managers pose questions to their problem owners about the nature of the problem and the best available counter-measures. Doing this automatically transfers responsibility for the problem from the higher- to a lower-level manager, who is closer to the problem.

In authority-based management, the higher-level manager maintains the illusion of being in control and accepts responsibility for subordinates' results, even though the best thing to do is usually impossible for the higher-level manager to know.

Plans vs. Experiments

Modern managers make grand plans, on the assumption that they will work because they are lengthy and detailed. The lower-level employee's job is then to carry out the plans, which should work because they have been carefully devised by knowledgeable people. This approach often leads to a focus on measuring compliance and determining who to blame when a plan fails.

Lean managers treat every plan as an experiment, with rigorous and continuing PDCA. This approach leads to a focus on discovering quickly how the plan is working (the C) and then—the truly important action (the A)—rapidly devising and implementing countermeasures as the plan, if it is like most plans, encounters problems.

Formal education vs. Gemba learning

Modern managers seek formal education to advance their careers, often outside the firm in management schools or inside the firm through executive education at a corporate "university."

Lean managers pursue gemba learning within their organization by participating in frequent A3 cycles throughout their careers, mentored by managers at the next higher level with longer experience in the enterprise.

Staffs improve processes vs. Line managers and teams improve processes

Modern line managers improve processes by outsourcing problems to staffs or consultants.

Lean line managers improve processes by directly leading improvement activities in dialogue with everyone touching the process, bringing in staff or consultants only as necessary on major technical issues. This practice is how lean managers gain deep knowledge of the process they are managing, and it seems so obvious that I marvel that I need to write it down. Yet I have walked through company after company in recent years where the line managers had neither the knowledge nor the intention to improve anything. They did, however, have advanced skills in delegating to staffs and outsourcing to consultants!

Decisions made remotely with data vs. Decisions made on the gemba with facts

Modern managers make decisions remotely, analyzing data, usually in conference rooms far away from the gemba. (This is often called "conference-room management.")

Lean managers make decisions on the gemba at the location of the problem, turning data into verified facts. The now famous mantra of "Go see, ask why, show respect" captures the spirit of gemba-based decision-making.

Standardization by staffs vs. Standardization by line managers and teams

Modern managers standardize processes by relying on staff experts. Or, more likely, they never make any serious effort to standardize the processes they are managing or their own management practice—which is itself a process requiring standardization.

Lean managers standardize processes through hands-on engagement with all of the people touching the process, using outside expertise only as necessary.

Go fast to go slow vs. Go slow to go fast

Modern managers go fast to go slow, because problems are never fully understood and the quick countermeasures put in place don't (and, in fact, can't) address the real issue, leading to time-consuming rework.

Lean managers go slow to go fast, by taking time at the outset to fully understand the process and its purpose, through dialogue with everyone involved (often including the customer and the suppliers) and by fully understanding the root cause of problems and the most promising counter-measure before taking action.

Since childhood I've had friends and colleagues who were "fast studies," seemingly able to analyze problems and take action faster than I could. And for years I felt bad that I seemed to be so slow. Then it suddenly dawned on me that these jackrabbits were mainly fast at driving into ditches because they never understood the problem with a process or even its purpose. They were jumping to solutions and then moving on before the results could be evaluated. So I was delighted when a lean manager in a company I was visiting finally formalized these alternatives for me.

Vertical focus vs. Horizontal focus

Modern managers focus vertically on the organization, with all the functions and silos oriented toward the CEO at the top. This fits in perfectly with authority-based management, my first point of contrast above.

Lean managers focus horizontally on the flow of value across the organization, from the initial concept for the product and the raw materials to the customer. This can only work by utilizing responsibility-based management where lean managers think horizontally to solve problems by dialoguing with many departments and functions over which they have (and can have) no authority.

Note that this last contrast is not just a matter of thinking. It must also be the way that managers act every day if value for the customer is going to be optimized by engaging all the people touching the process in steady improvement. It is the key to creatively fusing purpose, process and people in a lean enterprise.

November 2010
(original essay for the first edition)

Managing and sustaining a lean enterprise once created is a daily challenge. But creating such an enterprise in an organization grounded in modern management is a larger and different challenge. I view the former task as the role for management. The latter task calls for leadership, which by its nature is transformational. In the next section of essays I tackle the many aspects of lean transformation and leadership.

TRANSFORMATION

The U.S. Supreme Court Justice Oliver Wendell Holmes Jr. remarked at the end of the 19th century that "the life of the law has not been logic; it has been experience." He meant that people, including judges, change their views over time about the way things ought to be conducted in society, based on new experience. And the law ought to change (live) in response.

Let me paraphrase and shorten Holmes for present purposes by stating that "the life of lean is experiments." Lean practice must necessarily change over time as experimental evidence accumulates about tools, management methods, and the best approach to transformation. In the essays in this section you will find that I have gradually changed my views on lean transformation over the past decade—based on continuing observation of many experiments.

In particular I have adjusted my primary focus from applying tools to changing management behavior as the key issue in transformation. And I expect I will continue to modify my views in the future as evidence continues to accumulate. I hope this is your expectation and practice as well. Otherwise lean risks dying as a creative movement, becoming instead an arid dogma of rules to follow.

Shopping for a Sensei

This essay addresses a question about transformation that I was asked repeatedly in the early years but much less frequently today: "If I and others in my organization do not possess the needed lean knowledge to pursue our transformation, how do we find someone to teach us?" The question is still important, but I believe that many members of the Lean Community have gained access to enough knowledge to move beyond it. Nevertheless, I decided that this essay merits inclusion for those who are at the start of their journey.

I get a lot of requests to help companies find lean expertise. Unfortunately, I can't do what many of you would like: find just the right person to join your company or just the right consultant to share his or her learning curve with you. What I can do is to suggest guidelines for finding the lean "sensei" (Japanese for "teacher") you may need.

1. Start by asking whether you want to hire a senior manager to lead your lean leap as an employee or whether retaining a consultant would be better. The third approach is simply to do it yourself with the managers you have now, using the many available workbooks and learning resources.

2. If you want to hire someone, look at successful lean firms and figure out who was responsible for the transformation. (A good headhunter specializing in lean may be able to help you find good candidates.) But be careful: I have seen many cases of a lean firm like Toyota or Danaher where managers really only need to *maintain* a system set up by others some time ago. Taking these "steady-state" managers— very successful in an established lean environment—and asking them to create order out of chaos in your environment may be asking for more leadership than they can deliver. So be sure that both the lean skills and the ability to create change are equal to the job before you make an offer.

3. If you want to hire a consultant, ask yourself whether you want (a) an expert in what Mike Rother and John Shook call "process kaizen" who can apply specific techniques to specific problems (like cell design or 5S or standardized work), (b) an expert in what Mike and John call "flow kaizen" who can tackle entire value streams, from a single model line to a whole company, or (c) what I call a "kaikaku" specialist (a real revolutionary) who will show you the big picture by tackling all of your value-creating activities, horizontal and vertical, as a system to challenge all of your assumptions about your organization (including your management system) and thoroughly stir things up. Possibly you can find one person who can do all three, but be sure what your priorities are or you are likely to be disappointed with the results.

4. Once you are sure of what you want in a consultant, check the previous work of your candidates carefully by visiting the gemba at firms where they have been involved for a considerable period of time. Did they get sustainable results? And could they diffuse their knowledge across the client company? Or did they behave like classic skilled tradesmen who will solve a problem but never tell how it was done so it will always be necessary to call them back? (We call this latter phenomenon "consultant dependency.")

5. Once you are sure you have the right consultant or transformation leader, ask yourself how you are going to internalize their knowledge and diffuse it across your business. I continue to be amazed at how many companies think that once they retain a highly skilled consultant or a manager with lean experience they can simply set the lean transformation on autopilot and wait for lean thinking to deepen and spread. By contrast, the smart company assigns some of its smartest people to follow the sensei's every move, records the techniques and methods, and then systematically diffuses it across the organization. (Even Toyota did this with Taiichi Ohno, who was highly resistant to writing down the principles and techniques of TPS. One of the early assignments of Fujio Cho, who rose to chairman, was to follow Ohno around and make sure everything was recorded and shared.)

6. As you systematically record what your transforming manager or sensei is doing, challenge him or her with more and more difficult assignments on harder and harder problems. Stated another way, never ask your sensei to solve the same problem twice. Instead have the sensei solve a specific problem once, then challenge your people to solve it the second time, perhaps with a bit of coaching. This is the way to get the best use of your sensei, and a good sensei will respond to the challenge.

These are simple rules, and we know that they work. Together they constitute a simple "process"—that magic word—for finding the help you need. I wish you luck in your shopping!

Dec. 19, 2001

The next question has been asked by members of the Lean Community more frequently in recent years. It's about the sequence to follow in implementing lean in their organizations. And they ask because they get different advice from different sensei. (See: "Dueling Sensei and the Need for a Standard Operating System" on page 105.) Members of the Community seem to deeply desire a simple answer, a single "right way" that justifies their actions and protects them from criticism. Unfortunately, as I observe in the next essay, the right sequence always depends on the situation and the resources at hand.

The 'Right' Sequence for Implementing Lean

Recently I've visited two truly interesting operations, one in the U.S. state of New Hampshire, and the other outside of Chennai, India. Together they provide an important lesson about the best sequence for lean transformations.

In New Hampshire I visited Freudenberg-NOK's Manchester molding operation, which I have seen a number of times over the years. This facility started its lean transformation at the beginning of the 1990s with kaizen breakthrough projects under the GROWTTH (Get Rid of Waste Through Team Harmony) program to cellularize operations, and then introduced smooth flow of product families through the facility from cell to cell. Doing this highlighted the problems with product and machine design and led to a 3P (Production Preparation Process) initiative to get the next generation of product and process technology right. And recently, the Manchester facility has gotten serious about six sigma, getting scrap down to 0.7% (and even lower on some processes) from around 7% overall at the beginning of the 1990s. Note that the sequence for the lean transformation was kaizen to implement TPS, 3P, and six sigma.

This summer in India I visited a remarkable air-brakes plant belonging to the TVS Group, which is one of the leanest operations I have ever seen outside of Toyota City. TVS started its journey in the late-1980s with total quality management (TQM), focusing on process capability. In 1996 its brake plant became the first outside of Japan to win the Deming Prize. It then worked very hard at total productive maintenance (TPM) to make every machine available to make good parts whenever needed. And in the past four years, it has cellularized all operations, introduced standardized work for everyone, inaugurated periodic materials movements with tugger routes, and initiated a pure pull system all the way through the large plant and back to all of its suppliers. Note that the sequence was TQM, TPM, and TPS—the reverse order from the Manchester transformation.

My conclusion is that all of us making a lean leap will need to deal with capability issues (TQM/six sigma) and with availability issues (TPM) while removing wasted steps and introducing flow and pull in every value stream (TPS). My further conclusion is that there is no "right sequence" to follow in tackling these problems. Rather it depends on the nature of the product, the nature of the process technology, and the nature of the business.

Where there is a "right" vs. a "wrong" is with leadership and management. Each of these successes was undertaken at the urging of a strong change agent—Joe Day at Freudenberg-NOK and Mak Mahesh at the TVS group—and both firms focused on getting everything right for entire product families running all the way through the company, by means of strong value-stream management.

Oct. 11, 2002

Substituting Money for Value-Stream Management

By the time I wrote the following essay I was starting to see a disquieting pattern in lean transformation efforts. Whether the sensei was good or bad, the sequence was right or wrong, or kaizen was applied in the appropriate context, the focus seemed to be on pursuing a rigid program without regard to its fit with the underlying management system. In particular I saw more and more evidence that the metrics for judging management performance, which are the foundation of modern management, were getting in the way of doing the right, lean thing.

I recently visited a household-name American company trying to create a lean enterprise across its whole business after starting with an all-out six sigma initiative.

What I found is a pretty common pattern. Technical experts have conducted hundreds of six sigma projects across the company, many involving detailed process analysis to remove wasted steps and increase inventory turns. Meanwhile the senior manager of each facility and of each administrative department has been given a set of key metrics—each with a stretch goal for this year—and motivated by a bonus to reach the goals.

So what's wrong? My discussions with several facility managers quickly highlighted the problems. Each manager has multiple value streams running through his or her departmentalized facility, but the metrics are at the department or facility level. Thus, natural conflicts have emerged between what's best for the department or facility and what's best for the product as its value stream flows from start to finish through many departments and facilities.

But this is not the only problem. At a report-out meeting at the end of my visit, I asked the managers how they felt. The key word was "exhausted." A typical comment: "We started with lots of excitement, but we've got so many projects underway that we can't seem to get many of them finished. And we have a problem of rapid regression once a problem is fixed and management attention shifts to the next problem."

I felt a lot of sympathy with the facility managers and hourly associates, but not much for the senior managers leading the company. They are committing three common sins the Lean Community should be getting beyond:

- They have no policy-deployment process to prioritize the improvement initiatives and to narrow down to a short list of what can reasonably be accomplished and stabilized each year.

- They have no value-stream managers to look at the entire value stream for each product family, to optimize the whole rather than the parts.

- They have relied on multiple and sometimes conflicting metrics to get their facility and department managers to do the right thing. Yet they have not given them any useful training in how to actually improve performance. (My saddest moment came at a lunch with an able and energetic facility manager, who brought along his "stretch goals" chart as I requested. He reported that he is working 60 hours a week and has many improvement initiatives underway, yet has only been able to reach the stretch goal for one of the 15 metrics tied to his bonus. As it turned out, this was the only metric completely under his control. The other 14 required the cooperation of many departments and corporate functions.)

In short, exhortation, money, and advice from distant experts have been substituted for the organizational changes (particularly with regard to metrics), policy focus, and in-depth training of line managers in lean techniques that can actually produce results.

I hope you don't see your firm in this example. And, if you do, I hope you will take the appropriate actions so you can sustain your progress.

Nov. 13, 2002

We Have Been (Lean) Thinking

The preceding essay's observations from my gemba walks found their way into a revised version (2003) of my and Dan Jones's 1996 book, *Lean Thinking*. This essay suggests revisions to the action plan for lean transformation proposed in that volume.

Since writing *Lean Thinking*, Dan Jones and I have had a lot of gratifying experience watching members of the Lean Community resolutely apply the five lean principles of value, value stream, flow, pull, and perfection. We also have been encouraged by the efforts we have seen to apply the 21-step action plan to achieve lean transformations in organizations and all the way up and down value streams shared with suppliers and customers.

Since publication we have confirmed the fundamental soundness of the action plan. But we have also gained additional, important insights about nine of the 21 steps that should be shared within the Lean Community:

Find a change agent: We hope this person is you or that you are lucky enough to work for one. However, we've discovered that there are really two roles involved in creating permanent change: pushing the old ways aside and firmly installing the new way as a business system. In the most successful implementations we've observed, the visible change agent (let's call this person the leader) was assisted by system builders. These are the lean managers—sometimes behind the scenes—who methodically put all the elements of organization and method in place so the new system continued to improve even after the change agent moved on. In the absence of system builders, results often last only as long as the change agent/leader is in charge.

Get the knowledge: In a parallel finding, we've discovered that we are moving beyond the need for isolated process knowledge—how to create truly continuous flow cells, how to install simple pull systems—to the need for comprehensive lean system knowledge. That is, we are moving from process kaizen to flow kaizen, which is a job for line managers rather than lean experts operating in consultant mode or located in a lean promotion office. (These experts are still needed, but to solve higher-level process problems rather than to repetitively address lower-level process problems caused by a lack of effective line management.)

Seize the crisis: Moving all your manufacturing operations to the lowest piece-part cost location on the globe and operating there with traditional mass-production methods does not constitute seizing the crisis! You're probably creating the next crisis instead.

Map your value streams: The power of this simple rule is the most surprising thing we have learned in the past six years. We simply hadn't grasped how much help the average manager needs in learning to see the value stream or how eagerly managers would embrace Toyota's simple method for mapping information and material flows. Now if only every manager and every mapping team can achieve and sustain its beautifully drawn future state!

Reorganize your firm by product family and value stream: This is a great idea—if you can do it without creating enormous disruption. In the past six years we've discovered that some firms really need to send a message to their functions (e.g., engineering, purchasing, sales) to get behind value-stream thinking. A dramatic reorganization of this sort is certainly one way. However, we've also discovered the power of a different way: Appoint a value-stream manager for every product family's value stream and have this person take responsibility for defending the product's interests as it goes through a functional organization. Then create a chief value-stream manager (perhaps the chief operating officer) to aggregate the problems being discovered by the individual value-stream managers (which will probably be very similar) and take up these problems with the chief executive in conference with the function heads.

A chief executive wanting to confront a firm's functional sclerosis without the chaos of a total reorganization may be able to get the same effect through this method. And, by the way, this is how Toyota runs its predominantly functional business through the mechanism of the chief engineer for each car line who determines what engineering, purchasing, operations, and the other functions need to do to make the product a success for the customer and for the company.

Create a lean promotion function: We are now even more certain that every firm needs such a function, where its senior experts on every aspect of a perfect value stream—from quality to equipment availability to continuous flow and pull—can be located. However, we also know that the lean promotion group can never substitute for widely instilling lean skills in value-stream managers and function leaders. We've watched all too often as the "lean team" came to the scene in firefighting mode to push muda out of the way, as line managers, function heads, and production associates passively watched. We've also observed as competing experts within the lean group gave conflicting advice and thoroughly confused even those line managers who wanted to be actively involved. Our hard-won advice is to keep the lean team small and its message completely consistent. Then, as time goes on, focus it on higher-level problems as line managers become lean managers for routine tasks.

When you have fixed something, fix it again: This is an obvious point. Every future state for your value streams, as it is achieved, must become the new current state as you start the improvement cycle over again. But firms seem to forget the importance of this simple maxim. Recently we were delighted to look at a process at Freudenberg-NOK where five successive future states had been achieved over a full decade, with each future state moving the operation decisively ahead in terms of cost, quality, flexibility, and competitiveness. This firm provides striking evidence that if you think you can, you really can manage toward perfection.

Utilize strategy deployment: We have found this step the hardest to master even in our own nonprofit organizations. And we've also found that a failure to rigorously define and deploy strategy at the outset has been the root cause of every failed initiative. Our conclusion is that this truly is the key heavy-lifting job for the CEO and that it never gets easier as long as an organization is traveling through a changing market (which surely defines the path we all must follow).

At the same time, we've found that the plans so laboriously developed in the deployment exercise are soon in need of modification.

As a senior Toyota executive once pointed out, "Planning (in the form of policy deployment) is invaluable, but the actual plans are soon worthless." His point was that the real gain from the rigorous planning process is that every part of the organization is forced to become aware of the effect of its own actions on every other part. The result is that unworkable projects are deselected at the outset and all approved projects are developed with a viewpoint for the whole organization.

Convince your supplier and customers to take the steps just described: In the past six years we've gone through one more management fad with the dream of an infinite supply base managed with web-enabled reverse auctions. (Remember that the web can magically create a nearly infinite supply base for everyone if bids are accepted from practically anyone practically anywhere.) And we've learned again what we all should have known: Margin squeezing is easy but of little value while real cost reduction is highly valuable but hard.

To help entire value streams moving down the low-cost, high-quality, high-flexibility path, we have worked hard these past six years to create ways for firms sharing a value stream to hold a civilized conversation with each other. This conversation must focus on accurately determining the current state of the shared value stream and thinking creatively about successive future states, leading eventually to an ideal state. We think we've got the tool with extended value-stream mapping, described in *Seeing the Whole Value Stream*, and we are hopeful it will gain a wide audience.

Since *Lean Thinking* was published in 1996, it's amazing how much has changed. We've abruptly transitioned from a world where every new business model seemed promising and practically anyone could make money, even in manufacturing. Now we find ourselves bogged down in a world where most new business models seem foolish. And everyone in every business is struggling just to get by. The one constant in this sea change is the set of lean principles combined with the action plan. These ideas worked then and they work now for any firm in any industry willing to try them.

May 21, 2003

Additional reading:

Dan Jones and Jim Womack, *Seeing the Whole Value Stream* (Cambridge, MA: Lean Enterprise Institute, 2011).

Mike Rother and John Shook, *Learning to See*, (Cambridge, MA: Lean Enterprise Institute, 1999).

Jim Womack and Dan Jones, *Lean Thinking*, Second Edition, Chapter 15, *Institutionalizing the Revolution* (New York: Free Press, 2003).

Despite my confidence in the core lean principles of value, value stream, flow, pull, and perfection, and progress in refining the action plan, I continued to encounter situations I describe in the next essay: lean transformation efforts thwarted by abstract arguments between competing sensei about the single best way to proceed. This flies in the face of the simple proposition that the life of lean is experiments. All authority for any sensei flows from experiments on the gemba, not from dogmatic interpretations of sacred texts or the few degrees of separation from the founders of the movement. In short, lean is not a religion but a daily practice of conducting experiments and accumulating knowledge.

Dueling Sensei and the Need for a Standard Operating System

Recently I witnessed a sight I've seen too many times before. I was visiting a company when a new sensei arrived to advise on the firm's lean conversion. The first thing the sensei said to the vice president for operations was, "My method has nothing in common with the method of your previous sensei. You must now do everything my way."

The sad part was that both the new sensei and the previous sensei have strong Toyota Production System experience and approach most issues the same way. But the impression was quickly created that "lean" is not necessarily "lean," and the leaders of the company were thrown into confusion.

It's hardly surprising that sensei act this way. They maximize their power by insisting that only they understand lean thinking. What I do find surprising is that so many companies still depend on an outside source to define (and redefine) their fundamental operating system, their approach to process management and improvement. And if they do have a consistent approach they fail to write it down clearly and simply so that all managers can approach the same problem the same way.

Companies are not unaware of this issue, and many in the past have written lengthy manuals—the Ford Production System comes to mind—to set down the company's methods. But these were usually so lengthy and complex that few managers ever mastered the details. In addition, there was too big a gap between the high principles and the essential, day-to-day operating methods. Recently the trend seems to be toward shorter and more precise operating systems—GM's Global Manufacturing System comes to mind—that managers find easier to follow and that seem to be producing better results.

But most firms still have a long way to go. To judge how your firm is doing just ask yourself a few simple questions:

- "Do we have a standard, lean way to conduct plant operations that everyone understands and agrees on?"

- "Do we have a standard, lean way to interact with our suppliers on an operational level that everyone understands?"

- "Do we have a standard, lean way to interact with our customers on an operational level that everyone understands?"

- And most important, "Would a new manager just arriving at a facility or in a new area of responsibility immediately know what to do, as prescribed by our operating system, and do it the standard way?"

Please note that this is not a recipe for rigid, top-down rules, developed by a staff group and unrelated to actual conditions. Rather, it is a prescription for a top-down, bottom-up process—led by a company's senior operations managers—to precisely define a company's operating system, to get agreement from everyone that it is currently the best known way to conduct operations, and then to teach it to every manager.

Of course, it is then important to continuously conduct experiments —that's what kaizen is—to search for better operating methods and to incorporate new methods in the standard system once they are proved superior. This is where an outside sensei is often most helpful, to spur thinking about better methods.

Sept. 11, 2003

As a result of more gemba walks, in which I observed organizations trying to implement lean methods on a foundation of chaos, I started to wonder if most transformation efforts were starting in the wrong place and, therefore, never moving far beyond their starting point. The next essay tackles this problem.

Mura, Muri, Muda?

When my first daughter was born in 1986, the young men I supervised in MIT's International Motor Vehicle Program went dashing out of the office to buy her a gift. They returned shortly with a pink T-shirt, size one, with the stenciled message on the front: "Muda, Mura, Muri."

My wife was bewildered—"Is this how guys welcome a baby girl?!" But I could understand. We had made an intense effort that summer to grasp these new Japanese terms for waste (muda), unevenness in demand not caused by the end customer (mura), and overburdening of people and equipment (muri). These terms had entered our lives when John Krafcik joined our team from NUMMI, the Toyota/GM joint venture in California. The boys just wanted to share their enthusiasm and took the first opportunity at hand.

Our understanding at that time was that "muda, mura, muri" was a logical improvement sequence for lean thinkers. And we suggested starting with muda, which is any activity that is waste because it doesn't add value for the consumer but does consume resources.

Conveniently, Taiichi Ohno at Toyota had long before provided a list of the seven types of muda that was an excellent guide for action. So we urged managers to immediately tackle overproduction (beyond what the next customer currently needs) plus unnecessary waiting, conveyance, processing, inventory, motion, and correction.

An additional virtue of starting with muda was that many types could be removed from a narrow area without the need to coordinate with the larger organization or across firms. For example, machines could be moved together quickly in a kaizen exercise to create a cell—to eliminate the muda of waiting, conveyance, inventory, and motion. And this could be done without disturbing (or getting the permission of) the broader production system. We believed that the progressive elimination of muda would pave the way for tackling mura and muri.

That was the theory. But now it's striking to me how much effort we've expended on eliminating muda and how little attention we have given to mura and muri. As a case in point, the American car companies announced [in July 2006] new incentive schemes that will sell a large number of vehicles over a brief period, running down excessive inventories. This will lead to additional overproduction at the factories, which will lead to more inventories, which will lead to more incentives, which will lead to ... [as we now know but I strongly suspected then, the collapse of Detroit and the ultimate mura].

Meanwhile this unevenness in sales and production that is quite unrelated to any desires being expressed by customers (a common type of mura) will undercut the efforts of the entire organization—from sales to purchasing—to eliminate muda (waste).

And in most companies we still see the mura of trying to "make the numbers" at the end of reporting periods. (Which are themselves completely arbitrary batches of time.) This causes sales to write too many orders toward the end of the period and production mangers to go too fast in trying to fill them, leaving undone the routine tasks necessary to sustain long-term performance. This wave of orders—causing equipment and employees to work too hard as the finish line approaches —creates the "overburden" of muri. This in turn leads to downtime, mistakes, and backflows—the muda of waiting, correction, and conveyance. *The inevitable result is that mura creates muri that undercuts previous efforts to eliminate muda.*

In short, mura and muri are now the root causes of muda in many organizations. Even worse they can put muda back that managers and operations teams have just eliminated.

So I would give some different advice to the boys at MIT if they were preparing that T-shirt today. I would tell them to have it read "Mura, Muri, Muda." (Although the mother wouldn't be any less bewildered.) And I have the same advice for managers—especially senior managers—trying to create lean businesses:

Take a careful look at your mura and your muri as you start to tackle your muda. Ask why there should be any more variation in your activities than called for by customer behavior. Then ask how the remaining, real variation in customer demand can be smoothed internally to stabilize your operations. Finally ask how overburdens on your equipment and people—from whatever cause—can be steadily eliminated.

This will be hard work, and will require courage because it will often require you to rethink longstanding sales, management, and accounting practices that create the mura and muri. However, if you can eliminate mura and muri at the outset to create a stable environment for your sales, operations, and supply-management teams, you will discover that muda can be removed much faster. And once removed it will stay removed.

July 6, 2006

The one thing most lean practitioners have seemed to agree on is that kaizen is the path to transforming processes and organizations. And kaizen is a wonderful thing. But as I walked through organization after organization, observing their kaizen efforts, I began to see that there was an additional dimension to transformation and a proper context for kaizen. This is the subject of the next essay.

Kaizen or Rework?

I recently visited a contract electronics manufacturer with a striking capacity for kaizen—the steady improvement of every step along its key value streams. Dozens of kaizen events were being performed across the company to eliminate wasted steps and to remedy quality, availability, adequacy, and flexibility problems in each value stream. At the same time, kaizen teams were trying to speed continuous flow and to perfect pull systems when flow was not possible.

The managers were pleased with their work, and I had to admire both their technical skills and their enthusiasm for rapid improvement involving the employees touching each value stream. However, I also noted that most of the value streams being improved were for products that had been launched recently. I wondered why so much kaizen was necessary.

Indeed, I pondered whether the kaizen effort was analogous to old-fashioned, end-of-the line quality inspection in mass-production organizations. Value streams for new products were being put in place without adequate thought to lean principles or sufficient rigor in thinking through the details of every step and action. Kaizen teams were then inspecting the processes once in operation, finding them far from lean, and launching waves of corrective action.

Given that many bad practices had been built into the value streams, these kaizen efforts were necessary and highly productive. But why wasn't the organization performing lean process design as an integral part of the development process? And was the organization's skill in after-the-fact kaizen—that is, its talent for process rework—actually reducing the pressure for the hard conversations about lean process development that ought to be taking place during product development instead?

As I've reflected on this situation, I've wondered if the practices of Toyota and other lean pioneers have been misunderstood. Kaizen is an important activity at Toyota and involves all employees. But new processes launched at Toyota are usually extraordinarily lean to begin with, and postlaunch kaizen is a small part of Toyota's competitive advantage.

The secret lies in Toyota's product/process development system that focuses on creating "profitable operational value streams"—to use a favorite phrase of the late Allen Ward. These streams have been thoroughly "prekaizened" by examining every step in the proposed production and fulfillment process long before launch.

The first step is to make sure someone is responsible for thinking about the whole process needed to bring a new product from order to delivery. By thinking about the production process at the same time the product design is being evaluated, it's possible to optimize both.

The second step is to lay out the process on paper and consider the different ways that it might be conducted. For new types of products requiring new processes it is particularly important to consider a number of different ways the whole process and each step might be conducted and to conduct simple experiments to see which way works best. (This is the process development analogue of the set-based concurrent engineering methods used to evaluate different approaches to the design of the product. It's also a key element in the Production Preparation Process (3P) now conducted by advanced lean organizations.)

The third step is to test new ways of conducting process steps with simple prototypes—even cardboard mockups—to learn how well they actually work. (Another element of 3P.) The knowledge gained from these experiments then needs to be written down and turned into the experience curves of the sort Toyota develops from experiments with simple prototypes of new products.

(In fact, this knowledge is Toyota's great advantage in concurrently and rapidly developing new products and processes. At this point, most of Toyota's production processes are highly standardized and fully documented. Most new product designs only need to comply with well-understood process requirements to launch as smoothly flowing streams. By contrast, most organizations I visit have poorly documented processes with weak standards and little real knowledge of tradeoffs in designing a process one way vs. another. They will need a lean leap in consciousness and practice in order to catch up.)

Once the best process is determined, which may result in changes to the product design as well, the next step is to finalize equipment designs and information management systems.

Finally, it's time to develop standardized work for every step in the value stream and standardized management for the whole value stream. This includes a training plan for every employee, a plan for every part, and a maintenance plan for every piece of equipment.

If all of these actions have been completed by the start of production, the value stream should be very lean from the first item delivered. Kaizen will still be important, based on hansei (reflection) about the performance of the process once operating. But it can start from a higher level in a more stable process so that additional rapid improvement is actually easier.

It's my feeling that many organizations are now ready to elevate their level of play. As I hope I've made clear, this does not entail de-emphasizing the idea of kaizen, but rather performing the PDCA process that is at the heart of kaizen inside the development process. This will insure that every new value stream for every new product commences its productive life as a lean stream.

Given the steady reduction in the length of product lives, I believe that it will become ever more important to achieve "process quality at the source." Otherwise, the product may be ready to go out of production before process problems are ever addressed through kaizen as rework.

Aug. 22, 2007

Additional reading:

Allen C. Ward, *Lean Product and Process Development* (Cambridge, MA: Lean Enterprise Institute, 2007).

The Worst Form of Muda

By this point in my observation of transformations I was seeing very clearly that to get off dead center and move down the path, it is necessary to remove a special type of waste. This essay presents a striking example.

I recently traveled to India where I added some new souvenirs to the collection I have assembled from every country I have visited: special reasons why lean is impossible in local conditions.

At a series of conferences on lean thinking, a number of senior Indian managers explained that their organizations don't have the discipline to create and operate a lean enterprise. Others solemnly told me that a lean logistics system would be quite impossible on India's chaotic and crowded roads. The media—who everywhere seem to focus on bad news and impossibilities—seemed to agree. Every interviewer started by asking me how undisciplined Indian managers using chaotic Indian infrastructure could hope to copy Toyota, Honda, and other lean organizations.

This is all part of what I think of as the worst form of muda: Thinking you can't. This of course guarantees you can't. Henry Ford probably said it best when he noted, "Whether you think you can or whether you think you can't, you're right." Thinking you can't is the worst form of muda because it thwarts your tackling the other, more-familiar forms of waste.

The fun in collecting these defeatist sentiments is that it is always possible to demonstrate at some place in the country in question that they are completely wrong. Indeed, this is one of the most important tasks of the lean institutes around the world.

As part of my Indian trip I visited the WABCO-TVS manufacturing facility outside Chennai. (See "The 'Right' Sequence for Implementing Lean" on page 96, for my reactions on an earlier visit.) The managers there decided in 2000 that they could create a lean enterprise. I first visited this facility in 2002 and found that they were well on their way. And I am happy to report that because they thought they could and continue to think they can, they have largely succeeded in the manufacturing portion of their business.

At the outset they retained a few foreign advisors with good lean educations but quickly internalized what those advisors had to teach. They then embarked on a rigorous strategy deployment exercise to determine which steps should be taken in what order, based on business needs, to transform what had been an orthodox mass-production manufacturing operation.

Eight years later they have achieved basic stability (capability plus availability) in each manufacturing step. This has permitted them to successfully cellularize and introduce single-piece flow in all machining and assembly operations, accompanied by precise standardized work. It has also permitted managers to install a pull system throughout the facility using kanban and water spiders moving products and information at frequent intervals, with very little work-in-process inventories. Meanwhile, visual controls have been installed to a remarkable degree, 5S is maintained, and every production employee from top to bottom participates in a kaizen activity every week.

What I always find the most fun in manufacturing transformations is when I encounter machines and tools made by the plant that are right-sized, capable, available, flexible, and cheap. As C. Narasimhan, the former head of the operation and the force behind the transformation, remarked during my tour, "Why do 'catalogue' engineers buy fancy machines that immediately need unnecessary kaizen in order to work properly in their context? Why not just build them right from the beginning?" And this facility has done just this, with many examples across the operation.

Meanwhile, downstream toward the customer and upstream to suppliers, WABCO-TVS has been introducing frequent deliveries to precise customer need using milk runs on chaotic Indian roads. A small amount of safety stock is needed beyond what would be required in a less taxing environment. But the system works just fine, reducing total inventories and costs while improving quality through rapid feedback.

WABCO-TVS is not perfect or complete. The lean transformation in product development, supplier management, and business processes outside of production still lies in the future. And a problem-solving culture at every level of management is a work in progress. Therefore the management team has a list of additional actions to be taken in the next year, even as the company grows steadily to meet rising demand. These actions are clearly shown on simple charts in a situation room, broken out by specific tasks for each area of the organization. This makes visual one of the most comprehensive and disciplined strategy deployment processes I have found.

Future challenges notwithstanding, the operations aspect of WABCO-TVS is "lean" by any reasonable definition and getting steadily leaner. This remarkable feat has already been achieved in a country where many managers still think it will be impossible.

Let me conclude by hoping that you and the management of your organization think you can. Every company in every country can come up with unique reasons why it can't. Yet all we need do to remove the world's most harmful form of waste—the one that prevents our tackling all of the others—is to reboot our thinking and point ourselves resolutely in the right direction by acting on the deeply empowering belief that we can.

Aug. 14, 2008

Constancy of Purpose

After more years of watching experiments on the gemba, it became clearer to me that one of the admonitions in the original action plan for a lean transformation that Dan Jones and I enunciated in 2006 was in need of modification. It turns out that even the most able transformational leaders need more then the five years we had allotted to complete a lean transformation. It follows that sticking to it is a critical element of success, as discussed in the next essay about constancy in pursuing organizational purpose. Getting the right thing done—whatever it might be—through constancy of management focus is critical to a successful lean transformation.

The first of Dr. W. Edwards Deming's 14 Points is "create constancy of purpose for continual improvement of products and service to society." When I first read this many years ago it seemed so simple and obvious. How could anyone not have constancy of purpose?

Now that I'm older and wiser, or at least older, I have discovered that this simple attitude is often the missing element when managers set out to create a lean enterprise. Organizations start with the best intentions, launch a lean program, gain some initial results, lose their focus (perhaps as a result of an economic crisis when many employees are let go?), and backslide to their original state of performance. They then set off again with the best intentions. The power of constancy of purpose hit me with particular force recently when I visited a firm that started its lean journey 14 years ago and has truly practiced Deming's first point. I found the story so compelling that I would like to share it.

It's about Bob and Ed, although these are not their real names. In June of 1995 Bob approached me at a conference I had organized and announced emphatically that he was going to create a true lean enterprise. Because I had heard this statement of good intentions many times before and because Bob was only a plant manager in one business unit of a corporation with many business units and plants, I told him frankly that I doubted he would get anywhere. But I pointed out a few other people at the conference he might talk to if he needed specific advice on how to get going. And I never expected to hear from him again.

About two months later Bob called to announce that he and his controller Ed had gotten started in their plant and that they wished me to inspect what they were doing. Then they wanted me to give a pep talk at a business-unit-wide operations event for all plant managers as their first step in spreading the word.

I went with some trepidation. There is nothing more awkward than visiting eager managers in the first flush of lean enlightenment who need to hear how little they have actually done and how far they need to go.

But at least I was not disappointed with the opportunities at hand. Their massive facility was organized in process villages for all fabrication activities. An inaccurate MRP scheduled all operations, there were turnbacks everywhere for rework (not planned by the MRP), there was no visible standardized work, and there were large inventories between each processing step and assembly step. The facility had approximately 0.5S (as opposed to 5S), the primary workforce was disengaged, and the management team below Bob and Ed was firefighting with no focus on the big issues. The predictable results were long lead times, poor on-time performance to customer schedules, costs much higher than necessary, and a company in financial distress. In sum, everything that could be wrong was wrong with the exception of a few model areas where Bob and Ed had tried their first experiments.

The one thing the plant did have going for it was Bob and Ed's constancy of purpose. As I walked through the operation, I quickly realized that I had been wrong at the conference. As I met the team they had formed, saw the boldness of their initial experiments, and felt their extraordinary intensity, focus, and tenacity on the gemba, I knew they would get somewhere and that it would be worth my while to observe. So I have been back four times over the years to check on their progress.

What did they do? Their first step over the first four years was to identify the basic product-family value streams and to create flow by removing unnecessary steps and lining up the remaining steps adjacent to each other in process sequence.

As they did this they soon learned that they needed to create basic stability by making each step both capable (in terms of good quality every time) and available (in the sense that every piece of technology was able to run when it needed to run to support flow in the process.) Achieving this by introducing rigorous standardized work, quality at the source, and a plan for every machine was their second step. This was pursued not just in one plant but across the business unit as Bob and Ed were promoted to lead Operations and Improvement for all of the subsidiary's facilities.

Four years into their transformation (which was already much longer than most lean journeys last), Bob and Ed were ready for a dramatic third step, which was to introduce rigorous strategy deployment at every level of the company. (Today their strategy-deployment process is the most rigorous and comprehensive I have seen. As I recently talked with those working on this year's strategy deployment in different streams, I realized again that if strategy deployment isn't driving you crazy, you aren't doing strategy deployment. This is because the whole idea is to flesh out for resolution the contradictions and conflicts between value streams and functions that remain well-hidden in most organizations.)

As the organization rolled out strategy deployment, it also instituted a rapid problem-resolution process, and redoubled the focus on standardized work. These are versions of the three key lean management techniques we advocate at LEI: Strategy deployment cascading from the top with feedback loops to set direction and gain alignment. A3 analysis to deploy the policy initiatives from above, resolve problems in day-to-day operations, and evaluate proposals from below. And standardized work with standard management and kaizen to sustain capability and availability while steadily improving performance.

As a fourth step in their transformation, Bob and Ed then reorganized the entire $1 billion business into a number of horizontal value-streams with dedicated engineers, production teams, purchasing, etc.

Their two final steps in creating a lean enterprise were to transform the product and process development process to incorporate lean principles and to convert a very conventional purchasing organization into a lean supply management team. The last step is just being completed after a 14-year journey.

With the complete lean business system now in place, the current challenge facing the management team is to globalize operations and the supply stream. Their objective is to better support customers around the world without losing the hard-won, line-of-sight ability to deal with problems in real time.

A final challenge lies not far ahead—one few organizations have faced. How can Bob, now the president of the business unit, and Ed, now the vice president of operations, hand off the lean journey to the next generation of management as they approach retirement age?

Bob and Ed's journey is inspiring. Indeed, as I look at the last 14 years, I ask what would have happened to the world economy if every plant manager and controller had had their constancy of purpose to completely transform an entire management and business system. What if by doing this every manager in every firm had increased labor productivity nearly sixfold, cut the needed space per unit of output by 75%, achieved nearly perfect quality with 100% on-time delivery to customers, steadily improved margins, and rapidly grown sales? We would be living in a very different and much better world. So following their path must be the challenge for the rest of us.

As we set off, I need to emphasize one additional point, perhaps the most important. Bob and Ed started their journey in the trough of a major recession in their industry. As their firm struggled to fund development programs in 1997, it was acquired by a giant firm completely unaware of what they were doing and managed on different principles. Most managers would have been completely distracted—like most managers today at this traumatic point in history? They would have lost their concentration, just trying to get through the day under new ownership. But these managers had set a course, and they sailed steadily ahead through some rough seas.

This is the real challenge for all of us now—to seize the current crisis, set a steady course, and turn today's chaos to a useful end.

Feb. 11, 2009

Now that Bob and Ed have started giving public presentations about their journey, I can reveal that Bob is actually Greg Peters and Ed is actually Martin Lodge of Goodrich Corp. Subsequent to the writing of this essay Greg was promoted to leadership of the operational excellence program for the entire Goodrich Corp., while Martin continues as the vice president of operations at Goodrich Aerostructures. The latter is the business unit where Greg and Martin conducted their many experiments starting in 1994 when Greg was a plant manager and Martin was the plant's controller.

After walking the gemba on every continent except Antarctica, I'm still pondering why transformation is so much harder than it should be. In this last essay on transformation I arrive at my current hypothesis about the root cause: the horizontal nature of the lean thought process in a vertical world. Stated another way, it's a matter of the needs of the process (as reviewed in the set of essays on process) running into the needs of traditional organizations and managers (as described earlier in the essay "Making Everyone Whole" on page 41). What's needed to bridge this gap and continue the transformation is the value-stream manager, a currently rare species.

Becoming Horizontal in a Vertical World

One of my favorite value-stream walks is with the senior managers of several organizations who share and jointly manage a value-creating process that stretches all the way from raw materials to the end customer. I've been taking walks of this sort for more than 20 years, and I usually see the same thing: smart, hard-working managers, each trying to optimize their portion of the value stream. They also wonder why there is so much inventory, interruption, and waste along the stream and why it is so hard to truly satisfy the customer waiting at the end.

This is what I usually see because we live in a world where everything is oriented vertically—departments, functions, enterprises, and, very important, individuals—despite the fact that the flow of value to the customer is horizontal across all the departments, functions, and enterprises. And—here's the really odd part—every manager and employee touching the value stream knows intuitively, just below the surface, that value flows horizontally and that customers have no interest at all in the vertical constraints interrupting the flow.

So what's the problem? Why is it so hard for us to act horizontally rather than just work around (or simply ignore) the enormous problems of being vertical?

I hate to say, but the problem begins with you and me. We are all points along the stream, standing tall in our own estimation, and our first objective is to optimize ourselves, our own point! Given this, it's not surprising that we first seek to optimize our department (where our boss, our personnel evaluation, and our career path reside) and then our function and then, maybe, our enterprise, with no energy left over for optimizing the whole stream.

But let's not be too hard on ourselves. Our personal objectives, compensation, and career trajectories strongly direct us to look up, for fear of falling down, rather to look from side to side, in hopes of doing better. We aren't so much bad people —at least I'm not!—as good people working in a bad management process. However, unless we can devise a new framework for thinking together about the horizontal flow of value in a way that makes everyone better off, we will all continue to act as we always have. The predictable result is frustrating work lives and an exasperating experience for customers.

How can we do better? The first step is simple. Take a walk together along the stream to see, and to reach agreement on, what is really happening and the problems the current state causes managers, employees, and customers. Then draw a map that everyone touching the stream can see, and post this as the baseline. This step always produces amazement and then relief that all of the dysfunctions and conflicts are finally out in the open.

Next, make someone responsible for leading a team involving every function and firm touching the value stream to envision a value-creating process that better solves customer problems while saving time and money. Then ask why this can't be created and seek the root cause. Part of the problem may be technical, and some outside help may be needed when skills are lacking. But in my experience, the critical problems are more likely to be organizational across multiple functions and enterprises. For example, money may need to be spent at one point (for facilities, equipment, training, new packaging of goods, etc.) and behaviors may need to change at this or other points to create a better result for the whole stream.

But why would the managers of the factory or the warehouse or the retailer do this when all of the benefit goes to one or a few points elsewhere along the stream? And why would employees cooperate in rethinking work when they may individually have more work or no work at all? The answer, of course, is that they won't, and everyone involved will spend their time instead on explanations of why the failure to improve performance is everyone else's fault. A classic prisoner's dilemma in which everyone gets to stay in their vertical jail!

So the job of the value-stream manager—who it should be noted has no authority over most and perhaps all of the departments and firms involved—is to take responsibility for the performance of the whole value stream and discover ways to make everyone along the stream whole as the stream is improved. In the end, the senior leaders of all the departments, functions, and firms will need to agree with the plan, arrange compensation mechanisms for those who would otherwise be losers, and make sure that everyone touching the stream has incentives aligned with the goal of optimizing the stream.

But the first steps are to raise consciousness, create the vision, highlight the problems to be overcome, identify the costs of improvement along with the benefits of success, and describe the ways to offset costs with benefits to achieve a positive-sum solution. Without taking these initial steps, starting with a simple walk together, we will all continue along our vertical path, where value-stream performance is a stagnant, horizontal line.

May 18, 2010

DIFFUSION

Transformation, as I used this term in the previous section, is about leaders converting individual organizations from modern to lean. By diffusion I mean something quite different, notably the spread of lean concepts from their point of origin in manufacturing operations to every process in every organization and to every sector of the economy.

Transformation is mostly the work of individuals. Sometimes a few heroes really are needed as well as a lot of farmers. But diffusion is better thought of as a social process in which new ideas originating on the manufacturing gemba influence practices in other parts of manufacturing firms and in sectors of the economy far from manufacturing.

In this section I examine the process of diffusion—remember that transformation and diffusion are both processes—in the office inside manufacturing firms, in the upstream activities of the supply base, and in the downstream activities of the service organization. Then I look at the process of diffusion to activities far beyond manufacturing, ranging from air travel to healthcare. Finally, I ask why entrepreneurs can't start and sustain every new business as a lean enterprise rather than creating a traditional business that soon needs transformation.

Lean Beyond the Factory

Lean thinkers have made big strides in recent years in creating smoothly flowing product family streams running horizontally across production operations. However, these primary processes in the factory are only a small fraction of the total value-creating processes within manufacturing firms. And until recently the lean movement has had little to say about the other processes, often hidden from view in the "office."

About a year ago [in 2003], I spoke to the senior management of General Motors about the challenge of "leaning" the office. The occasion was the launch of an ambitious effort to apply the lean-thinking principles of GMS (their Global Manufacturing System) to every office process in GM. It is hardly possible to quickly "lean" every process in a vast business like GM, but the results to date have been quite remarkable and have caused me to think about broadening the focus of the lean movement to include the entire range of business processes.

I hadn't pursued this before because of horrible memories of business process reengineering. This consulting phenom-enon came roaring through North America and then Europe during the recession of 1991–92, when many big companies were desperate to cut costs at least as fast as sales were falling.

The idea—as popularized by Michael Hammer and James Champy in the best-seller *Reengineering the Corporation*—was for special teams of process reengineers (often led by outside consultants) to analyze key processes, identify the waste, and quickly remove it to create smoothly flowing processes at much lower cost.[7]

The problem was that most of the reengineers lacked a credible method or any experience, and they gained little cooperation from employees. In the end, many employees were laid off to meet consultant promises to management for almost instant paybacks on investment. But few processes were successfully reengineered. In fact, the most enduring

7. Michael Hammer and James Champy, *Reengineering the Corporation: A Manifesto for Business Revolution* (New York: HarperBusiness, 1994).

effect of this episode was the American comic strip *Dilbert*, created by Scott Adams, whose beleaguered protagonist first came to public attention as the dogged survivor of reengineering efforts in his office.

This experience was so negative that I was reluctant for the lean movement to tackle office processes until experience was gained about how to improve processes the right way, using a rigorous method and with employee buy-in. During the past year, as I have watched the GM experiment, I also have heard frequently from lean practitioners around the world who are moving from the factory into the office. As a result, I have concluded that we now have the knowledge, and that it's time to expand our scope.

As with any lean effort, the key steps are to:

- Identify the key processes to tackle (in the same way we draw up a product family matrix in the factory).

- Draw an accurate current-state map of each process.

- Apply the key lean principles to envision a leaner future state for each process.

- Implement this future state in a way that can be sustained.

However, there is a special challenge at the very outset. This is to clearly identify the value emerging from each office process, most of which are support processes with no cash-paying customer outside the organization. In one notable instance at GM, senior management concluded that an expensive process consuming many hours of management time actually created no value for anyone. Rather than improving it, the answer was to eliminate it. As you contemplate leaning your office processes, just remember that in the absence of value, everything is muda.

March 23, 2004

Manage the Contract or Improve the Value Stream?

The previous essay describes the challenge of diffusion across entire manufacturing firms, but diffusion is also needed upstream to every supplier. This has proven remarkably hard to do as witnessed by the fact that I hardly ever encounter a truly lean purchasing organization. This is the case even in firms that have made great progress in leaning their production, product and process development, and offices processes. The challenge of upstream diffusion is the topic of this essay.

As much as I would like to, I can't walk along every type of value stream frequently. As a result, it has been a while since I've walked along the extended value streams shared by customer firms with their suppliers. So when several firms recently offered me a chance to take multi-organization walks—from the point of customer use back to the beginning of the suppliers' manufacturing processes—I was delighted to put on my walking shoes and stride along with teams from the customers and suppliers.

As I walked I was quickly reminded of how easy it is for all of us to focus on formal measures of value-stream performance as written in contracts: defects delivered to customers per million opportunities; price per piece, often without reference to what is happening either to customer volumes or upstream materials costs; and delivery performance, often to a materials-requirements planning (MRP) schedule that has little relation to actual customer needs at the point of use. These indicators can sometimes be useful, but they always measure results after the fact, when mistakes have already been made. More important, they say nothing about causes of problems or how to eliminate them.

As I walked I also was reminded how hard it is for customer purchasing organizations and the supplier sales organizations they usually interact with to talk in specifics about their shared value-creation process and the root causes of problems, ideally before they occur. In times of gyrating customer volumes and raw materials costs for suppliers, the result is often a zero-sum ritual of customers making threats (based on penalty clauses in contracts) and suppliers making promises to do better (based at most on a hope and a prayer).

This is actually all shadow boxing because without careful attention to the shared design and production processes, little improvement in performance is possible. In the short term, the customers have nowhere else to go, and the suppliers can't do any better. So both sides get the satisfaction of some cathartic mud wrestling while nothing actually changes.

How can we all do better? Well, first, we can't instantly. The short-term future is determined by decisions made long ago. So contracts with their penalty clauses rule. But we can do better in the intermediate and long term if we shift our focus from wrangling over contracts (reflecting arms-length, abstract legal relationships) to managing shared value streams by jointly observing the actual supply process.

To do this the customer needs to take the first step. Taiichi Ohno at Toyota believed that the shop floor is a reflection of management. Let me add a corollary: the supply base and the performance of value streams shared with suppliers are a clear reflection of the customer's purchasing management. A brilliant supply base with superior prices, quality, delivery, flexibility, and product performance doesn't happen magically. And it can't be bought off the shelf instantly by visiting some virtual "supplier supermarket." It is created over time by a brilliant purchasing organization. Indeed, creating a brilliant supply base is the real (and only?) value created by purchasing.

So how do we begin the transition from managing contracts to improving value streams? First, the customer needs a "plan for every supplier," just as a lean organization has a plan for every part, every machine, every employee. This means determining the right suppliers to work with over the long term and then understanding the current state of every supplier's design and production process for the items supplied.

Many years ago, when I first visited Toyota in Japan, I had dinner with the purchasing director. I asked how he could be sure that Toyota was getting good performance from its suppliers when only two suppliers were employed for a given category of need and when Toyota relied on target pricing rather than supplier bids. "How," I asked, "do you know you aren't getting ripped off?" After an incredulous look, he answered, "Because I know everything—every aspect of every value-creating process—running from raw materials at suppliers through Toyota's operations. That's my job."

In practice, achieving this means continually determining the performance gap between what the supplier's value stream is capable of delivering and what the customer needs. Then it requires a future-state plan for who will do what when—both at the customer and at the supplier—to achieve a future-state value stream adequate to the customer's current and future needs.

But creating a lean supply stream also means that purchasing needs to look inward for a bit of organizational hansei (critical self-reflection) inside its own company walls. Why are schedules from production control so erratic and inaccurate? Why aren't orders to suppliers leveled? Why are the logistics to get items from suppliers to the point of use so loosely managed? Why are design requirements for supplied items frozen so late in the development process? Why is the customer's production process so poorly designed and in need of immediate kaizen after launch, upsetting the production process at the supplier (whose process also is poorly designed, in part due to the lack of customer attention)?

The typical reaction of purchasing organizations when I make these points is to say, "Wait a minute. We just obtain needed items from available suppliers and bargain hard to get good terms in contracts that we can enforce. We have no mandate to look downstream into our organization or upstream into what suppliers actually do in their value streams to meet our needs. And we certainly can't afford to build long-term, stable relationships with suppliers as markets continually gyrate." And I respond, "Well, fine, but you will always have a lousy supply base with poor performance, and you will spend your time chasing parts."

So it's really a matter of what purchasing organizations think they should do and what they think they can do. Perhaps you remember Henry Ford's aphorism that you can think you can or you can think you can't, and you will be right (see "The Worst Form of Muda" on page 113). (But please forget that Henry actually thought he couldn't create a brilliant purchasing process and, therefore, vertically integrated instead!)

In today's world, we know that vertical integration won't work. Deintegration is here to stay. Purchased items account for half or more of most organization's total costs plus a large fraction of their quality, delivery, and responsiveness problems. So we all need to think that purchasing organizations can create and sustain brilliant supply bases.

Doing this will take time and upfront investment, but the cost of not acting is far greater over time. So wherever you are in your organization and whatever your organization's current relation to its suppliers, I hope you will lend a hand to help with the diffusion of lean supply.

Sept. 16, 2008

Even when organizations successfully diffuse lean thinking upstream, they are still far from what I would call "lean enterprises." This is because value is defined by the end customer. The mura, muri, and muda in the value stream needs to be removed all the way to the customer, and the customer's definition of value must be respected before any organization has a right to label itself "lean." The next two essays tackle this problem, which has proved to be as difficult for lean leaders like Toyota and Honda, in their operations outside of Japan, as for other firms.

Even when organizations and their upstream partners in value creation are willing to take an extended walk along their shared value streams, I find that following the stream all the way to the end customer is often the greatest challenge. This is because production and customer support are often conducted by independent organizations. But it also is because confusion about value and purpose becomes more important and apparent as we approach the end customer.

In the next essay, I talk about this pervasive problem in today's world, even in the case of the best companies, and suggest a tool for addressing it—the end-to-end, value-stream map.

Thinking End to End

Every value stream runs from raw materials all the way to the end customer. And value for the customer is only delivered at the very end.

In many service industries, of course, the "raw material" is information rather than molecules—like the data in the claim application processed by an insurance company. But the situation is the same. Value is only delivered at the end of the stream.

Today I see a lot of progress in applying lean thinking to segments of value streams, even across functions within firms. But optimizing the entire stream as it flows *between* firms—to truly solve the customer's problem while helping all the providing organizations to prosper—still seems to be elusive.

Take the case of motor vehicles. As customers, we want to obtain a physical object called a car or a truck. But the real problem we are usually trying to solve is personal mobility: We want to get places cost-effectively with no hassle or wasted time. So the processes of buying the vehicle and then keeping it running through an extended life are critical parts of the complete value stream. This total stream must link the car manufacturer's design and production processes to the car dealer's sales and service processes.

I've been looking at the data collected by J.D. Power and Associates on customer satisfaction, by brand of vehicle, with the car-buying experience and with the car-service experience in the United States. And I've been comparing this information with data on satisfaction with the vehicle itself. Not surprisingly, Toyota continues to capture top scores for satisfaction with the vehicle among brands sold in the United States. Its Lexus brand was No. 1 in 2006, while Toyota was No. 4 despite some recent problems with recalls. These data are for problems encountered with the vehicle in the first three months of ownership, and the results are similar after three years. Lexus buyers report the fewest problems while the Toyota brand is in fifth place among the 37 brands in the market.

But the service experience at Toyota dealers—as tracked by the Power Customer Service Index—ranks 27th among 37 brands. (Lexus is

No. 1.) And the buying experience at Toyota dealers—as shown by the Power Sales Satisfaction Index—ranks 29th out of 37. (Lexus is No. 2.)

What's worse, as Dan Jones and I report in our recent book, *Lean Solutions*, (where we provide data collected by the International Car Distribution Programme) all 37 brands are terrible at meeting customer needs *cost-effectively*! Thus Toyota dealers are performing poorly in a race where no one is doing well.

In sum, Toyota solves half the customer's problem by delivering high-quality vehicles. But it is still struggling to solve the whole problem by perfecting the entire value stream of the vehicle plus sales and service.

How can this be? And how can Toyota's performance in its largest market—the United States—be so different from its performance in its home market in Japan where the Toyota buying and service experience is legendary for the customer satisfaction it provides?

The heart of the problem, I think, is that Toyota dealers in Japan are co-owned by Toyota. So applying process thinking to the selling and service processes is much easier: The dealer really must listen. In the rest of the world, car dealers, for all brands including Toyota, are independent businesses. And, in my experience, most car dealers—certainly not just Toyota dealers—are "hunters." They focus on making the sale at an advantageous price and moving on to the next sale. What's needed instead are "farmers" who carefully study their selling and service processes to completely solve every customer's problems throughout the life of the vehicle.

So the simple fact is that, because Toyota dealers have had a superior product to sell, they could afford to treat the customer poorly. The combination of a high-quality vehicle plus inferior sales and service—which comprise the total customer experience—was still competitive in the marketplace. What's more, the dealers erroneously believe that creating a superior buying and use experience must cost them money.

Lexus dealers, by contrast, treat their customers well. But they seem to achieve this by spending more on sales and service, not by creating smooth-flowing, lower-cost value streams. With a higher-priced product, they can afford to do this despite the waste in their processes.

We now know that the belief that better sales and service costs more is simply wrong. *In fact, better sales and service, like better quality in products, actually costs less.* This is because large amounts of wasted time and effort for dealers and customers can be eliminated through careful process analysis. Dan Jones and his colleagues at the Lean Enterprise Academy in the United Kingdom have clearly demonstrated this through their work with the GFS car-dealing system in Portugal, where one-third of the cost of providing a given amount of service was removed even as the level of customer service was dramatically improved.

Now that other manufacturers are closing the gap with Toyota brands on delivered defects and product durability—look, for example, at the recent progress of Hyundai—Toyota needs to "lean" its value stream all the way to the customer. And I don't doubt that Toyota will try, given its long tradition of brilliant process thinking. But what about the rest of us, whatever industry we are in? Almost all firms in today's deintegrated world either reach their end customer through other firms or obtain the items they need to solve their customers' problems from many suppliers. The end customers—that's you and me in our role as consumers—are only interested in the value delivered at the very end of the value stream. And we certainly don't want to hear about the difficulties that retailers, distributors, manufacturers, and suppliers are having cooperating with each other to solve our problems.

So the challenge now for all of us—no matter which customers we serve—is to begin conversations across firms about optimizing total value streams. The best approach is to take a walk together, backward from the end customer (or, even better, *with* the end customer), in order to draw an accurate map of the total value stream with all its short-comings. Then it's time to talk seriously about how to create a smoother-flowing, higher-quality, lower-cost value stream that can be a win-win-win for providers, their suppliers, and consumers as everyone learns to think end to end.

Aug. 11, 2006

Additional reading:

James P. Womack and Daniel T. Jones, *Lean Solutions* (New York: Free Press, 2005).

The Missing Link

Even when there is a will to walk all the way to the end of the value stream, there is still a need for a rigorous method for analyzing and improving the customer support process. Fortunately, several lean thinkers have taken on this challenge, which is the topic of this essay.

I have a great stove, not that I cook that much. It's shiny, sophisticated, and full of capabilities, most of which I never use. I've been very happy with this brilliant object and its manufacturer for more than five years. Until, that is, the last few weeks when it needed its first repair.

I called the service organization of the manufacturer and arranged a technician visit after a number of calls and callbacks. When the technician arrived it was easy to identify the problem. Indeed, I had accurately described the problem over the phone. But the technician hadn't gotten the information and didn't have the right replacement parts. So a second visit was arranged.

On the second visit the technician thought that the parts were right but the installation instructions were somehow incomplete. After a lengthy phone discussion with the technical-support organization at the manufacturer—which I was paying for because the technician was charging by the hour—the parts were installed. And they promptly failed. They weren't the right parts after all. So a third visit was arranged.

"Three times perfect" is a common expression in English, although as mysterious in its precise number as the Five Whys, six sigma, and seven wastes. And this seemed to be the case this time. The new parts were installed, the stove worked properly, and the job was finished. Except that the technician—who finished up the job while I foolishly stepped away to do some work—forgot to align the heavy, hard-to-move stove properly with the kitchen counters, leaving it sticking out with a large gap at the rear. So a fourth visit was arranged. (So much for the magic of three.)

Now everything is fine. But look at the unnecessary time and cost, both for me as the customer and for the service organization. And I see this sort of drama all the time: Faltering technical support for computers and IT links at the office. The inability to keep those moving jetways, walkways, and escalators at the airport actually moving. The brilliant "lean" machine I examined on a recent value-stream walk in a very lean factory that was unavailable due to a mysterious series of breakdowns.

My conclusion: There is a missing link between the world's brilliant objects—now cheaper and better in many cases because of lean thinking applied to their design and manufacture—and support for these objects in customer hands through their useful lives.

Lean thinkers now need to bridge this gap, and I am happy to report that Dave Brunt and John Kiff at the Lean Enterprise Academy in the United Kingdom, in collaboration with Dan Jones, have recently formalized a process for highly effective customer support. They have conducted a series of experiments to apply lean thinking to car repairs, and what they have learned deserves to be widely known because it is so powerful and so useful to anyone in any customer support business.

The place to start is by drawing a map of the current state of the car-maintenance process. This consists of all of the steps—value-creating and wasteful—currently required from the time the customer calls for an appointment until the vehicle is given back to the customer at the end of the repair cycle.

Once the map is drawn, it is time to ask how well the process is performing to deliver value to the customer as well as good business results for the provider. Determining this requires going far beyond typical customer satisfaction measures ("rate your satisfaction with your dealer's service on a scale of 1 to 10") to discover how frequently a service job is performed right the first time on time (RFTOT).

RFTOT is rarely measured by dealers or car companies but is the underlying basis of "satisfaction." And be prepared for the worst: surveys across the world by the International Car Distribution Program consistently show that car repairs are only performed RFTOT in six cases out of 10. That's 1.75 sigma!

No process can be improved if the work needing to be done is a continuous surprise with no opportunity to plan. Fortunately, by careful "prediagnosis" of vehicles coming in for repairs it is possible to predict which vehicle will need what type of service and to preorder parts. Prediagnosis involves a careful telephone or email discussion with the customer about the nature of the problem using a checklist administered by a staff member with sound technical knowledge. A second customer contact just prior to the service confirms there are no new problems (and also increases the likelihood the vehicle will be brought in on time). And an inspection of the vehicle the moment it arrives at the dealer confirms the diagnosis and provides the customer with the precise cost of the repairs.

A few types of jobs account for a large fraction of total car repairs. For example, mileage- or time-based tuneups on vehicles that are otherwise running fine. By creating different value streams—one for high-volume jobs which can be done quickly, another for more complex jobs that can be accurately prediagnosed, and a third for jobs where the problem is not known prior to detailed investigation in the service bay— it is possible to smooth and speed the flow of work for most jobs with tremendous benefits for customer response time and process productivity.

Even with the best prediagnosis and assignment of jobs to the correct value stream, flow can still be disrupted if the right parts, tools, technical information, and technicians aren't available at the moment the work needs to be done. (Note my frustration with my stove repair. Even when I tried hard to help the provider prediagnose my problem, the right parts and information still weren't available. This brought the job to a halt and necessitated a time-consuming restart.) So the provider must have a robust system for pulling all the needed items to the point of use at just the right time.

And finally, every step in the process must be capable, in the sense of perfect quality at the source, in order to increase velocity while avoiding rework at the end of the process or once problems are discovered by the customer.

Achieving all of these objectives requires that someone be responsible for the performance of the entire service process and that visual measures be put in place, such as schedule and progress boards, so that the status of the process is instantly visible and any problems are traced to their root causes.

The consequence of creating a lean stream is that maintenance and repairs can be done RFTOT in a vastly higher fraction of cases at dramatically lower cost. David Brunt and John Kiff have recently verified this hypothesis through their experiments with car dealers in Europe, raising RFTOT on vehicles that could be prediagnosed from 60% to 94%, and cutting the cost of the typical repair by 30%. A win-win for the customer and the service providers.

So instead of being fatalistic about the potential for lean maintenance and repairs in the organization where you work, I hope you will help take the lead in applying lean customer-support techniques. You will be building a stronger enterprise. And as other organizations follow your company's example, there will be an extra benefit. You will have helped build a more satisfying life for yourself as a consumer.

Feb. 7, 2008

Additional reading:

Dave Brunt and John Kiff, *Creating Lean Dealers* (Goodrich, UK: Lean Enterprise Academy, 2007).

If we allow ourselves to dream for a minute, we can easily imagine creating lean enterprises running from the customer back to raw materials in the world of manufactured products. But this great achievement would still leave the great majority of the world's value-creating activities untouched. Diffusion really becomes a serious and powerful phenomenon when the Lean Community turns its efforts to transforming the world of services. I have therefore devoted a number of my essays to lean diffusion in different sectors. Air travel has been one of my favorites, perhaps because I have written most of these essays while flying to and from my gemba walks. However, diffusing lean further and further from its point of origin will never be easy.

Lean Thinking for Air Travel

Recently I got a call from an aide to the chairman of American Airlines. This person wanted to apply lean thinking to air travel and asked what I thought about their "lean" idea.

It turned out that American was making plans to smooth the flow of passengers and aircraft through their major hubs in Dallas and Chicago. The idea was to spread out arrivals and departures so that planes would come and go at a fairly steady rate through the day, rather than in the massive waves required by classic hub-and-spoke systems. (They apparently thought this was some type of heijunka.) The new approach would require fewer gate staff, and airplanes would wait in shorter queues to take off (possibly permitting the airline to squeeze in one more roundtrip per plane per day). What the aide wanted was for me to certify that this was "lean" air travel.

I responded, as I always do, "You should start with value from the standpoint of the customer. Does this proposal make the passenger better off, and will the passenger be willing to pay for it?" And it turned out that rolling pulses are actually designed to make better use of airline assets. The traveler arriving in a hub to change planes could now expect somewhat smaller crowds, a somewhat shorter takeoff queue, and … a longer wait in the hub to make connections. Who knows whether travelers would think this is a good trade, but no one at the airline was even asking about customer value in a period when cost reduction seems to be most airlines' only approach to survival.

So let me apply lean thinking to air travel by asking the two questions American should have asked:

What does the traveler really want? My answer is that there are two distinctly different types of travelers. One—the leisure, price-sensitive traveler—wants the lowest price to get safely from A to B. The opposite type—the executive traveler who thinks his or her time is worth a lot of money—wants the fastest way to get safely from A to B. (And note that each of us may shift from being one type of traveler to the other, depending on the purpose of our trip.)

The problem with hub-and-spoke airlines is that they are trying to serve both types of passengers with practically the same product, adding a slightly wider seat, free drinks, and an airport hub club for the executive traveler. As a lean thinker would state it, they are comingling value streams that really ought to be separated. Even worse, these airlines charge the executive traveler, who can't book ahead or stay over a Saturday, several times the price for practically the same product.

Hub-and-spoke airlines have built enormous amounts of waste into their value streams for both types of travelers because to take a trip anywhere the traveler needs to make two flights—one from the origination point to the hub for cross-docking (or self-sortation in this case) and the second from the hub to their destination. When you add in the long changeover times for current aircraft designs (where hundreds of passengers must squeeze through one tiny door to get on and off) and the massive capital and operating costs for the sortation centers (where I think of myself as a package with feet), it's not surprising that most travelers are unhappy, either because the product costs too much or because the trip takes too long.

What would the lean thinker propose instead? It's actually pretty simple:

1. Disaggregate the value streams for price-sensitive and time-sensitive travelers.

2. Fly everyone point-to-point using different types of equipment.

3. Develop aircraft types that can be quickly turned (changed over) between flights.

Southwest, JetBlue, Ryanair, and easyJet have been moving steadily ahead to introduce point-to-point travel for the price-sensitive traveler. And we can expect their efforts to continue in the years ahead. However, as I experience these carriers, their efforts have only gone half way. They only serve markets where they can generate five roundtrips per day with aircraft carrying 90 to 150 passengers. And their turn times have slipped steadily from the 15 minutes Southwest originally claimed to 30 minutes today. Why can't they offer the same service cost-effectively with smaller jets so they can serve many more points, and why can't they work with aircraft makers to design planes that can be turned in 10 minutes or less. (Dr. Shingo's SMED applied to aircraft-setup reductions!)

At the same time, why doesn't someone—anyone, please!—use smaller commuter jets in a way that actually makes sense by offering scheduled business-class, point-to-point service for executive travelers from the secondary airports (grossly underutilized) in every metropolitan area? If travelers could park near the plane, go quickly through security, and avoid takeoff queues, it ought to be possible to cut turn times and airport waits to only a few minutes. Indeed, by using small terminals, arriving only a few minutes before the flight, and flying point-to-point, it should in many cases be possible to cut total trip times in half compared with hub-and-spoke systems even though the airplanes fly no faster.

These are simple ideas: Ask what the passenger truly values and where the waste lies preventing the provision of this value. Then rethink operating methods and staff roles. (Purpose, then process, then people!) It's amazing how easy lean thinking can be if only managers can forget about their existing assets and traditional methods for a moment and give themselves the freedom to dream.

May 5, 2003

After many years of trying—I even spent a lot of time some years ago brainstorming with an entrepreneur trying to create a "lean" airline for business travelers—I'm forced to admit that to date there has been no progress. (About the only good thing to say about this is that my travel time never seems to get shorter, so I have plenty of time to write.) However, before declaring defeat, let's examine a different type of service activity—healthcare—that until a few years ago struck me as equally hopeless.

Creating Lean Healthcare

In 1997 I made a visit to the Mayo Clinic's large medical complex in Rochester, MN. I was not there as a patient. Instead I was a sort of lean anthropologist. I was making my first foray into a major medical organization to examine its thought process and behavior from a lean perspective.

The trip was arranged by Dr. Don Berwick, the founder and president of the Institute for Healthcare Improvement in Boston. [Don was recently appointed Director of the Centers for Medicare and Medicaid Services by President Obama.] Don had just convinced me that I should start LEI as a replacement for my former home at MIT. He asked me to ponder a simple question: How would a major medical system go about implementing lean thinking across all of its activities? (As Don put it, "In healthcare we have no Toyota to copy. We don't even have a Yugo. So where do we start?")

As always, I took a walk. Over two days I followed a number of patient pathways as well as pathways for medical supplies, patient schedules, and specimens going through the laboratories. (Call these pathways value streams if you prefer.) And I soon reached a diagnosis: severe sclerosis of patient and support pathways.

At Mayo (and in the many medical organizations I have visited since), I found brilliant doctors who were point optimizers, focusing solely on their narrow activity without much thought (or patience) for how it meshed with the other activities around them. The hospital's administrators, by contrast, were asset optimizers, trying to keep every expensive machine, hospital room, and specialist busy, even if this meant delays for patients and heavy burdens for staff. The nurses were the members of the organization thinking about patient pathways and about core support processes like handling supplies and drugs. But they were doing this intuitively and reactively to somehow keep things moving. They lacked recognition of the importance of their task and a rigorous methodology.

Together, the brilliant doctors, diligent administrators, and long-suffering nurses were providing healthcare that cost too much, took too long, and often produced less than optimal outcomes. To make a lean leap, everyone in the organization would need to change their way of thinking and acting.

My prescription was simple: Identify all major patient pathways as well as support streams. Map them from end to end. Then ask how each pathway can be cleared of its blockages, backflows, and cul-de-sacs for the benefit of the hospital, its staff, and its patients. Finally, and most important, ask what changes in management will be required to keep the pathways clear.

What troubled me was not the diagnosis or the prescription. I was pretty sure I was right. What I worried about was the prognosis. My recommendations would require everyone—doctors, nurses, and administrators (and suppliers, too)—to change their behavior, their organizational lifestyle. And as medical professionals know, lifestyle change is usually the hardest part of any treatment.

Given the difficulties involved, I ended my first venture into healthcare in May 1997 thinking it was premature to hope for much progress toward lean healthcare. I didn't return to Mayo until last week [April 2007], when I spent a day with Dr. Henry Ting, a cardiologist with a natural instinct for process thinking. We looked carefully at the work his team has done recently to speed patients from the point they suspect they might be having a heart attack—usually far from a hospital—to the point where all appropriate treatments have been applied.

The results are quite dramatic. Rethinking this pathway saves lives—many lives—because the more quickly appropriate treatments are applied the more likely the patient is to survive and to survive without major heart damage. And here's the really encouraging news: a lean pathway reduces costs for the hospital and makes life better for the staff. It's a win-win-win. My skepticism on my previous visit was replaced with hope after this visit.

But I also realized while flying home that Dr. Ting's team had performed a brilliant procedure on one of the easier problems to fix and sustain. They had analyzed a single pathway, one where the value of saving time is so overwhelmingly obvious that any medical organization will find it hard not to change its behavior once the sclerotic state of the existing pathway is clearly revealed. (In fact, this new approach is now being successfully applied throughout Mayo's cardiology practice and by similar pioneers along other pathways in many healthcare organizations across the world.)

The hard part for all of us is to tie together these pioneering, single-pathway efforts—which seemed beyond our grasp only 10 years ago. We need to create a complete lean enterprise in which all pathways have been permanently cleared and the lifestyle of the organization has been changed as well. This will require more than lean techniques. It will require new management methods and a new type of transformative leadership.

These are the most important value streams in our lives. Indeed, they often determine the length and quality of our lives. As I told an Australian healthcare audience recently, "Toyota takes better care of car parts than most healthcare organizations take of their patients." This is not right! We know how to do better and have a moral obligation to do so.

So I'm deeply encouraged that lean thinkers in the healthcare community are at last tackling the world's most important value streams. But I'm also concerned that we will stop short, with single-pathway interventions. And I'm worried that improvements in individual pathways can't be sustained because the organizations in which they reside have not changed. What the patient—the whole healthcare system—really needs is to rethink management and leadership so we can truly create and sustain lean healthcare.

May 3, 2007

The Tipping Point?

The previous essay was written at a time when lean thinking was just getting a widespread hearing in healthcare. I find it quite amazing that only three years later there has been an explosion in interest driven by the realization that the current system can't deal with cost and quality challenges as the baby-boom generation approaches retirement and economies stagnate in all of the developed countries. One of the many dramatic experiments underway is described in this essay.

Because of my longstanding desire to apply lean thinking to healthcare, I was overly optimistic about the first experiments, beginning with hospitals in Seattle in the mid-1990s. (See "The Problem of Sustainability" on page 68, for a brief description of what happened.) When these efforts faltered I was overly pessimistic—despite telling myself to practice emotional heijunka—and began to wonder if perhaps healthcare was immune to the lean virus. But experiments continued (see previous essay, *Creating Lean Healthcare*) and, gradually, after many more false starts, ideas born in the factory were adapted to the bedside.

It took even more time to develop lean management methods in a craft industry with no standardized work, few publicly reported outcomes, and little ability to think horizontally about the flow of patients through the diagnostic and treatment processes. And, until recently, the economic context of healthcare had not changed. Governments and insurers were willing and able to pour unlimited amounts of money into healthcare providers to pay for services, and they demanded little in the way of better outcomes in return. So why should healthcare organizations tackle the daunting challenge of lean transformation when the mediocre providers could survive and even prosper?

Now the context has totally changed. The United States spends more than 16% of its gross national product on healthcare—twice the level of other advanced economies. Yet the demand for healthcare will spiral rapidly upward as 24 million additional citizens enroll for subsidized health insurance and the baby boom marches resolutely toward a life stage where healthcare needs multiply. Given the spending limits the U.S. government is facing and voter resistance to additional taxes, the only alternatives in the absence of dramatic service-delivery reform are price controls, rationing, and denial of the care just promised.

Fortunately lean thinkers, after 15 years of experiments, now have the tools to reform healthcare delivery. In the last few years lean healthcare proponents have demonstrated that costs can be dramatically reduced as outcomes and patient experience are dramatically improved—a feat traditionally thought to be impossible. They have also shown that steady progress can be sustained in complex healthcare organizations.

One of the best demonstrations is the experiments at the ThedaCare medical system in Wisconsin, recently described by Dr. John Toussaint and Roger Gerard, PhD, in their book, *On the Mend*.[8] I believe this volume will have a profound effect by summarizing the principles of lean healthcare, documenting their benefits with striking examples, and providing an action plan for other healthcare organizations to follow to achieve similar results.

The four principles that John and Roger have applied over the past decade are simple and they work:

1. Focus on the patient (not the organization and its employees, the insurance industry, the drug companies, etc.) in order to determine the real value desired. Then,

2. Identify the value streams (or patient pathways) that provide this value in order to identify where value is actually created while removing massive amounts of waste (including the large numbers of errors causing rework that drives up costs).

3. Reduce the time required to go from start to finish along every pathway (which always creates more value at less cost).

8. Dr. John Toussaint and Roger Gerard, PhD, *On the Mend* (Cambridge, MA: Lean Enterprise Institute, 2010).

4. Pursue principles 1, 2, and 3 endlessly through continuous improvement that engages *everyone* touching the patient pathways—doctors, nurses, technicians, managers, suppliers, and patients *and* their families.

Humans will try anything easy that doesn't work before they will try anything hard that does work, and that's where we have been in healthcare. But all the easy fixes have now been tried and only the hard things that work are left. And the hardest part of the hard work ahead is that everyone has to change their behavior:

- The doctor accustomed to craft methods with no rigorous outcome measures;

- Medical device makers accustomed to providing new equipment without regard to cost or clearly demonstrated benefits;

- Nurses hoping that daily workarounds in the delivery process will somehow make fundamental problems go away; and

- Administrators hoping that somehow costs can be reduced with higher capacity utilization by simply running the same broken processes harder—regardless of the effect this may have on patient and staff experiences and errors (which dramatically increase costs).

The final challenge is that everyone in healthcare must learn to think horizontally [as discussed in several previous essays]. Managers, doctors, and nurses must learn to see patients flowing across complex organizations rather than reverting to their traditional vertical thinking where every department and activity is a castle with its moat, thwarting the patient's quest for more value with less time at lower cost.

Despite the hurdles ahead, I'm hopeful once more that the availability of proven lean methods will push providers past the tipping point on the journey to lean healthcare, now that all the easy fixes have failed and there is no other option.

June 10, 2010

Additional reading:

Dr. John Toussaint and Roger Gerard, PhD, *On the Mend* (Cambridge, MA: Lean Enterprise Institute, 2010).

Marc Baker and Ian Taylor, *Making Hospitals Work* (Goodrich, UK: Lean Enterprise Academy, 2009). (For a provocative treatment of the issue of horizontal, end-to-end patient flows through complex, vertical organizations.)

It is important to emphasize that these are still early days for lean healthcare. Most of the important experiments are just underway or are still to be run (in the case of end-to-end value streams). And we would not want to make the mistake that many healthcare practitioners have fallen into in the past of ignoring the scientific method while claiming that victories have been achieved but with no rigorous outcome measures.

It would be so much easier if we could just start from scratch with no assets, no bad habits, and no malfunctioning organizations. But with a few exceptions—ThedaCare, for example, has built a completely new hospital starting with a clear statement of purpose and fashioning a building to support visual control and the horizontal flow of value—we can't. But when we can, we should, which requires diffusing lean thinking to one last frontier —the startup entrepreneur. This is the topic of the final essay in this section.

The Joy of a Greenfield

Last spring on a trip to Central America, I encountered that wonderful sight for process improvers, a "greenfield." And I literally mean a green field. It was behind a hospital operated by a nongovernmental organization (NGO) where I was volunteering my time. The problem I was assigned was to dispose of 15 years of personal medical records in a country with no recycling. The standard way to dispose of waste in this country was to simply dump it down a ravine to form a landfill without any top cover. But this, thankfully, was not acceptable for medical records containing personal information about past patients at the hospital.

So what to do? The correct thing, of course, would have been to create a lean recycling program of the sort Lean Institute Brasil (*lean.org.br*) recently established. (It's in a poor Sao Paulo neighborhood and provides employment to residents with difficulties entering the formal labor market, such as persons being released from prison.) But I had only a week to complete several tasks at this NGO, and this was not going to be possible.

Upon reflection, the least bad thing to do was to burn the records. So I soon set out with the hospital's warehouse manager (who had been keeping the records in a storage building bursting at the seams) and a small team to figure out how to do this. The manager suggested that we use the open field of scrub grass behind the hospital since there was no incinerator on the grounds.

In the spirit of going to see and asking why, we went to the field, and I asked the small team what we should do. Their answer was to remove the records from their folders (which could be reused), scatter them on the ground, and light them. Pretty simple. But this soon proved to be completely ineffective unless we were going to stand around burning documents one page at a time. Dropping burning documents on the ground more than one page deep caused the fire to smolder and go out.

Fortunately, there was an old oil drum in the trash pile at the edge of the field plus a couple of concrete blocks and a steel pry bar. Within a few minutes we had created a simple incinerator and the team was happily dumping the records in the top of the drum. Indeed, they were dumping stacks of documents so energetically that the fire soon went out for lack of oxygen.

A second round of "go see and ask why" led to the realization that the documents needed to be crumpled to let air reach each page, not dumped in batches. And they needed to be fed into the drum steadily to exactly match the combustion rate if we were to keep the fire burning smoothly and minimize the time needed to get the job done. But how to do this with the least human exertion? (It was a very hot day.)

The answer was to divide the labor. One person removed the records from the folders, a second and third person crumpled the papers and threw them into the fire, a fourth person stoked the fire with the steel rod to knock the ashes out the bottom and keep air flowing, and a fifth person fetched and opened more cartons of records. As it turned out, if the barrel was placed in the sun away from the nearest tree but everyone else stood in the shade of the tree, it was possible to have a hot fire and a cool workforce. Soon—after a third round of experimentation to standardize and balance the work—voila! We had created a lean destruction line and all of us working together at a steady pace got the job done in hours rather than the expected days.

This was a small-scale but still satisfying example of applying process thinking to the world's work. But what was really striking to me was how easy it was to create a relatively lean process almost instantly. The reason was that no inappropriate assets and no managers and work team with carefully learned bad habits stood in the way. (This situation, of course, is what most members of the Lean Community face every day.) Why can't it always be this way?

This summer in Boston I had a second experience that raised this same question on a much larger scale. Three young entrepreneurs called to ask how a lean thinker would go about starting a greenfield business. They invited me to a test site for a new restaurant chain they are raising funds to start, and we thought through the application of lean thinking to the core processes of this business. These include staff selection and training, work design including the daily work experience of staff, logistics to get materials into stores and the waste out, setup of new stores (because they want to grow fast with minimum cash tied up in stores not yet open), and the customer's consumption process and experience (which interacts with the store's production process and staff experience). In only a couple of hours it was easy to think of ways to launch the business with robust, lean processes that would also require less capital.

Why, I thought, doesn't every startup start lean, rather than growing to considerable size before management realizes that key processes are broken or balky, interfering with continued growth and profitability? And in mature businesses, why doesn't every new product requiring a new production and delivery process start lean at Job One?

The answer, I think, is that most of us in the Lean Community learned our skills by reworking broken processes. That's what we feel most comfortable doing. And maybe we even have a financial and psychological bias: it takes a lot less effort on our part to get the job done right from the beginning than it does to do kaizen as rework to get it right much later.

But mainly, I think, we simply have never learned how to speak to the entrepreneur starting a new business or the chief engineer leading a team to launch a new product with a new production process. These folks generally have only a weak awareness of the importance of rigorous process design and the power of a truly lean process from the very beginning. And most that I have spoken to are convinced that creating lean processes from the beginning would cost more and take more time. I'm certain that these views are based on ignorance and lack of reflection, but until we start conversations to explain why, a great opportunity for the Lean Community and for society will be wasted.

I'm now engaged with a number of "system design" experiments to create new, lean processes to address new or changing consumer and societal needs. So I hope to do my part in raising consciousness by publicizing these experiments. I hope you also will give thought to this important issue so we can all create more value with less process rework in brownfields that should have started and stayed bright green.

Aug. 24, 2010

THE GREAT RECESSION

The brightest news about diffusion in the previous section came unexpectedly from the world of medical science. But now we need to turn to a different science—the truly dismal science of macroeconomics—to focus in this section on The Great Recession and what it means, both good and bad, for the lean movement.

Mega Mura Bubble Trouble

I started writing my monthly eletters in October of 2001 to speak to the worries of the Lean Community as the world economy slid into recession. So this month [November 2008] marks the end of one complete cycle—seven years of bust, boom, and bust—as the world endures a new recession.

When Dan Jones and I wrote *Lean Thinking* in 1996, we believed that the spread of lean production would damp the business cycle. Economists have long thought that at least half of the depth of recessions is due to companies working off their inventories and delaying the purchase of more materials from suppliers. Because lean firms have much lower inventories of raw materials, work in process, and finished goods in relation to their sales, we thought the adoption of lean inventory management would have a recession-damping effect on the whole economy. And perhaps we were right. The 2001 recession was modest compared with the previous recession of 1991.

In any case, we do face a major recession even if lower inventories make it shallower than it might otherwise be. I think of these events as a form of mura (variation), indeed as "mega mura" affecting the whole economy.

By contrast, the type of mura that has drawn most of the attention of lean thinkers is day-to-day and hour-to-hour variations in the volume and mix of products demanded by a downstream customer. Let's call this "mini mura." This phenomenon also includes gyrations in orders progressing up a value stream to suppliers—even when end-customer demand is smooth—due to the internal dynamics of the value stream. Lean thinkers learned years ago to deal with this type of mura by introducing heijunka to level demand at some pacemaker point, with smoothed pull signals upstream from there.

Mega mura by contrast applies to large and lengthy shifts in total demand by external customers across the economy. Unfortunately, a boom in demand—caused in the current case by low interest rates and relaxed lending standards for homes—always leads to a bust. The sad part of these episodes—which are as old as market economies—and the reason we can fairly call them mura is that they don't involve fundamental changes in consumer desires. Millions more Americans and Europeans didn't suddenly want to own a home or buy a bigger house in the years after 2001. They had always had these desires, but they lacked the money or credit to act on them.

What we really need as an antidote is macroeconomic heijunka ("mega heijunka"?) in which governments level demand to avoid both booms and busts. And economic stabilization policies toward this end—fiscal and monetary—have been pursued by every modern government.

Unfortunately, we have learned that stable growth is hard to achieve as a political reality. The lure of making short-term windfalls through financial engineering is very strong. And regulators, like generals preparing for the previous war, are always putting mechanisms in place to prevent the last crisis, not the next one. In my mind's eye, the folks who thought up the credit default swaps, the collateralized debt obligations, and—my favorite—the synthesized collateralized debt obligations that fueled the recent boom, are now sailing their yachts on some tropical sea thinking up the next lucrative boom. And I wouldn't bet against them.

Fortunately, the recessions that follow bubbles can be great spurs to lean transformations, the necessities that birth innovations. Toyota only decided to comprehensively embrace lean enterprise after the bust of the Japanese economy brought the company to the brink of bankruptcy in 1950. And in 1990–91 Lantech (Chapter 6 in *Lean Thinking*) and Wiremold (Chapter 7) embraced lean thinking as the economy foundered. A creative crisis was handed to managers ready to seize the opportunity and they made the most of it. So perhaps some good will come from the present recession as new lean enterprises emerge.

However, as the lean movement matures and more firms embrace lean enterprises, a different problem presents itself. A lean enterprise at its heart is a group of people (including downstream customers and upstream suppliers) who have learned together how to take initiatives to remove (mini) mura, muri, and muda while solving shared problems with their shared processes as they arise. It is this set of skills more than specific lean techniques that create the remarkable effectiveness of these organizations.

The problem with a recession is that it challenges lean organizations as they try to protect their problem-solving employees. It also challenges them as they try to defend the problem-solving relationships built over time with downstream customers and upstream suppliers. The temptation in any crisis, of course, is to go back to point optimization in which it is each person and each firm for itself.

So how does a lean enterprise think about protecting itself and its people from the mega mura that is likely always to be with us? Here is a short list of ideas:

- Rethink recruitment policies to create a pool of entry-level temporaries who can be a buffer in severe downturns (defined as those where the survival of the enterprise dictates layoffs). Gradually convert temporaries to permanent employees—who can be protected through practically any conceivable downturn —as they prove their fit with the organization's problem-solving methods and as they prove their commitment to the organization. The alternative is to fire people in some random way, often starting with higher-paid employees with more seniority. This sends the message that loyalty doesn't count and squanders valuable team skills.

- Create companywide bonuses for all employees, based on profitability, to adjust wages through the economic cycle and defend core employees from layoffs. Most firms still have all-or-nothing compensation for everyone except those executives on a bonus plan. This gives no flexibility in downturns, meaning compensation is constant for those who stay and zero for those who are let go. With variable compensation it is more likely that everyone can stay.

- As the lean transformation proceeds, convert physical inventories into cash but keep an inventory of cash to buffer the firm during the down cycle. From the standpoint of modern financial thinking, this seems suboptimal. Shouldn't all of the freed-up cash be put aggressively in play in the financial markets? But in the current crisis, firms with stable cash reserves can keep new programs on schedule and will surge in the upturn as competitors who delay or cancel new projects fall behind.

I realize that these steps work best if taken well before the bubble bursts. So what do lean enterprises that have recently transformed themselves but not taken these steps do to get through the current crisis?

- Take back work from suppliers that are not going to be part of the core supply group going forward. This can defend jobs in the company and increase the level of understanding of what goes on in the supply base. And it need not disrupt relations with the remaining suppliers if it is clear that the firm will be working on a continuing basis with fewer but more talented suppliers in the future.

- Look at every product to ask how it can be offered more effectively. For example, at LEI we are asking hard questions about online learning and other methods to more cost-effectively deliver training.

- Look at every product and its value stream to see how it can be offered more efficiently by leaving out wasted steps and unnecessary expense. The hope, of course, is that careful targeting of waste can support price reductions to customers that will capture additional sales, so there will be no need to reduce the number of employees.

The very last thing to consider is the one thing managers seem to embrace most readily: cost cutting. This means leaving out steps and features that actually create value from the perspective of the customer and removing employees who are actually needed to get the job done right using the current process. The hope, usually wrong, is that the customer won't notice.

This last expedient is the one I most fear, because it is likely to be justified in the name of "lean." Every recession seems to produce a major cost-cutting campaign sold by traditional consultants. Their key promise is rapid financial payback, even within one quarter, and the only practical way to achieve this is layoffs. I truly hope that this will not be known to history as the "lean" recession, and everyone in the Lean Community should vow to avoid the cost-cutting urge in their own organizations.

To avoid the need for cost cutting, I hope that every would-be lean enterprise will assign someone responsibility for developing a "recession A3" that carefully reviews the background situation. The critical step in the A3 process will then be to develop a set of counter-measures that can protect the organization and its people through the current recession while laying the groundwork for a sustainable lean enterprise in the future.

Nov. 13, 2008

A Large Enough Wave Sinks All Boats

Perhaps the most shocking consequence of the financial tsunami was that no enterprise, no matter how lean, seemed to be immune. Understanding this unpleasant fact and what it means is the subject of this essay.

We all know the phrase, "a rising tide lifts all boats," and this was true during the world economic bubble of the last few years. Almost any firm could survive, even with mediocre performance and no improvement.

Unfortunately, there is a corollary. A rapidly falling tide—following a financial tsunami—can at least briefly tip even the sturdiest boat. The painful evidence for the Lean Community is the recent announcement that the world's most consistently successful and financially stable organization—Toyota—is now losing money for the first time in 70 years.

How can this be? And what does the financial tsunami mean for the lean movement?

The root cause of Toyota's current problems is the decision in the late-1990s to step on the gas and gain No. 1 position in the global auto industry. Toyota added enormous amounts of capacity around the world and passed GM as the global sales leader. However, doing this chewed up cash, required borrowing beyond Toyota's modest historic levels, and made the firm vulnerable to a steep drop in demand. A sales collapse was apparently not anticipated, but Toyota more than any firm should have respected its hard-earned knowledge that forecasts—particularly optimistic forecasts—are usually wrong.

Despite the collapse in demand in every major market, Toyota is not in the desperate straits of many of its rivals. It still has a sterling credit rating and can borrow to keep its new product programs and R&D on schedule. Indeed, if things somehow get so bad that only one car company is left operating, that company will be Toyota.

But the happy era of boundless expansion is now over, and Toyota has doubtless been spending a lot of time on hansei. My colleague John Shook has been very articulate in observing that Toyota from its beginnings always wanted to be the best at solving customer problems using the least resources so it could survive. But in the mid-1990s it changed course to embrace the common view in business that growth of any sort is good and that being biggest is best. This is not the lean way, and I predict a return to Toyota's traditional view of its purpose. I also predict that the current downturn will prove a blessing by giving Toyota time to replenish its stock of lean managers. Its breakneck growth seriously diluted its managerial experience level and was becoming a grave risk to its long-term success.

But what about the rest of us? The simple fact is that this adversity will force all of us to confront difficult issues in our organizations and in our markets, issues that we would rather avoid and probably have long avoided. For those who reflect carefully, determine root causes, and take focused, creative actions, the future will be brighter.

Let me cite Toyota's history as evidence. This is not the only financial wave Toyota has confronted, but instead is the latest of many:

- The collapse in demand in the Japanese market in 1950.

- The oil shock of 1973 that again depressed demand as the yen soared.

- The world recession of 1981 when both North America and Europe imposed trade restraints that depressed Toyota's exports and required massive investments in foreign markets.

- The yen shock of the late-1980s that dropped the value of the yen against the dollar from 240 to 120 in only a few months.

- The collapse of the Japanese economy leading to a decade of stagnation after the real-estate bubble burst in 1990.

By reflecting carefully, tracing problems to their root causes, and taking bold action, Toyota emerged stronger every time. Despite the gloom of 2008, I therefore have an optimistic view. Those in the Lean Community who confront root causes and take decisive action will be stronger and more vibrant once the storm subsides. And there will be more of us as desperate times cause many additional organizations to embrace lean thinking.

Dec. 31, 2008

Additional reading:

John Shook, *Lean Management* column, www.lean.org.

MISUNDERSTANDINGS

Many years ago when the MIT car team launched the term "lean" in the world, it was the best label we could devise. It was designed to capture what lean does, which is create more value with less of everything. But we knew then that we could not control the term and that it would be subject to misunderstanding. We were aware as well that many of the concepts and terms accompanying lean would also be vulnerable to misconstruction. And we were right. This section of essays explores how so many things have been gotten wrong, with the hope that public discussion will gradually lead to everyone getting them right.

Deconstructing the Tower of Babel

In the summer of 1987 in my office at MIT, I witnessed a magic moment when a new term was born. We were getting ready to publish the first article on the findings of the International Motor Vehicle Program and we needed a label to describe the phenomenon we were observing in our comparative study of performance in the global auto industry.

After trying out a lot of terms that didn't seem quite right, John Krafcik, one of our young researchers, suggested that we name the system—including its product and process development, fulfillment (from order through production to delivery), supplier management, customer support, and general management elements—for what it does.

So we wrote on a whiteboard the performance attributes of a Toyota/Honda-style system, compared with traditional mass production. It:

- Needed less human effort to design, make, and service products.

- Required less investment for a given amount of production capacity.

- Created products with fewer delivered defects and fewer in-process turnbacks.

- Utilized fewer suppliers with higher skills.

- Went from concept to launch, order to delivery, and problem to repair in less time with less human effort.

- Could cost-effectively produce products in lower volume with wider variety to sustain pricing in the market while growing share.

- Needed less inventory at every step from order to delivery and in the service system.

- Caused fewer employee injuries, etc.

After a moment of looking over this list, John said, "It needs less of everything to create a given amount of value, so let's call it 'lean'." And the term was born. [John, by the way, came to MIT from the Toyota-General Motors joint-venture in California. He went on from MIT to 14 years at Ford, where he eventually was chief engineer for large sport-utility vehicles, and is now president of Hyundai Motor America.]

It seemed so simple at the time. But we soon learned that creating a new term is like launching children into the world. The parents have clear ideas about how they want their offspring to behave, but the kids have minds of their own!

As the years have gone by, we seem to be building a lean Tower of Babel. I hear the term applied vaguely and used to mean many things: goals (highest quality, lowest cost, shortest lead time), general methods (just-in-time, jidoka), specific tools (kanban, poka-yoke), and the basic foundation (heijunka, standardized work, and kaizen, built on process stability).

This is fine, but I get upset when I hear the term used inaccurately or in some narrow way that excludes part of its core meaning. Recently, after reading an article in which a prominent expert on production systems stated that lean doesn't involve standardized work, I thought I should say something. So here's what lean means to me:

- It always begins with the customer.

- The customer wants value: the right good or service at the right time, place, and price with perfect quality to solve their problem.

- Value in any activity—goods, services, or some combination—is always the end result of a process (design, manufacture, and service for external customers, and business processes for internal customers).

- Every process consists of a series of steps that need to be taken properly in the proper sequence at the proper time.

- To maximize customer value, these steps must be taken with zero waste. (I trust you know the seven wastes of overproduction, waiting, excess conveyance, extra processing, excessive inventory, unnecessary motion, and defects requiring rework or scrap.)

- To achieve zero waste, every step in a value-creating process must be valuable, capable, available, adequate, and flexible, and the steps must flow smoothly and quickly from one to the next at the pull of the downstream customer. (This is how we eliminate the seven wastes identified by Toyota many years ago.)

- A truly lean process is a perfect process: perfectly satisfying the customer's desire for value with zero waste.

- None of us has ever seen a perfect process nor will most of us ever see one. But lean thinkers still believe in perfection, the never-ending journey toward the truly lean process.

Note that identifying the steps in the process, getting them to flow, letting the customer pull, etc. are not the objectives of lean practitioners. These are simply necessary steps to reach the goal of perfect value with zero waste. And note that kanban, poka-yoke, and other specific techniques are aids to performing these steps. They are the critical tools for making the general methods work.

And here is where I think we often get confused. "Lean" must include all of these: They can't work without each other. We need to utilize all of the goals, methods, techniques, and foundation elements in combination. For example, no process can be capable, available, or smoothly flowing without standardized work. And there will be no improvement in any process without rigorous kaizen. It's only when we deploy the whole arsenal in pursuit of the perfect process that can create perfect value for the customer that the term "lean" becomes magic.

Oct. 7, 2004

If what "lean" means is confusing, so is its relation to a number of other terms addressing the same set of issues. Understanding the similarities, differences, and what's important is the subject of the next essay.

How Lean Compares with Six Sigma, BPR, TOC, TPM, Etc.

It amazes me, but I still get lots of questions about how lean compares with TPS, six sigma, Total Productive Main-tenance, business-process reengineering, demand flow, the Theory of Constraints, and other approaches to improvement. And I always give the same answer: At the end of the day we are all trying to achieve the same thing: the perfect process providing exactly the value the customer wants with zero waste. Here's how I think about it.

To create value for the customer—which I hope we agree is how we should be earning our living—a series of steps must be conducted properly in the proper sequence. These steps collectively are what we call the value stream (process) for each product. As I walk through any value stream I ask the following simple questions about each step:

Is the step *valuable*? Would the customer be equally happy with the product if the step could be left out? For example, is there any type of rework? If so, it's what I call Type One muda. Get rid of it as soon as you can! (There is another type of muda that lean thinkers often term incidental work. It involves activities that create no value from the standpoint of the customer—for example, moving product from one disconnected batch process to another when the current design of the process doesn't permit its removal just yet. I call this Type Two muda. It should disappear, too, but it often takes much longer to address.)

Is the step *capable*? Can it be conducted with the same, good result every time? This is the starting point, but never the end point, for six sigma.

Is the step *available*? Can it be performed whenever it is needed, or is the step subject to breakdowns and varying cycle times so you are never sure what will happen? This is the starting point, but, again, not the end point, of Total Productive Maintenance.

Is the step *adequate*? That is, is there capacity to perform it exactly when the value stream requires it, or is there a bottleneck? Bottleneck analysis is, of course, the starting point of the Theory of Constraints. Or, and more likely in the current era, is there too much capacity? Lean thinkers try to avoid this by adding production capacity in small increments rather than in big hunks, increments whose production volume also can be flexed by adding or subtracting employees.

Is the step *flexible*? Can it shift over quickly from making green ones to making red ones? And can it change over without compromising capability, availability, and adequacy? Flexibility is the key to rapid response to changing customer desires while avoiding the inefficient production of big batches. This ability is a hallmark of the Toyota Production System (TPS).

If all the steps in your value streams are valuable, capable, available, adequate, and flexible, you are well on your way. What remains is to perfect the linkage among the steps.

Does the product *flow* from one step to the next with no delay? Henry Ford pioneered "flow production" in 1914 by moving the process to the product rather than the reverse. This is how he created nearly continuous flow not just on the assembly line but also in component fabrication at Highland Park. Unfortunately, he found flow hard to sustain in a world with changeable demand and wide product variety. That's where Toyota came in with TPS to create smooth flow in lower-volume production with wide variety.

Does the product only flow at the *pull* of the next downstream step? This is the central point of JIT, one of the pillars of TPS: Products should only flow at the command of the next step downstream.

Is the flow *leveled* back from the customer to the fullest extent possible, with a standard inventory of finished goods if necessary? Leveling permits every step in the whole value stream to operate smoothly while an inventory at some point in the process provides the flexibility to provide the customer with exactly what is needed exactly when it is needed. This is another hallmark of TPS.

None of us, of course, has created a perfect value stream. Probably we never will. But energy expended on comparing and criticizing improvement methods rather than pursuing the perfect value stream is surely Type One muda. That's the type of waste we can get rid of immediately!

July 14, 2003

Just-in-Time, Just-in-Case, and Just-Plain-Wrong

The misunderstandings just discussed mostly occur within the community of process practitioners. A different set of confusions occur in more popular commentary, particularly in the business media, and the concept of just-in-time seems to be particularly confounding to the public.

When I started my eletters immediately after Sept. 11, 2001, it was partly as a response to the many commentators asserting that JIT could no longer work due to the risk of disruption in supply chains. They argued that large inventories were needed everywhere along value streams to permit rapid response to chaotic conditions.

I knew that this was a complete misunderstanding of the situation. Counting on finished units and parts lying around at many locations to somehow respond to disruptions in transport links or at key production facilities would be ineffectual as well as harmful to production organizations and society.

Since that time I've been keeping a media file on reasons why JIT supposedly can't work in today's world. The latest reason comes from a front-page article in *The Wall Street Journal* that carries the headline "Just-In-Time Inventories Make U.S. Vulnerable to a Pandemic."[9] The key sentence in the article describes the problem as follows: "Most fundamentally, the widely embraced 'just-in-time' business practice—which attempts to cut costs and improve quality by reducing inventory stockpiles and delivering products as needed—is at odds with the logic of 'just in case' that promotes stockpiling drugs, government intervention, and overall preparedness."

So if anyone was foolish enough to think JIT was a good idea after 9/11, surely they will come to their senses at the prospect of avian flu! Let me take a minute to see if I can set the record straight.

9. Bernard Wysocki Jr. and Sarah Lueck, "Just-In-Time Inventories Make U.S. Vulnerable to a Pandemic," *The Wall Street Journal*, Jan. 12, 2006.

First, what is JIT? It's a simple idea formulated by Kiichiro Toyoda at Toyota in the late-1930s. Each step in a value stream should pull precisely what it currently needs from the previous step in the value stream. This pull should be the signal for the previous step to immediately make new items to exactly replace those just withdrawn. The idea is to replace complex scheduling systems—depending on centralized accumulation of information and complicated formulae—with simple, reflexive systems that work much better while dramatically reducing the amount of inventories along a value stream.

Toyota implemented its pull system by means of simple rules. One was that between every step in a value stream it is critical to accurately calculate *standard inventory*. This is the amount of material that must be in place so that the downstream customer is never disappointed. This inventory consists of three elements: Buffer stock, safety stock, and shipping stock:

- *Buffer stock* is goods already finished and kept on hand to deal with sudden spikes in demand from the downstream customer.

- *Safety stock* is finished items or raw materials maintained to protect the output of the process if upstream suppliers fail to respond to the pull signal in a timely manner or if the process itself encounters problems (e.g., bad quality, broken equipment).

- *Shipping stock* is goods being built up for the next shipment.

A second critical rule is to select one point along a value stream as the pacemaker step and to add additional buffer stock there to deal with normal fluctuations in consumer demand. *This buffer is sized to deal with all reasonable variations in commercial demand, so the customer is never disappointed.* By doing this, every step back upstream from this "pacemaker" can operate smoothly with leveled demand for extended periods. This, of course, is heijunka. When done properly, leveling demand largely eliminates the need for the buffer stocks between each step and reduces total inventories along the value stream dramatically.

So what's the problem, and why do commentators keep suggesting that JIT can't work in a chaotic world? The problem is that *severe disruptions driven by geopolitical events and natural-biological catastrophes must be dealt with outside the framework of JIT.* Only muddled thinking results when normal commerce and extreme emergencies are combined.

How should these issues be uncoupled? Let's look at the Avian flu, where a major worry is the shortage of ventilators to help victims breathe until their strength returns. Governments need to make a decision now on just how many spare units—completed and ready to run—need to be kept on hand to deal with a sudden, enormous surge in demand. (The *Journal* article states that the U.S. government does have a stockpile of 4,500, but that tens of thousands of additional units may be needed very quickly from an industry that currently produces only a few thousand units per year.)

These goods should be held separate from normal commercial inventories, under government control, and called by their proper name: *emergency stocks.* These are simply a physical version of an insurance policy, except that the policy is for society rather than an individual.

Proposing instead that old-fashioned, just-in-case inventories located along the ventilator value stream could solve the problem is naïve: The real problem is the lack of capacity to assemble the parts quickly into finished units. And thinking that companies on their own will maintain a buffer stock of finished units adequate for a true emergency is equally naïve. They would go bankrupt if they tried.

(Governments also need to decide how to distribute the emergency stocks when needed, because normal market price allocation can't work in a panic. Looking at the bright side, as the Katrina hurricane emergency showed, modern logistics firms like FedEx and Walmart are capable of delivering needed items quickly in chaotic conditions, even when government efforts falter.)

The key point to note is that with emergency stocks in place, as we should all hope they will be, JIT works just fine. It helps production systems deal with normal variations in commercial demand at the lowest cost with the highest quality with maximum responsiveness to the customer's desire. Indeed, the cost savings from JIT—which we've only started to achieve across the entire economy—are a good way for society to afford the cost of emergency stocks.

So, please, whenever you hear well-intentioned but muddle-headed people attacking JIT when they really should be confronting our lack of emergency stocks, do what you can to set the record straight.

Jan. 22, 2006

Looking more broadly, beyond lean terms, I find many misunderstandings of simple concepts and words used by everyone every day where a bit of lean thinking can provide real clarification and insight. These are the subjects of the remaining essays in this section.

Move Your Operations to China? Do Some Lean Math First

Most organizations I visit don't seem to understand math. It's not that they don't do math to calculate the cost of designing and producing products in one place or another across the world. But their math seems to leave out many of the costs. In this essay I tackle this misunderstanding by describing the type of "lean" cost counting needed to get the right answer for where to locate activities in today's world. Without doing lean math at the beginning of process-improvement activities it is easy to improve the wrong things in the wrong places.

I recently got a phone call from a reporter for *The Wall Street Journal* with a simple but provocative question: "If you are a manufacturer in a high-wage country such as the U.S., can you ever be lean enough that you don't need to relocate your operations to China?"

The reporter's reasoning was that China has an enormous labor pool in its coastal development zones, with 300 million additional migrants to these areas expected in the next 10 years. So labor costs may stay at their current low levels for decades.

He further reasoned that a large fraction of the cost of manufactured goods is ultimately wages (for touch labor plus support staff, managers, and engineers, and the workers designing and making process machinery and extracting and processing raw materials). He then concluded that no matter how much cost an American or Japanese or German firm removes by getting lean, costs in China (or, if you prefer, India) based on cheap labor will always be much lower. Hence, "Won't you need to relocate?"

My answer to this simple question also was simple: "Do some math before you move, and make sure it's lean math." Here are the items you need to include in your calculation:

- Start with the piece-part cost for an item where you are.

- Compare this with the piece-part cost for the same item in China or India or Vietnam or Burkina Faso or … (It will almost always be much lower.)

- Add the cost of slow freight to get it to your customer.

Note that you have now done *all* the math that many purchasing departments seem to perform. Let's call this "mass-production math." To get to lean math, you need to add some additional costs to piece-part plus slow-freight cost to make the calculation more realistic:

- The overhead costs allocated to production in the high-wage location, which usually don't disappear when production is transferred. Instead they are reallocated to remaining products, raising their apparent cost.

- The cost of the additional inventory of goods in transit over long distances from the low-wage location to the customer.

- The cost of additional safety stocks to ensure uninterrupted supply.

- The cost of expensive expedited shipments. (You'll need to be careful here because the plan for the part in question typically assumes that there aren't any expediting costs, when a bit of casual empiricism will show that there always are.)

- The cost of warranty claims if the new facility or supplier has a long learning curve.

- The cost of engineer visits or resident engineers to get the process right so the product is made to the correct specification with acceptable quality.

- The cost of senior executive visits to set up the operation or to straighten out relationships with managers and suppliers operating in a different business environment. (Note this may include all manner of payments and considerations, depending on local business practices.)

- The cost of out-of-stocks and lost sales caused by long lead times to obtain the part.

- The cost of remaindered goods or of scrapped stocks, ordered to a long-range forecast and never actually needed.

- The potential cost, if you are using a contract manufacturer in the low-cost location, of your supplier soon becoming your competitor.

This is becoming quite a list—and note that these additional costs are hardly ever visible to the folks in senior management or purchasing who relocate production of an item in a low-wage country based simply on piece-part price plus slow freight. However, lean math requires adding three more costs to be complete:

- Currency risks that can strike quite suddenly when the currency of either the supplying or receiving country shifts.

- Country risks that also can emerge very suddenly when the shipping country encounters political instabilities or when there is a political reaction in the receiving country as trade deficits and unemployment emerge as political issues.

- Connectivity costs of many sorts in managing product handoffs and information flows in highly complex supply chains across long distances in countries with different business practices.

These latter costs are harder to estimate but are sometimes very large. The only thing a manager can know for sure is that they are low or nonexistent if products are sourced close to the customer rather than across the globe.

If you do the lean math, will it always mean that you don't need to relocate? Absolutely not. For example, if you are planning to sell within high-growth, low-wage markets like China or India, you will almost certainly need to locate most or all of your production for those markets within those markets. This is simply because lean math works in the opposite direction as well. Transport, inventory, and connectivity costs, and country and currency risks are much lower if you produce within the market of sale.

However, in my experience, a hard look at the true cost situation will suggest that relocation is not the first line of defense for producers in high-wage countries. Rather it's to get truly serious about a lean transformation through the entire value stream for the product in question.

If you find that you do need to relocate, even after doing lean math and applying the full complement of lean methods, my experience is that moving all of the steps in the value stream for a product to an adjacent location in a low-wage country within the region of sale—Mexico for the United States, Poland for Germany, and China or Vietnam or Thailand for Japan—is likely to provide the lowest total cost.

Jan. 10, 2003

Recently, with wages rising in China and the controlled Chinese currency facing demands from the U.S. government for upward realignment, I'm hearing that factory-gate prices are rising in China and will soon rise more, and that the need to relocate operations is decreasing. I think this would be good for the world economy if it occurs gradually, and I hope it proves to be true.

However, it is important to add one last element of cost to the math. This is the rate of currency and wage increases in relation to the lean learning curve of managers in China and other low-wage locations. From recent visits to both China and India I know (a) that lean methods work as well in these countries as anywhere in the world and (b) that current labor productivity in China and India is abysmal. Thus it should be possible to dramatically boost productivity in the years ahead by applying lean thinking to largely offset strengthening currencies and rising wages. It is not time yet for manufacturers elsewhere to relax and slacken their own quest for lean operations.

The next essay examines the misunderstanding of two simple words—value and waste, a confusion that seems to confound economists and the public.

Gross Domestic Product vs. Gross Domestic Waste

I've always been fascinated by how humans count, especially the way we always seem to count the wrong things. Recently I was looking at the American counting of gross domestic product (GDP). The U.S. government reports that GDP was up 2.6% in the second quarter of 2006, after rising 5.8% in the first quarter, and the economists offering commentary seem to think this is good. We are producing more goods and services (domestic product) per capita, meaning economic output is growing faster than population. That means we should be getting wealthier.

Governments in every country across the globe do this same sort of counting with the same thought process. The universal view is that growth in domestic product is good. End of discussion.

But for the lean thinker this should just be the start of the discussion. GDP simply counts all economic activity in the economy. Any goods produced or services provided that someone paid for is "product." Thus the surge of growth in online and telephone helpdesks—to aid consumers using products they can't understand how to install, that won't work with their other products, or that simply won't turn on—counts as growing domestic product. So does increased spending on recalls of defective products. So does new warehousing for needless inventory. How about construction of massive airports to cross-dock passengers at Point C when the passengers really just wanted to go directly from Point A to Point B? Or additional spending on mega-medical centers to warehouse patients waiting for the next step in their treatment when the flow paths are blocked? More growth in gross domestic product!

Clearly the problem here is that one measure called "product" comingles two very different things: value and waste. What we really need is to measure gross domestic value (all of the "product" that actually creates value as perceived by the consumer) and compare this with gross domestic waste (or maybe GDM, for gross domestic muda). We want the former to grow but the latter to shrink.

This counting problem actually has two additional dimensions. First, even in the case of goods that clearly create value for the consumer, such as the new computer that actually works without resort to a help desk, the processes of designing, making, and delivering the item are a mixture of value and waste. For example, assembling the parts is clearly value while reworking the finished unit in the factory to a point where it finally works properly is waste. But the consumer has to pay for the value and the waste together.

A second issue is that externalities imposed on the environment by value-creating processes are currently counted as economic product. For example, a recent study by the Chinese government's environment ministry estimated that of the officially recorded 10% growth in Chinese GDP in 2004, 3% was actually expended on trying to deal with the environmental damage to human health and agriculture caused by the other 7%![10] In this case the internalities, in the form of the goods and services produced for consumers' personal benefit are confused with externalities: the burden of their production on the environment and the general public. Both are counted as GDP.

We are all familiar with product labeling that tells what fraction of the product was made domestically, what fraction uses recycled materials, what fraction is fat, protein, carbohydrate, and so on. How about labels that show how many of the steps involved created value and how many were actually waste from the standpoint of the consumer? That is, an accounting of the steps the customer was happy to pay for compared with those the customer was forced to pay for because of the poor design or performance of the processes involved? And what about "green" labels that show the costs to the environment that ought to be subtracted from the value of the product?

But actually this would be a mistake if it was just another counting exercise. Unless waste was actually removed as result, this type of counting would just be more muda.

---

10. "Green GDP Accounting Study Report 2004," issued by the State Environmental Protection Administration of China (SEPA) and the National Bureau of Statistics of China (NBS), Sept. 8, 2006.

What I propose instead is that lean thinkers help others with less vision to see that growth is good but only the growth in value, not the growth in waste. And then I hope we will all reexamine every process we touch to clearly distinguish value from waste. That, of course, is just the necessary preparation. The value of the exercise lies in removing the waste, not just counting it.

My ultimate hope is that someday our current method of counting GDP will become completely accurate even if we don't change it. We will really be counting gross domestic value, whatever we may call it, because we will have removed our gross domestic waste.

Oct. 23, 2006

If value and waste are confusing, it turns out that cost and value are even more confusing, particularly to accountants. Sorting out this confusion is the topic of the next essay.

Adding Cost or Creating Value?

I was out on tour this past week, listening to companies' stories as they try to achieve a lean transformation. And I was struck, as I often am, by confusing terminology. The companies I visited thought they were "adding value," but I mostly watched them adding cost. So let me try to clarify things.

I always use the term "creating value" rather than the more familiar "adding value" because the former is the voice of the customer while the latter is the voice of the accountant. Companies add up their costs—both bought-in materials and internal spending on capital and labor plus their margins—then subtract the cost of their purchased items to determine how much "value" they have "added." The problem is that this leaves out the customer, the only one who can determine value. Often, what a company really means by "adding value" is "adding cost." Whether the extra cost creates any value is known only to the customer, and many managers never ask!

A quick example: Let's suppose a company buys some nuts, some bolts, and some widgets, and assembles them into a simple product. These purchased items clearly are costs. Then let us suppose the company uses a lot of labor to store these parts, take them to the point of assembly, assemble them, rework the defective items, store the assembled goods, hunt for missing items, and then ship them. Finally, let us suppose that the bought-in items cost 50 units and the selling price for the finished product is 100 units. Clearly the company must have "added" 50 units of "value." Right? Wrong!

From the customer's standpoint this company may only have added 50 units of "cost," including its margin, and created very little value. The reason is simply that most of the steps consuming the resources—storing the parts, hunting for them, reworking them—added cost but no value from the perspective of the customer. Customers actually would have thought the product was more valuable (and been willing to pay more) if these steps had been left out and the product had been delivered faster!

Because products come as a bundle of value and costly waste and because the firms in most industries currently mix the two, customers often have no choice but to purchase the waste along with the value. But what if some lean thinking firm in your industry separates value from waste and eliminates the waste? If that isn't your firm, watch out!

Words aren't a substitute for action, but the wrong words often get in the way of the right actions if managers can't tell the difference between value and cost. So I hope lean thinkers will sharpen their language to focus on actually creating value, often by eliminating unnecessary costs.

March 4, 2004

Creating Value or Shifting Wealth?

A final confusion I often encounter lies in the interchangeable use of the terms "value" and "wealth." The former is meaningful to the consumer whose problems are solved by some use of resources, while the latter is meaningful to the owner of the resources. I find this a damaging confusion, and this final essay in this section attempts to sort it out.

How do we judge the progress of the lean movement? One critical indicator is our success in extending lean thinking to new industries and activities. In recent years I have been greatly encouraged that lean thinking is moving far beyond its origins in manufacturing to distribution, retailing, maintenance and overhaul, consumer services, construction, and—perhaps most striking—healthcare. Indeed, the latter may be the most energetic area of lean practice today.

However, I have been concerned about our prospects for changing the thinking of investors, and specifically the giant private-equity investment firms that now control large parts of the economy. While we have gained a strong foothold in financial services, this has been at the operating level. Most efforts to date have focused on how value streams within financial firms can be made lean—for example, those for processing loans or making credit checks. This is important work but it is on a different level from how financial firms think about investments and specifically how they might instigate lean transformations in the firms they control in many industries.

I was therefore delighted recently when I was contacted by one of the largest private-equity firms, an organization with dozens of firms in its investment portfolio garnering perhaps $100 billion in total sales. This type of firm pools private investment funds to buy companies, in hopes of quick "turnarounds" with resale of these firms at much higher prices.

The partner contacting me noted that conditions in this industry have changed with the credit crisis and weak equities markets. Instead of selling firms after two or three years it may be necessary to hold onto them for a long time, even a decade, before they can be sold to advantage. His question was a simple one: "Given that we may now need to hold firms for many years, how can we take the long view. Indeed, how can we turn firms into lean exemplars in order to maximize their price when they are sold?"

I was delighted to engage in this conversation. But to avoid any misunderstanding, I needed to start by comparing a traditional private-equity "turnaround" with a "lean trans-formation." In the former, the objective to this point has been to go quickly to produce a dramatic bottom-line result.

This has often meant:

- "Rolling up" two or more companies in the same industry to reduce competition and increase prices to consumers.

- Negotiating lower wages and benefits.

- Cutting spending on long-term development projects not critical to the firm's short-term performance.

- Reducing headcounts in activities judged nonessential.

- Restructuring the balance sheet to add bank debt, often creating instant dividends for the private-equity firm in the form of management fees but high levels of long-term debt for the firm once it is sold.

- Renegotiating prices with suppliers on threat of loss of business.

These actions quickly shift *wealth* from customers, employees, suppliers, and former owners to the new owners. This may do more good than harm, because otherwise the firm in question may completely fail. But it is often unclear that any additional *value* has been created in the sense of better satisfying customer needs with a given amount of human effort and capital investment. And, from society's standpoint, the only way to increase living standards is to change the ratio of human effort and capital going into firms to the amount of value coming out. Otherwise the outcome is basically zero-sum, with some winners and some losers.

By contrast, the objective of a lean transformation is to analyze the core value-creating processes of organizations in light of customer needs (which may have changed), then figure out how to create more value with the same resources so the organizations can grow and society can prosper. It's the difference between shifting wealth from one party to another and creating more value, ideally value that can be shared with customers, employees, suppliers, and owners. I was relieved that after a frank discussion of the differences between traditional and "lean" private equity, the firm in question was still interested in pursuing lean. Indeed, this firm has now launched a wide range of experiments to "lean" the processes of its portfolio firms, and other private-equity firms are now following its lead. It is far too soon to know how much progress will be made along this new path. But I'm heartened that an industry I feared I would never hear from is now actually listening.

May 1, 2008

MISADVENTURES

Many years ago the management writer Peter Drucker penned a wonderful autobiography titled *Adventures of a Bystander*.[11] In his introduction, he noted that he had been a ringside observer at a number of great moments in management history, including at General Motors when GM took its final form as the exemplar of modern management immediately after World War II. (As he explained in his classic volume, *The Concept of the Corporation*,[12] he was given unrestricted access to every gemba at GM in order to observe, but only to observe, management behavior.) But he was never directly involved in decision-making and was, thus, always a bystander. I have often felt the same way as I walked along the gemba of organizations where I was merely a visitor.

Fortunately, I've also had several opportunities to be more directly involved. As I trust I have made clear by this point, I believe that the life of lean is experiments. And I have confirmed in a number of experiments the adage that you learn the most from mistakes. In the two essays that follow I describe two "misadventures" where things did not go exactly as planned and describe the lessons learned. The first involves my very brief career as a capitalist.

11. Peter F. Drucker, *Adventures of a Bystander* (New York: Harper & Row, 1979).
12. Peter F. Drucker, *The Concept of the Corporation* (New York: The John Day Co., 1946).

The Value of Mistakes[13]

Several readers of the second edition of my and Dan Jones's book, *Lean Thinking*, have emailed me with an interesting question: "Whatever happened to the bicycle company you talk about in Chapter 3? Why isn't its success mentioned in the new Chapter 14 in the same breath as the other companies in the book?" Here are the answers:

In 1995, I partnered with a number of investors to buy a small, bicycle-frame manufacturing company in the Boston area. My role as an investor and board member—not an employee—was to introduce appropriate lean knowledge for improving operational performance.

As we got started it looked amazingly easy: The firm built its high-end titanium bike frames to confirmed customer order and had a reputation for shipping within a week or two of receiving an order. However, to do this the company had created four months' of almost-completed frames, which underwent final fabrication and adjustments just before shipping. In addition, because of the batch mentality of its key supplier—the firm making the titanium tubing—the bike company had four months' of tube stock on hand. Adding four months to four months, it was easy to see that throughput time for a piece of tubing, from entering the company until shipment to the customer, was eight months, and that this was where all the operating capital was tied up. (The cost of the tubing was 40% of the total shipped cost of the bike, so this was big money.)

Our plan was to eliminate the four months' of partially completed frames and the four months' of tube stock while maintaining the ability to ship almost immediately to customer specification. To do this we transformed the process-village layout of the facility to create three cells for tube fabrication, tube welding, and final machining and adjustment. (We got some terrific advice from a number of sensei, ranging from Bill Moffit to Hajime Ohba, so any mistakes were strictly my own doing.)

---

13. Originally titled, *Beach Reading*.

Then we ran down the inventory by reducing throughput time from the first cut on a tube to customer shipment to only two days for a custom frame. This permitted us to eliminate the storage areas and rent out half of the plant to another firm. Because we also increased productivity, while making a successful effort to find jobs for the folks who were no longer needed—an easy task in the boom economy of 1996—it looked like a win-win-win!

Then I made some mistakes:

The first was a technical effort to create a completely flexible welding fixture for any bicycle so that the welders could switch over from one bike to the next practically instantly, and we could run bikes through the plant in the exact sequence of customer orders. It was a splendid thing to behold—and lingers in my memory much like Mark Twain's mechanical typesetting machine that consumed his entire fortune and never worked! We were so obsessed with lean purism—in which I was determined to make bikes in the exact sequence of customer orders— that we forgot some technical limits and the fact that many of our customers were not actually that concerned about waiting a bit for their bike. Indeed, some reported that if we could make a custom bike within two days of receiving an order, we must not have any business or their bike was really taken from inventory rather than custom built. Either way, we were not delighting our customers, who, like Harley Davidson buyers, seemed to place positive value on waiting. So ... we purposely added two weeks' of lead time to custom frames!

The net result was that we tied up a lot of the capital freed up by the inventory reduction in a technology effort designed to serve a customer need that only we were feeling and that we were never able to complete. In the end, we had to accept the reality that small batches weren't always a sin. The business takeaway: Never put lean purity ahead of what's realistic or what the customer actually wants.

Our next mistake was simple hubris on my part: I decided I would visit the titanium tube supplier—the only firm in the world able to make tubing that did not crack in our benders. I would make such a persuasive case for converting their tube mill to lean methods with faster setups for smaller batches that we would get better service with much smaller lots and lower pricing. (I was young back then.) It was only when I got to their tube mill in Louisiana and looked at their technology that I realized it was a lost cause. I asked if I could simply sit and watch while they did a complete tool changeover on their big machine, but they pointed out that since I was only in town for 24 hours I wouldn't have time to watch the whole process! Then they asked if I wanted to buy their company, too, since they were underwater and on the market! (They were soon bought by a financial turnaround firm with zero interest in operational issues.)

Reality began to sink in when we realized that the tube mill had only four customers—Boeing, Pratt & Whitney, GE Aircraft Engines, and us —and that a remarkable boom in the aircraft industry was just taking off. As a result, the supplier shipped us whatever they wanted to ship us whenever they wanted to ship it, and the best we could do was to get them to store the excess in their distribution warehouse near our plant. Because nothing fundamental had been done about costs and their plant was sold out for several years to come, it wasn't surprising—indeed, we were lucky—that prices didn't move. The business takeaway: The extended value stream is critically important, but fixing it is always a lot harder than fixing your own operations. So don't count on unrealistic short-term benefits.

Our next mistake was just bad timing: As a result of the bubble economy and the ease of IPOs, most of the big bike companies went public in the mid-1990s. As they did this, they needed to greatly increase sales to meet Wall Street expectations for rapid growth. And the best way to do this was to offer retailers extremely favorable terms for putting bikes on the retail floor without paying carrying costs. That was one thing for $300 bikes but quite another for us with our $2,500 frames, yet retailers wanted us to match the terms of the big boys.

We had a brilliant idea in mid-1997, which was to take a giant gamble and shift our sales channel to the web. We designed a site where buyers could build their own customized bikes on the screen and with just a few clicks send us a lot of money! The problem was that making a dramatic channel switch required both cash to get through a probable short-term drop in sales—as traditional dealers realized the rules had changed and dropped their franchises—as well as to advertise the new channel in high-end publications like GQ.

So our president went to our bank and explained that we wanted to borrow to create a new business model. This quickly led to a discussion of collateral. In our two years running the business, we had gotten it from chronic losses to small profits, but we had also eliminated almost all of the assets. Work-in-process had gone from eight months to less than a week. Receivables on finished products were zero since we shipped cash-on-delivery (COD). Our equipment inventory had actually shrunk as we replaced fancy new machines with simple old machines (led by the "ancient reamer" whose manufacturer's plate confirmed that it was a century old). And we had eliminated half of the plant space. In short, we had created low-capital manufacturing, which is precisely where the world should be heading.

As our president went through the logic of our business model with the bank, their rejoinder was simple: "So you are asking us to lend against a business that has no assets by design?"

"Right, this is the future of manufacturing!"

"Well … the future isn't here yet. Good-bye."

The business takeaway: Don't expect traditional financing sources to understand what you are trying to do with your lean transformation!

So we concluded we couldn't get there from here and called a broker. In short order we sold the company to a multinational sports equipment maker wanting to pick up another high-end brand. And that was that, except for one dispiriting final detail: The new owner immediately concluded that more inventory would be needed to support rapid response to customer orders and went back to making large batches of partially completed frames! They couldn't make any money with this approach—surprise, surprise—and soon sold the company to another big firm where it now only exists as a marketing device, one badge among many.

On the brighter side, a number of the employees of our firm broke away to found a new firm and have made a solid success in the custom bike industry using the manufacturing methods we introduced. And for me the experience was invaluable in converting from a lean dreamer to a lean realist: I invested very little going in; I received very little coming out; and I got an invaluable education in what it really takes to transform a business.

I hope that your lean education is proceeding as well and that you have a higher ratio of gain to pain!

Aug. 12, 2003

After I sent this eletter I was struck by the reaction. A number of readers wrote back to complain that since I had made mistakes I had no standing as any sort of authority on lean transformation. One leader of lean implementation at a large aerospace company even wrote in to assert that I had no right to write anything further, having proved my ineptitude. My reaction was that this mindset is one of the key reasons that large organizations find it so hard to improve: There is zero tolerance for failure and, therefore, reluctance to try anything new that might possibly fail. Yet experiments are the only way for humans and for organizations to learn, and all worthy experiments contain some possibility for failure.

My brief career as a capitalist taught one set of lessons. Trying to help lean a mighty corporation taught another, as described in the next essay.

Necessary but Not Sufficient

One of the hardest things in my line of work is seeing a company make enormous strides in getting lean and yet fail to prosper. Today's heartbreak is Delphi, the giant American auto-parts company that was one of the founding sponsors of LEI and which has been a test bed for our ideas and publications over the past eight years. As you may know, Delphi filed for bankruptcy on Oct. 8, 2005, and is now in reorganization.

I have walked through dozens of Delphi facilities in many countries, and in my recent walks I have seen some of the leanest practices I have ever found outside of Toyota City. Delphi retained the very best ex-Toyota sensei, pursued kaizen and kaikaku with a vengeance, and took billions of dollars out of operating costs. At the same time quality was dramatically improved (down to defects-per-million-parts in the single digits), responsiveness to changing customer requirements was enhanced, investment requirements for a given increment of capacity were slashed, and inventories shrank. In short, Delphi took all the necessary steps to transform its production system, but these steps alone weren't sufficient.

So what went wrong? Delphi was caught in the middle between promises made to employees as it departed General Motors and demands from its largest customer (GM) as it struggled to adjust to today's hypercompetitive world economy. When Delphi gained its freedom in 1999, the hope was that there would be enough time to make the transition. Delphi would honor wage and pension agreements with existing employees working on GM business in North America while it steadily diversified new business away from GM, which initially accounted for 90% of Delphi's sales. Then as Delphi's unionized workers in the United States, working at high "GM wages" retired, they would be replaced by young workers with "Tier One" wages comparable to those at Delphi's competitors in the supplier industry. At the same time, GM would acknowledge Delphi's cost problem on its GM business and keep price-reduction demands in line with Delphi's ability to remove costs.

For five years, as Delphi steadily increased its productivity through its lean initiative and as its high-wage workers retired, it seemed that the equation might work. But then energy prices zoomed, the big SUV and pickup segments where GM still made good margins stagnated, and lean competitors like Toyota launched products in each of GM's remaining profitable niches. GM responded by pushing harder and harder on Delphi's product pricing to a point where Delphi losses soared. (The irony for lean thinkers is that lean-leader Toyota beat GM, and GM responded by beating up Delphi, which had become one of Toyota's most eager pupils. If only Delphi had had Toyota as its major customer!)

Something had to give, and Delphi decided that bankruptcy was the only way to deal with money-losing activities in the United States—even as the company had good financial performance elsewhere in the world, aided in every case by lean production.

So what's the takeaway for lean thinkers? Simply fixing operations may not be sufficient if managers wait too late to start and factor costs (principally wages and healthcare costs these days) are too far out of line. Delphi will now go through a reorganization process in which the bankruptcy judge rather than senior managers, union leaders, or customers will decide how to divide the pain. And here is a contrarian prediction: I believe Delphi has a great future as the world's leading car parts supplier once promises made in a much less competitive past are addressed. This is because the lean foundation for success has already been laid.

Many observers assume, of course, that a key step for Delphi will be to move practically all U.S. and Western Europe operations to low-labor-cost countries. And this may be part of the solution. But again, let me be a contrarian and point out that this step, although necessary in selected cases, can never be sufficient.

After all, anyone can chase labor. If Delphi simply moves all operations to China (see "Move Your Operations to China? Do Some Lean Math First" on page 174)—assuming that this is the global low-cost location—but runs its operations like a mass producer, how can sustainable competitive advantage be gained as competitors pursue the same strategy at the same rate? In fact, sustainable advantage lies in combining truly lean practices in product design, operations and logistics, purchasing, and customer touch with appropriate labor costs at the right location to serve specific customers.

What these costs are and where activities should be located depends on the specific customers to be served. (You'll need some "lean math" to get the right answer.) But I predict that in many cases the right location for Delphi will be closer to the customer than most observers believe today. In any case, and for any company in any industry, only lean processes in the right location will prove both necessary and sufficient.

Oct. 17, 2005

Looking back five years later, my hopes for Delphi have been confirmed and thwarted. The company emerged from bankruptcy, but only after four years during which the entire North American auto industry was transformed by the collapse of GM and Chrysler. And it has now returned to profitability with prospects for a stable future. But the bankruptcy and those of its largest customers resulted in half of the company's operations being sold off or closed. Delphi is now only half its prebankruptcy size and few of its surviving operations are in the United States or Canada. At the same time, the lean lessons learned in the years before the bankruptcy have been remembered and even pushed further ahead in Delphi's remaining operations across the world.

Despite companywide disruptions from closing plants and relocating the remaining employees, defects per million parts delivered to customers fell from 5.6 in 2005 to a remarkable 2.7 in 2010 (which is better than the 3.4 level required for six sigma). At the same time Delphi continued to deliver on time to customers at or above the 99% level, inventory turns improved by 10% even as volumes fell, and the lost-work-day rate for employees due to on-the-job injuries fell from 0.36 in 2005 to 0.15 in 2010.

Soon after Delphi filed for bankruptcy, I heard from several readers that the failure of Delphi was proof that "lean doesn't work," a reaction to be repeated a few years later when Toyota stumbled. But the problem was not lean concepts, which work just fine whenever applied in the proper context. And they did work brilliantly in every operational area at Delphi. The problem was the unique circumstances in which Delphi found itself as two business systems collided in North America, which is the topic of the next set of essays.

THE GREAT CHASE

The Delphi story from the previous section is one small part of a much larger drama. It ran for 60 years from the point in the late-1940s when Toyota's senior managers decided they could catch up quickly in productivity and quality with General Motors, then the world's largest and most successful company. And this drama is only a part of a still greater competition between two very different business systems— modern management vs. lean management. The story of this great chase in the period after the publication of *The Machine That Changed the World* in 1990 is told in this set of essays.

A Tale of Two Business Systems

In the fall of 1990, Dan Jones, Dan Roos, and I coauthored *The Machine That Changed the World*, our description of lean enterprise. On page 253 we forecast that 1991 or 1992 would be the moment of crisis as the full power of lean (represented by Toyota and Honda) threatened to topple mass production (defended by General Motors). And in the recession of 1991–1992 GM nearly did go bankrupt.

However, as usually happens with forecasts, we were off in our timing. The moment of truth was actually delayed 15 years. What now seems certain is that Toyota will pass GM in 2006 to become the world's largest industrial enterprise and that GM and Ford will undergo a profound transformation, whether led by current managers or by someone else.

Recently, as I've listened to industry executives and the media grapple with this momentous event, I've been struck by the manifest irrelevance of most efforts to find the root cause. The crisis is not due to misaligned currencies, subsidies from "Japan, Inc.," or spiking energy prices (although the latter has affected the precise timing). And it is not a simple case of too many retirees for the present workforce at GM and Ford to support. (Indeed, this gets cause and effect backward: GM and Ford have too many North American retirees for current workers to support because both companies have lost half of their North American market share over the past 25 years and have hired hardly any new workers in a quarter century.) *The root cause of the crisis lies in a clash of two business systems, and the better system is winning.*

As we pointed out in *Machine*—devoting a chapter to each point— a lean enterprise consists of five elements: a product development process, a supplier management process, a customer support process, an overarching enterprise management process, and a production process from order to fulfillment. And each of these processes is superior to the processes employed for the same tasks at a mass producer.

The lean product development process permits a company to produce vehicles with fewer hours of engineering and fewer months of development time with fewer defects while investing less capital and making customers happier. The key tools are the chief engineer concept, concurrent set-based design (which is simultaneous as well), and high-speed prototyping with tradeoff curves so that reinvention is avoided.

Lean supplier management creates a small number of highly capable suppliers in long-term partnership with their customers. Suppliers work to demanding customer targets for cost, quality, delivery reliability, and new technology, and achieve these targets *by jointly examining the development and production process they share with their customers*. The lean approach has dramatic and predictable benefits, but if GM and Ford even understand these concepts, their perceived need to save themselves by bleeding their suppliers has made implementation impossible.

Lean customer support creates customers for life while reducing distribution costs by working backward from the customer's desired experience and forward from the production system's needs. In fact, although Toyota has deployed these concepts brilliantly in Japan, it has stumbled so far in applying them in the United States. Its Lexus dealer system has created a very high level of customer satisfaction but at substantial cost. Achieving high satisfaction *and* low cost is a key topic in my and Dan Jones's recently released *Lean Solutions* book, and provides a terrific opportunity for GM and Ford to move ahead of Toyota by using its own methods. Or, if they fail, this could be the final act in the tragedy as Toyota finally makes its retailers lean in the next few years, the way it transformed its service parts operations in the 1990s.

A lean management system involves managers at every level framing the key problems that need to be solved and asking the teams they lead to discover and implement the answers. This practice of asking the correct questions rather than providing the correct answers (which high-level bosses can never know in any case) is perhaps the starkest contrast between lean thinking and orthodox modern management and the hardest to remedy.

Putting these four elements together, it's not surprising that lean exemplars Toyota and Honda are steadily advancing, as recovering mass-producers GM and Ford steadily retreat despite adopting parts of the lean system. And note that I have not even mentioned the fifth element of a lean enterprise—production operations—because GM and Ford are now nearly competitive on this dimension in terms of labor productivity and assembly-plant quality. The root cause of the current crisis is not in the factory. It is in the rest of the value-creation system.

What must happen soon for GM and Ford to resolve this crisis?

Rewrite the social contract. As Toyota learned when it went bankrupt in 1950 and fired a quarter of its workforce, no company in a truly competitive industry can make promises to employees (or retirees) that are not sustainable in the market. So Toyota made a deal: Right-size the company at one go, tie compensation and benefits to market conditions (with bonuses of all employees geared to profits and with defined-contribution pensions), and try very hard to defend every employee willing to embrace the new value-creation system. Over more than 50 years—by carefully following these rules—Toyota has been able to steadily increase its competitiveness while defending its employees. But everyone at Toyota understands that continuing employment with good compensation depends on continually creating more value per employee. That's why everyone worries so much and thinks so much about continually improving every process. "Life-time employment" is a consequence of creating value, not a precondition or an entitlement.

Introduce all of the elements of lean enterprise. This includes product development, supplier management, customer support, and lean management. These practices have permitted Toyota and Honda to get the right products to market first in North America with substantially higher selling prices within each segment and with substantially lower costs. This is even though its employees in North America are being paid wages and benefits comparable to GM and Ford—except for unsustainable early-retirement plans and defined-benefit pensions—and its suppliers make adequate margins as well.

Simplify market offerings. GM and Ford do have a special problem, never faced by Toyota, in their plethora of brands. But the solution actually lies in GM's past. President Alfred Sloan worked miracles in the early-1920s by rationalizing the welter of overlapping and immemorable companies and products he inherited from founder Billy Durant. But where is the new Alfred Sloan who can either explain what Buick, Pontiac, Saab, Saturn, and GMC are (and Mercury, Mazda, and Jaguar at Ford), or get rid of brands only adding costs? Toyota's North American lineup of Scion (a buzzy, "what's new?" brand), Toyota (a bread-and-butter brand for people who love great, hassle-free transportation but actually don't care much about cars), and Lexus (for those needing status or image with their transportation) comprises as many brands as a car company today can support.

What's the prospect if lean production is uniformly embraced? After a moment of truth—involving employees, retirees, suppliers, and investors—followed by dramatic restructuring at each company, equilibrium could return to this massive industry. GM and Ford could survive as independent companies, although considerably smaller, and Toyota would find that it needs to work even harder to improve every process as competitors embrace lean thinking. And that would be good for the whole world.

But what will actually happen? That's for the managers, employees, and investors at GM and Ford to decide and decide soon. Dan and I learned in 1990 that lean thinking provides a great way to identify the root cause of the problem but that lean thinkers shouldn't put any confidence in forecasts!

Feb. 7, 2006

The Lean Way Forward at Ford

I've been reflecting on today's remarkable headlines [Sept. 16, 2006] about the latest retreat by the Ford Motor Co. as part of its "Way Forward" campaign. While reflecting, I have found it useful to think about the history of lean thinking at Ford, going back nearly 100 years. I believe it offers many useful lessons for our current-day lean journey and Ford's immediate choices.

The historical record is clear: Henry Ford was the world's first systematic lean thinker. His mind naturally focused on the value-creation process rather than assets or organizations. And he was the first to see in his mind's eye the flow of value from start to finish, from concept to launch, and from raw material to customer. In addition, Ford was history's most ferocious enemy of waste. (Except, possibly, Taiichi Ohno at Toyota, who claimed that he learned what to do from reading Henry Ford's books.)

Ford relentlessly emphasized the need to analyze every step in every process to see if it created value before finding a way to do it better. Otherwise the step should be eliminated. (This was Ford's greatest criticism of Frederick Taylor and Scientific Management. Why, asked Ford, was Taylor obsessed with getting people to work harder and more efficiently to do things that actually didn't need to be done if the work was organized in the right sequence and location?) Then, when the wasteful steps had been eliminated, it was time to put the rest in continuous flow.

By 1914 at his Highland Park plant, Ford had located most of the manufacturing steps for his product—the Model T—in one building and had created very nearly continuous flow in many parts of the operation, using single-piece-flow fabrication cells for components in addition to the moving final assembly line. He had even devised a very primitive pull system by using "shortage chasers" on timed routes along the assembly line to check inventories at every assembly point and convey the information back to the fabrication areas. This speeded up upstream processes that had fallen behind and slowed down those that were getting ahead.

Equally remarkable, Ford had designed his Model T in only three months in one large room with a small group of engineers under his direct oversight. This surely was a high point in lean practice for decades to come.

Then it gradually fell apart. Ford's span of management control at Highland Park had been remarkably broad because he could easily take a walk to see the condition of every process in design, assembly, and fabrication. And he could train a cohort of managers to see what he was seeing and remove more waste. No abstract measures of performance were needed.

However, as the company grew, Ford's personal management method became impractical. But with what to replace it? Ford himself seems not to have had an answer except to link every step by conveyors—as he attempted to do at the massive Rouge complex completed in the late-1920s. By the 1930s the whole Ford Motor Co. was in a sense one linked process. (Ohno, of course, realized that lengthy conveyors governed by a central schedule are a push not a pull system, but this was much later.) Did this mean that the founder believed the company needed only one manager—Ford himself—even as it became the world's largest industrial enterprise?

In any case, the system came crashing down in the 1930s as Ford tried to produce multiple products with multiple options in wildly gyrating markets. Only the staggering cash reserves from retained profits during the Model T era kept the company going until grandson Henry Ford II was able to take over in 1945.

But what management system should he impose on the chaos? Henry Ford II read Drucker's 1946 classic, *The Concept of the Corporation*, praising the General Motors management system, and quickly remade Ford in the image of GM.

What a different system it was! Henry Ford had managed by going to the gemba to inspect the value-creation process. GM executives managed by analyzing financial abstractions: for example, asset utilization (normalized for sales volume), days of inventory, cost of scrap, etc., in the factory and available engineering hours utilized in product design. Managers were then rewarded for making numerical targets using methods developed by staff experts that managers rarely understood. A good way to make many of these numbers was to make products in large batches in order to achieve high asset utilization and low cost per individual step. The total value-creation process from end to end —which had been so clear to Henry Ford—was gradually lost from view.

Soon Ford executives using the financial measures developed by finance czar J. Edward Lundy were even more rigorous in analyzing the performance of their area of control than GM executives. Robert McNamara and the Whiz Kids were the exemplars. And Ford did regain competitiveness as a GM clone, claiming a stable second place in the auto industry.

In addition, by the late-1940s Ford was one of three U.S. auto companies using the same management system in the same town with the same union. With high investment barriers to entry, a remarkable era of stability was put in place, lasting nearly 40 years until the transplant Japanese factories succeeded in the United States in the late-1980s.

When it suddenly became apparent at that point that the leading Japanese companies—Toyota followed by Honda—were using a different management system, it was very hard for Ford to respond.

In the late-1980s, as Dan Jones, Dan Roos, and I wrote *The Machine That Changed the World*, we were able to document that Ford had applied a number of lean techniques in its assembly operations and was making dramatic progress in manufacturing productivity. We took this to mean that at least one American company was applying lean principles and with good results.

What we couldn't report, because we had no way to measure it, was the status of the management system. And this was largely unchanged. Ford managers were still manipulating abstractions because the gemba consciousness of the early Ford Motor Co. had been lost. Even worse, in the product development and supplier management processes, no change had occurred at all.

But Ford could still be successful in its home market for another 20 years by developing large pickups and SUVs. These were essentially

America-only vehicles, suited to wide roads and low energy prices. They could only be challenged by Toyota and its Japanese emulators if they were willing to design vehicles specifically for the U.S. market and to locate production in North America.

In 1997, I got a call from Jac Nasser, who had just taken over Ford's North American Automotive Operations on his way to becoming CEO of Ford. He matter-of-factly told me that Ford's Explorer and F100 pickup series were the only Ford products that made serious money and that he calculated that he had four years to become as efficient and effective as Toyota. Otherwise, the large pickups and SUVs would be copied by foreign firms at lower cost with higher quality and Ford would be in terminal decline. "So," he asked, "how can Ford become Toyota in four years?"

We sat down to talk over just what this would mean—dramatically changing the supplier management system, the product development system, the production management system, what managers do—and he quickly concluded that it was just too hard. So he changed the management metrics, purged the poorest managers according to the metrics, and experimented with selling cars on the web! I was not asked back and had no desire to go back.

Ford actually survived for five years beyond Nasser's projected meltdown date—although Nasser didn't as CEO—to arrive at its current crisis. But my prescription for new Ford CEO Alan Mulally is the same: Fundamentally rethink the supplier management system. Fundamentally rethink the product development system. And fundamentally rethink the production system from order to raw materials and from raw materials to delivery, with special attention to the information management system. (Much can still be learned from Ford's Mazda subsidiary, which became an able pupil of Toyota after a crisis in 1973.)

Above all, fundamentally rethink what managers do and how they do it in order to regain the gemba consciousness that originally took Ford to world dominance. In brief, Ford needs to remake itself once more, this time in the image of the company that copied Ford's original system: Toyota.

In addition, finish rethinking the social contract as Ford becomes a normal company (not an oligopolist) in a normal town (where labor doesn't come from one supplier) that must live in a global market. Finally, rethink brand strategy to get rid of hopeless makes that can never make money—Mercury, Jaguar, Lincoln?—while refocusing the remaining brands on what customers really want—sophisticated, hassle-free transportation in every price range. (A hint: rethink the vast gap between the company and the customer to provide hassle-free mobility on a continuing basis to user-partners rather than selling cars to strangers in one-time transactions.)

Who knows whether this is doable in the time still available, but it is the lean way forward. It will be tragic if the originator of lean thinking is crushed in the end by failing to learn lean lessons from its most earnest pupil.

Sept. 15, 2006

Why Toyota Won and How Toyota Can Lose

Simon & Schuster has just reissued *The Machine That Changed the World*, which Dan Jones, Dan Roos, and I coauthored in 1990. Doubtless, our publisher has noticed the current Toyota boom when any book with "Toyota" on the cover sells.

Fortunately, *Machine* is still the best description of the complete lean business system—product and process development, supplier management, supporting the customer, fulfilling orders from raw materials through production, and management of the global enterprise. It still has a story to tell. As new CEO Alan Mulally remarked to Ford employees when he arrived in Detroit last fall, it is the best summary of why Toyota is winning.

But in fact Toyota has already won. It's just a matter of totaling units sold and revenues during 2007 to know exactly when to transfer the industry leader's jersey from GM to Toyota. Much more important from a business standpoint, Toyota won the profitability race years ago.

The interesting question for the future is not the precise day Toyota wins but how Toyota can lose. The conventional wisdom is that it may fumble on quality (as evidenced by recent recalls), go soft on costs, stumble in trying to make Lexus a truly elite brand, or fail to gain a stable production and sales base in the emerging markets of China and India.

And these could happen. But if they do they will be symptoms, not the root cause. Toyota's real challenge for the future is to introduce and sustain lean management at every point in a rapidly growing organization.

It's sobering to realize that many new employees at Toyota read Jeff Liker's *The Toyota Way*[14] and Jeff and David Meier's *The Toyota Way Field Book*[15] (which every lean thinker should read as well) to try to understand the company they have joined. Toyota's traditional way of creating managers by hiring them straight from high school or college and

---

14. Jeffrey K. Liker, *The Toyota Way* (New York: McGraw-Hill, 2004).
15. Jeffrey K. Liker and Dave Meier, *The Toyota Way Field Book* (New York: McGraw-Hill, 2006).

carefully coaching them over many years to become seasoned Toyota-style managers is being severely strained by Toyota's breakneck growth rate. There are too many new pupils and not enough mature teachers as Toyota opens new plants, engineering centers, and supplier development groups across the world.

Toyota's great risk—the way it can lose—is that its new managers and the managers in its new suppliers will revert to the old, modern-management mentality of the companies or schools from which they have come. If this happens, Toyota's management performance will regress toward the mean. Instead of moving the whole world to embrace lean management, Toyota will become just another company. And that will be a tragic failure for us all.

What does Toyota need to teach its new lean managers? Obviously, the specific methods (tools) for conducting production, product design, supplier management, and sales and service are important. But these are the easy part. The heart of the lean manager's knowledge is strategy deployment originating with senior managers, A3 problem solving for line managers in the middle of the organization, and standardized management of standardized work with kaizen for front-line managers.

And at every level Toyota needs to teach its managers to utilize these concepts by going to the gemba. There, they need to ask questions about the true business problem, the current condition causing the problem, a better condition (that is, a better process) that could address the problem, who must do what when to achieve this new condition (the future state), and what evidence will show that the problem has been addressed.

This means managing the organization's value-creating processes (value streams) by asking highly informed questions rather than managing results at the end of the reporting period. (The latter is simply another form of end-of-the-line quality inspection.) And it means not ordering people what to do next when matters seem to be getting out of hand.

Issuing crisp orders is the natural instinct of any boss. Indeed, most bosses seem to think that by virtue of their experience and authority, they should be able to solve any problem lower in the organization. But orders from the boss rather than informed questions take away the lower-level managers' responsibility for solving problems. They start a vicious circle in which lower-level managers wait to be told what to do by higher-level managers who are much further from the gemba where value is created and who inherently have less— not more—knowledge of the best thing to do.

Compared with the rest of us, Toyota has one major advantage. It never acquires companies or facilities. It expands by opening "greenfield" operations in new locations. So if it finds that it can't grow lean managers at the same rate as sales it can simply slow down. And my bet is that Toyota will slow down if it senses that its management values are being seriously diluted.

The rest of us face a harder problem. We already own and operate "brownfields" that urgently need a transformation in their management. Slowing down this transformation simply makes us fail faster!

In summary, Toyota can fail, and if it does the root cause will be a failure to propagate its management system. We also can fail. And if we do, the root cause will be a failure to transform our outdated modern-management systems. Thus it turns out that we all face the same challenge!

It follows that all of us in the Lean Community need to learn from each other about the best way to create lean managers. We don't want anyone to fail.

April 4, 2007

Additional reading:

James P. Womack, Daniel T. Jones, and Daniel Roos, reissue version of *The Machine that Changed the World* (New York: Free Press, 2007).

Jeffrey Liker, *The Toyota Way* (New York: McGraw-Hill, 2004).

Jeffrey Liker and David Meier, *The Toyota Way Field Book* (New York: McGraw-Hill, 2006).

This assessment of Toyota's situation, written in 2007, seems prescient in light of the events at Toyota in 2010. But the timing and magnitude of Toyota's difficulties were as big a surprise to me as they were to the general public.

What was not at all surprising was what happened to General Motors in the fall of 2008 and the spring of 2009, for I had long been convinced that the next recession would be the last for the old General Motors, as explained in the next essay. However, what was of much more interest to me at this juncture, and much harder to discern, was what the end of The Great Chase would mean for the Lean Community.

The End of an Era

When General Motors filed for bankruptcy yesterday [June 1, 2009] it marked the end of an era. The first truly modern, manage-by-the-numbers corporation, created by Alfred Sloan in the 1920s, was laid to rest as a viable concept. But what comes next?

This is not just a question for GM or large enterprises more generally. Yesterday also marked an end of the lean narrative that has been unfolding for 30 years, ever since GM first began to decline in the recession of 1979. David (in fact a team of Davids) finally felled Goliath just as Goliath was finally paying attention to the lean message. So we need to consider what happens next for the Lean Community as well.

What's Next for GM?

At the beginning of 2009, GM had three major weaknesses. It had too much legacy debt—bondholders and retirees. It had benefit (not wage) costs for current employees that were too high to compete with transplant operations in North America. And the money it received for its products in most segments of the market was far below average, partly as a legacy of decades of defective products and partly due to losing the pulse of the public on what the company and its products should mean for customers.

Ironically, GM also had considerable strengths. It had competitive factories in terms of productivity and quality and a competitive product development process when it could focus its energies (e.g., the new Chevy Malibu). After failing for 15 years to learn lessons from NUMMI (its California joint venture with Toyota), GM had in recent years developed a competitive and consistent global manufacturing system and rationalized its global product development organization. It had even taken impressive steps to lean its internal business processes. (See "Lean Beyond the Factory" on page 127.) But—as in the case of its cast-off parts supplier Delphi (see "Necessary but Not Sufficient" on page 194)—lean came too late.

The bankruptcy resets the trip odometer. The legacy debt has been written down to a manageable level, and the benefits costs for current employees will now be much more competitive. In addition, the company is dramatically retrenching toward a reasonable portfolio of brands with production capacity appropriate to its realistic share of likely market volumes.

So what is the problem? Simply that GM has now explained what it is not. It is not Saturn or Saab or Pontiac or Hummer. And GM is not a significant manufacturer in the United States outside of the Midwest. And GM is not, from a profitability standpoint, mainly a finance company. And GM will not have a dealer net blanketing every area of every city across the continent.

But what a company is not is of no interest to consumers. If General Motors is no longer "your father's GM" (to paraphrase its advertising line in the last years of Oldsmobile) or "the company that let you down" (as CEO Fritz Henderson phrased it at yesterday's news conference), then what is it? Why should any new customers care to shop GM products, much less pay the top-of-the-segment prices GM needs to flourish? And who can define what the new, appealing GM is?

Sloan's great genius in re-creating General Motors in the 1920s (after its second trip through reorganization—yesterday marked the third in 100 years) was to provide a compelling explanation of how GM fit into every American's life. He presented a complete range of vehicles from a used Chevrolet as a first car for the low-income buyer to a fully equipped Cadillac for those who had succeeded financially. And GM products were carefully arrayed in a status hierarchy with brilliant attention to the look and feel of each product in relation to American tastes. Indeed, as it gained massive size, GM was often the arbiter of American tastes.

So far the only message about what GM is is the Volt, its extended-range hybrid. Perhaps this is a start, although with enormous risks given the flux in technologies and in political and public perceptions about climate change and energy dependency. But even if it is a start, it is a very small start. Who can comprehensively define "your son's GM," or "the GM that never lets you down"? And what freedom will they have to do so?

It is easy to blame GM's recent management for its troubles. But the senior GM managers I have known—almost all of whom had strong finance backgrounds—were remarkably competent at running the company in the financially oriented, manage-by-results way that had produced success for generations. So the problem is not the individual competence of mangers but GM's irrelevant conception of what management needs to do. In the simplest terms, where is the new Sloan, the leader able to rethink GM's management and purpose and make it relevant to Americans again?

Clearly the hard part comes now, after bankruptcy, and we will all watch what happens. But let me make an exception for those readers—and there are many—who work at GM and who can take an active role in making it happen. I truly wish you the best.

What's Next for Lean?

For 30 years now the Lean Community has benefited from a strong tailwind. GM steadily declined as Toyota steadily advanced. All we needed to do was stand by and cheer! But this narrative is over.

GM and almost all large manufacturers have now accepted lean as a management theory, although the actual practice is always a struggle. As I noted above, GM was becoming a vastly leaner enterprise just as it collapsed, and I have confidence that it will continue to embrace lean principles and methods in the years immediately ahead.

At the same time Toyota has turned out to have flaws of its own in the current financial crisis. It barged ahead with capacity expansion across the world that outran its ability to create lean managers and defied reasonable expectations for long-term market demand. (As I have mentioned in previous essays, in the mid-1990s Toyota redefined its purpose from being the best organization at solving customer problems to being the largest, an objective of no interest to any customer.) This has been a real setback for the lean movement.

We in the Lean Community therefore find ourselves in the odd position of winning a battle of ideas without actually getting most believers to fully practice their new convictions. And we have as our ideal organization a company that is experiencing significant management and revenue challenges despite "winning" the great contest between modern management and lean management.

Even as this drama plays out within manufacturing, lean ideas are spreading rapidly to new fields, from the beleaguered financial industry to healthcare to government services. Yet we have not fully defined what lean means in these areas, much less how to implement and sustain it. So the dramatic events of recent weeks are not a time for self-congratulation. Instead, they are a time for modesty and self-reflection—hansei, if you will—as we all struggle with the economic crisis while trying to redefine our own purpose as a Lean Community for the new era ahead.

June 2, 2009

We continue to struggle with these latter issues, which I return to in the final essay in this volume. However, first I think it is useful to reflect on the long history of lean thinking—of which the great chase is but a small part—as a prelude to a consideration of the future. This long narrative is the focus of the three essays in the next section.

HISTORY THAT'S NOT BUNK

Henry Ford is famous for asserting that "history is bunk," bunk being a 19th century American term for worthless nonsense. I have often used this adage in my writing and speaking, taking it to mean that the dead hand of past practice must never be allowed to obstruct the search for better ways to do things in the future. And Ford surely did mean this.

However, Ford also meant that history as usually written—the business of assigning historical importance to the actions of a few elites and key individuals—is bunk of a different sort. As he understood history, it is actually the achievement of many people, working on the gemba, trying small and large experiments, usually anonymously, to move humanity ahead.

(I only became aware of this meaning recently, after reading about Ford's Fordlandia experiment in Brazil to create a reliable source of rubber for Ford's global production system. This was perhaps history's most spectacular failure to diffuse process thinking in a different culture.[16] By contrast, the Toyota-GM joint venture at NUMMI in California was perhaps history's most spectacular instance of successful lean diffusion, as explained in the last essay in this section.)

What Ford surely did not mean about history is that we should forget the many steps on our long journey of discovery as we find ever better ways to create value. (He preserved the apparatus required for a number of these steps in the Henry Ford Museum and at Greenfield Village in Dearborn, MI.) The essays in this section attempt to bring into focus this long, lean walk through history up to the present moment.

---

16. Greg Grandin, *Fordlandia: The Rise and Fall of Henry Ford's Forgotten Jungle City* (New York: Metropolitan Books/Henry Holt & Co., 2009).

A Lean Walk through History

In the first essay in this section I try to list and evaluate the many small victories, often anonymous, that have moved the lean thought process ahead, through a multicentury history that we ought to know better.

As you well know, I like to walk the gemba, along specific value streams, to see for myself how value is being created and how waste can be eliminated. Recently I took a wonderful, but dismaying, walk through a facility that no longer creates value, along a historic but vanished value stream. The experience set me thinking about the history of the lean movement and how we can preserve it.

The place in question was Highland Park, MI, a ghostly town with a ghostly factory—Henry Ford's extraordinary Highland Park plant where flow production was pioneered. In the older building on the site, I walked the floor along the exact path where the world's first continuous-flow assembly line started up in the spring of 1914. It's now empty, dirty, dark, dank, and uncommemorated.

In the six-story "new shops" across the street, I walked the exact path where the assembly line had been moved later in 1914. At that time, many continuous-flow fabrication operations worked on both sides of the line, and the upper floors supplied the parts needed by the line. Today, the new shops—all six floors and three skylit bays of Albert Kahn's glorious concrete structure specifically designed for flow production—also stand empty and uncommemorated, awaiting redevelopment or the wrecker.

It's my belief that this building was the site of the most important industrial and economic leap in human history. Yet Ford's descendents— and I include you and me since we have built much of our current lean knowledge on Ford's shoulders—seem to have misapplied one of his favorite aphorisms: "History is bunk." ("Bunk" is a 19th century American term meaning worthless nonsense.) We've ignored key moments and monuments in our past as we race toward the future.

How can this be? I think the root cause is that most of us don't realize that we are heirs to a remarkably long struggle in human history to see beyond isolated points in order to optimize the entire value-creating process. We tend to think instead that lean ideas were mostly created by Toyota a few years ago and that the history of lean thinking has been short and easy.

I was recently reminded of the length of our struggle when my colleague and coauthor Dan Jones visited the Arsenale in Venice, established in 1104 to build warships for the Venetian Navy. Over time the Venetians adopted a standardized design for the hundreds of war galleys built each year to campaign in the Mediterranean, and also pioneered the use of interchangeable parts. This made it possible to assemble galleys along a narrow channel running through the Arsenale. The hull was completed first and then "flowed" past the assembly point for each item needed to complete the ship. By 1574 the Arsenale's practices were so advanced that King Henry III of France was invited to watch the construction of a complete galley in continuous flow, going from start to finish in less than an hour.

The point I took particular note of from our visit was that the idea of continuous flow—which many in our community probably think was invented by Henry Ford—was being practiced more than 400 years ago, but then largely forgotten!

Once you are sensitized to the depth of lean history, along with its many advances and setbacks, it's easy to begin filling in some of the other milestones:

- By 1765 French general Jean-Baptiste de Gribeauval had grasped the significance of standardized designs and interchangeable parts to facilitate battlefield repairs. (Actually doing this cost-effectively in practice was another matter and required many experiments over another 125 years.)

- By 1807 Marc Brunel in England had devised equipment for making simple wooden items like rope blocks for the Royal Navy using 22 kinds of machines that produced identical items in process sequence one at a time.

- By 1822 Thomas Blanchard at the Springfield Armory in the United States had devised a set of 14 machines and laid them out in a cellular arrangement that made it possible to make more complex shapes like gunstocks for rifles. A block of wood was placed in the first machine, the lever was thrown, and the water-powered machine automatically removed some of the wood using a profile tracer on a reference piece. What this meant was really quite remarkable: The 14 machines could make a completed item with no human labor for processing and in single-piece flow as the items were moved ahead from machine to machine one at a time.

- By the 1850s all of the American armories were making standardized metal parts for standardized weapons, but only with enormous amounts of handwork to get each part to its correct specification. This was because the machine tools of that era could not work on hardened metal. Instead they machined soft metal, and the subsequent hardening process introduced warping of an unpredictable nature that had to be corrected by hand before parts would fit together. The expense was acceptable for military hardware, but unacceptable for most consumer goods.

- In 1914 Ford finally got all of these strands of thinking to come together with advances in cutting tools and a leap in gauging technology so that many suppliers could produce hardened metal parts that consistently fit perfectly in Ford's fabrication cells and on his final assembly line. This was the secret to truly continuous flow.

- By the late-1930s the German aircraft industry had pioneered takt time as a way to synchronize aircraft final assembly in which airplane fuselages were moved ahead in unison throughout final assembly at a precise measure (takt) of time. (Mitsubishi had a technical relationship with the German companies and transferred this method back to Japan where Toyota, located nearby in Aichi Prefecture, heard about it and adopted it.)

- By the early-1950s Toyota had integrated the idea of takt time with Ford's ideas on continuous flow and added the critical dimension of flexibility to make high-quality products in wide variety in small batches with very short lead times.

- In the early-1990s, the business process reengineering movement tried, but mostly failed, to transfer the concepts of standardized work and continuous flow to office and service processes that now constitute the great bulk of human activities.

Note that this very incomplete rendition of lean history involves contributions from Venice, France, England, the United States, Germany, and Japan at a minimum. And there may well have been advances pioneered in other societies that are unrecorded. To take two examples that Dan and I hope to explore someday: How did the Chinese build the vast armada of identical Treasure Ships that set out in 1421 to "unite the world in Confucian harmony"? Were they far ahead of Venice in their design and production practices? And what about the Romans, with all those sunken galleys in the Mediterranean with thousands of identical pots for oils and wine? What process was used to make them?

Whatever the final list of contributors, I feel strongly that our lean history isn't bunk. And Ford wouldn't have thought so either. Remember that he was a remarkable conservator of the pre-Ford industrial past at his Greenfield Village museum in Dearborn, MI. One of the things he meant by "history is bunk" was that established methods must never be used as an excuse or impediment to trying new methods. And Taiichi Ohno felt the same way in refusing to write down TPS. He believed that if it was strictly codified—put in a museum, in his thinking—it would be frozen and soon go backward.

None of us wants to embalm lean thinking in a museum. However, as long as we are determined to continue experimenting—with kaikaku and kaizen forever—then the history of how we got to our current state of lean enlightenment, inadequate as it is, becomes a precious legacy. It also can be an inspiring story that can sustain us through inevitable setbacks along the path to the future.

I hope you now have at least a bit of appreciation for the long struggle to perfect process thinking. But note the practically complete lack of commemoration. There are lots of *product* museums full of brilliant, breakthrough objects (like the Model T). And some—like the Henry Ford Museum in Dearborn, the Toyota Museum in Nagoya, and the Science Museum in London—include some remarkable process machinery displayed in isolation. But there are no *process* museums showing how value creation works as a whole. Shouldn't the Lean Community think about creating a place to showcase the long struggle from isolated points to optimized processes? And wouldn't Highland Park be a great place to start?

Dec. 7, 2004

Nice Car, Long Journey

Note from the previous recounting that only a few of the experimenters in lean hostory are known by name. Who made the breakthrough to flow at the Arsenale? Who thought up the idea of takt time? Indeed, who really invented flow assembly in Highland Park, and just-in-time and jidoka in Toyota City? The answer, I think, is not just anonymous individuals but anonymous groups of individuals collectively experimenting.

In this essay, I looked at one group of experimenters—at Highland Park in the period between 1908 and 1914—who pioneered many of the concepts that are central to lean thinking. However, my interest was not in the past for the sake of memorializing a few heroes of the lean movement, but rather in why it has taken us so long to apply lessons learned a century ago.

The year 2008 marks the 100th anniversary of the introduction of the Model T Ford. This truly is "the machine that changed the world," even if the title of a 1990 book might suggest otherwise! Nearly 16 million copies were built over 19 years of production as the world was motorized.

The Model T marks the beginning of the lean era. So I recently decided I should go to Detroit and learn to drive a Model T. I was pretty sure that I could do it—my father learned to drive on a Model T in 1918 when he was only 10 years old. But I'm still thankful to Don LaCombe and all of the folks at The Henry Ford Museum and Greenfield Village —which maintains a small fleet of Model Ts—for taking on my education. With their help I think I passed.

Let me say right away that it's a nice car: High and roomy like an SUV, great offroad performance in the mud, 20 miles per gallon on 60-octane gas (which would be a lot cheaper if you could find any today), great visibility (although windows and a top would be nice on some days), and easy to drive after only one lesson. (Starting the motor by turning the crank proved to be another matter.) The Model T was an extraordinarily sophisticated technical achievement in 1908, and I often say—to the irritation of my friends in Detroit—that there hasn't been a truly new idea in the auto industry since Ford's car introduced reliable personal transportation for everyone at an affordable price.

What is more significant for lean thinkers is that many of the product development methods we still struggle to implement today were pioneered by Henry Ford and his engineers as they designed the Model T in 1908. In particular, a design team huddled in one room with the chief engineer (a real obeya room!), working to a tight timetable (three months!), to design a highly modular vehicle that was easy to assemble and one with easy access to every part for maintenance.

Equally important, many of the methods employed in lean production were pioneered between the launch of the Model T in 1908 and the completion of Ford's Highland Park factory in Detroit in 1914. Ford's team achieved consistently interchangeable parts (for the first time in volume production), single-piece flow in fabrication by locating many technologies in process sequence, standardized work and precisely repeatable cycle times, a primitive pull system for parts supply, and a remarkably horizontal, value-stream focus for the entire production process that minimized total lead time. The innovation most visible to the public—the moving final assembly line—was actually introduced last—in the spring of 1914—and was only possible because of the previously pioneered innovations. Thus the Model T helped start us all on a long, lean journey.

But why has the journey been so long? How can it take a century to universally embrace some very simple concepts? Why has Ford's own company struggled to apply the full logic of the ideas prototyped between 1908 and 1914? And how can we go faster?

I've been thinking about these questions for a long time, and I don't have all the answers. But I do have a few observations:

Determine the right destination before you start the journey: As the length of the journey to a completed lean enterprise sinks in, I often hear the expression "it's the journey, not the destination." And it makes me grumpy every time I hear it. If we really have no expectation on our watch of creating a mature lean enterprise, but instead just want the pleasure of applying lean techniques to random processes, then let's take the next exit and do something else.

In fact, the reason the journey takes so long for many organizations is that they have no clear agreement on just what the right destination is. And in particular they make no connection between meeting the customer and business needs of the organization—the true purpose of any process improvement—and the right sequence of steps to take.

For example, I recently attended the beginning of a kaizen week in a large corporation. I played the role of an anthropologist by watching quietly from the rear. A team of earnest process improvers dove into applying a whole portfolio of lean tools to a process without any discussion of the needed payoff for the customer or the business. I don't doubt that they will be on their journey for a long time!

The key trick, as I now understand, is to pick an initial destination— an improvement in the performance of key processes that will permit the organization to prosper by addressing the customer's needs. Once that destination is reached, it's time to pick another, further along the path toward perfection, that materially benefits the organization. And so on.

This also suggests something about the very nature of "perfection": since the purpose of any process keeps changing as customer and organizational needs keep changing, perfection is a moving rather than a stationary target.

Management is more important than tools: Ford pioneered a concept for low-cost personal mobility and a series of lean design and production tools to make this concept practical. His problem was that he never created a management system that could sustain his methods. After his departure, a formal manage-by-results system was installed to replace the informal management-by-process approach of Ford's early days. And the company is only now returning to its roots, trying again to embrace process-focused management.

I see the same pattern in many organizations today. Lots of good lean techniques tied to a mass-production management system, without any awareness that you can't have sustainable lean processes unless you have lean management.

Good things do take time: When I first started visiting companies trying to make a lean leap in the 1980s, it seemed obvious to me that a transformation could be completed quickly. In retrospect, what's more obvious is that I could reach this breezy conclusion because I wasn't the one on the gemba doing the heavy lifting! I now understand that my happy estimate that a lean transformation could be completed in five years was far from the mark. The challenge is to make steady progress with clear interim objectives (successive destinations) that actually can be achieved, building momentum for further progress. Thus a better mantra is "it is the journey, but to the right destinations."

We really are making progress: I'm now old enough and have been observing the progress of lean thinking long enough that patterns are clear to me that many younger travelers with less experience may miss.

For example, I became interested in the Danaher Corp. as that firm started to embrace lean thinking 20 years ago. The path hasn't been along a straight line during this entire period, and observers of single points in time might easily have drawn the wrong conclusion. But the company has made continuing progress, driven by a very rigorous strategy-deployment process to decide on solid business grounds what the next destination should be. It is not coincidental that Danaher has been the most consistently successful American industrial company of the past 30 years.

To take another example, I recently visited Boeing Commercial Airplanes to check up on the progress of lean production for the 737 series, a family of airplanes assembled in the same room in Renton, WA, for the past 41 years. When I first visited this room in the early-1990s, the airplanes were assembled at stationary positions, parts shortages were the norm, and the total assembly time was more than 30 days. Now a moving assembly line takes planes from start to finish in only eight days. That's continuing progress—despite several severe downdrafts along the route—that provides great hope for the future.

Thus I see a pattern of organizations initially dabbling with lean tools—probably in the form of a "program." They gain some results, followed by backsliding, followed by a realization that management comes first and tools come second. This leads to a new round of progress and arrival at an interim destination. Then a new management team picks up the challenge, perhaps after a pause or even a relapse, and the organization sets off toward the next destination. It's not pretty to watch, and it's not "efficient" in terms of making the most progress in the least amount of time. But it is progress. So let's say a word of thanks to the humble Model T, on its centennial, for helping start us up this path.

June 6, 2008

The next great leap in lean thinking was in Toyota City in the period after World War II. In the next essay I review not what was learned in individual experiments but how the new learning was deployed across an extended value stream. As it turns out, the methods employed were not those of the large corporate program familiar in recent years in the lean movement. Instead it was a matter of many sensei (masters) teaching many deshi (pupils) through hands-on experiments on the gemba.

Respect Science, Particularly in a Crisis

The current recession is the fifth in my working career. And it is beginning to feel like the worst. I can't imagine that any manager or improvement-team member in any industry in any country isn't feeling a bit queasy at this point, as the world economy keeps recessing toward an unknown bottom. Where should we go to calibrate our North Star in times like these, to reassure ourselves that we are on the most promising path? Recently I've found one answer.

In carefully reviewing a new publication from LEI, I've had the opportunity to spend a lot of time with the "fathers of lean." By this I mean the small band of Japanese line managers who made the original breakthrough to create a lean enterprise and who were interviewed at length much later about what they did and why. The relevant point for this moment is that a small group of managers achieved a lean leap in a time of severe stress, making some of their boldest moves during the financial crisis of 1950.

As the Japanese economy entered a steep recession in that year, the Toyota Motor Co. ran out of cash, which was tied up in inventory for products customers no longer wanted. The company fell under the control of bankers who chopped the company in two, creating separate firms to divide the marketing and sales functions from the product development and production functions. (These firms were only recombined in 1982 to create the current Toyota Motor Corp.) Founding President Kiichiro Toyoda (new President Akio Toyoda's grandfather) was driven out in the process. The pursuit of what became the Toyota Production System, along with the product development, supplier management, and customer support systems, was the creative response to this crisis.

As I started to read these interviews I expected to discover that Toyota's managers had a clear plan all along. Surely leaders like Taiichi Ohno, Kikuo Suzumura, and Eiji Toyoda knew exactly where they were going and how to get there. I also expected to find a clearly chartered improvement team and a formal program to go with it. (Perhaps "Moving Forward," Toyota's recent tag line in its advertising?)

What I found instead was that a few line managers had some very simple ideas and an extreme sense of urgency: Minimize lead time from order to delivery (to free up scarce cash). Remove waste from every step in every process (to reduce costs and enhance quality). Take action now (because there wasn't much time). But what they also had—and this was critical—was a tight scientific discipline. While they did act quickly, they also took the necessary time to document the current state, to state their hypothesis very clearly, to conduct a rigorous experiment, to measure the results, and to reflect on what they had actually achieved, sharing their findings widely.

What they didn't have was a "program" or even a name for the system of scientific discovery they were creating. Indeed, the label "Toyota Production System" was only introduced in 1970—after the system had been fully invented—to explain it to suppliers. What they also didn't have was a program office or a dedicated improvement team. The fabled Operations Management Consulting Division was introduced at about the same time as the label "TPS" and only after TPS was deployed across the enterprise. Toyota's remarkable act of creation—based on a scientific process of systematic discovery—was conducted by line managers as the most important part of their daily work. And—here's the really inspiring part—they did most of their research in the midst of a fierce battle for survival.

In learning more about Toyota's achievements in the 1950s as the company struggled to survive, I've gained a new appreciation for the fact that we have no excuses in our current period of chaotic markets and falling demand. Systematic science works wherever it is applied to any process. And it is more and not less useful in the depths of a crisis. The only ingredient that may be lacking today is our determination to respect rigorous science in the current crisis. And that you can quickly rectify!

March 5, 2009

Additional reading:

Koichi Shimokawa and Takihiro Fujimoto, editors, *The Birth of Lean*, (Cambridge, MA: Lean Enterprise Institute, 2009).

In my view the last major historical milestone in the progression of lean thinking was the effort to diffuse it across the world from the leap made in Japan after World War II. The NUMMI experiment in California was the critical breakthrough, as explored in the final essay in this section.

The End of the Beginning

NUMMI closes today [April 1, 2010]. The General Motors-Toyota joint venture assembling motor vehicles in California lasted 25 years—a very long time for a joint venture —and about 8 million vehicles rolled off the line. For those working at NUMMI this is a truly sad day, and I hope our Lean Community will reach out to help many employees there find new jobs utilizing their advanced lean knowledge. But for the rest of the global Lean Community, this day is not just one of sadness. I think it marks the end of the beginning.

Honda first moved automotive manufacturing abroad from Japan in 1982, with a very similar production system to Toyota's. But NUMMI in 1984 was the first application of the complete lean system in a completely foreign environment using employees and line managers steeped in the tradition of mass production. And the best part was that the system the small band of Toyota managers brought to NUMMI from Toyota City was so systematic, visible, and easy to copy: The TPS house. The standard terminology. The methodical approach to human relations with a new, proactive role for teams, team leaders, and front-line management. The focus on problem solving and continuous improvement rather than fault finding and the status quo. And all of the support apparatus to handle information and material in order to create a smooth flow of value from end to end.

NUMMI could have failed to match the productivity and quality achieved in Toyota City (as many at Toyota feared it would). That would have left us with other things to do and talk about today. But instead it was a remarkable success in terms of quality, productivity, and the new way managers and employees were able to work together. It laid the foundation for all of the success lean thinking has had subsequently. So whatever happens to the NUMMI site in Fremont, CA, it surely should be designated a "world economic landmark."

Not only was NUMMI a remarkable success, it was an immediate success. From the start of production in 1984, it was only two years before our research team at MIT, in a remarkable paper by young John Krafcik,[17] was publicly reporting the revolution in product quality and productivity. And NUMMI also was an enduring success over its full 25 years through a number of phases of organizational renewal, proving that with periodic reflection and renewed management attention lean can truly endure for the long term.

Remarkably we were still learning from NUMMI at the end. John Shook in his recent Sloan Management Review article[18] explains how NUMMI showed that the best way to change and sustain an organizational culture is by first changing and sustaining management behavior, a lesson many transformation efforts still overlook. And toward the end even GM learned to manage in a different way with dramatic gains in productivity and quality, although too late to save itself. But now the launch party for the lean movement—continuing for all these years at NUMMI—is over. So where do we go from here?

(You can hear the sad story of how NUMMI failed to rapidly transform GM, including interviews with NUMMI workers, union leaders, and GM managers, on the March 26, 2010 installment of *This American Life*, downloadable from National Public Radio.)

Perhaps the hardest first step is to adjust to the fact that virtue isn't always rewarded. All of us in the Lean Community want to believe that a superior facility applying the best lean methods should be spared the forces of the global economy. But this isn't likely in a world where economic stability seems to lie always in the future. Sometimes making a product efficiently with few defects and strong team spirit isn't enough in a world of excess capacity and widely varying labor costs per hour.

And we would all like to think that a company like Toyota that has consistently shown the world a better way to do things would be treated generously when a few things go wrong. But this isn't the norm. Fault

17. John Krafcik, *Learning from NUMMI*, (Cambridge, MA: unpublished manuscript, MIT International Motor Vehicle Program, 1986).
18. John Shook, "How to Change a Culture: Lessons from NUMMI," *Sloan Management Review*, Winter 2010.

finding—the search for who is responsible—may have been replaced with root cause analysis—asking the Five Whys—in the lean management system, but the diffusion of this simple idea to the world at large is sadly lagging.

So we will have to move ahead in imperfect circumstances, doing the best we can on our watch. In my view, we are making progress and have dramatic opportunities just ahead despite the degree of difficulty:

- NUMMI proved once and for all that lean methods can be successfully adopted in the most difficult circumstances in tired facilities with aging workforces. (Just listen to the *This American Life* story and ask yourself if anything about your situation can be worse than the problems confronting a few Toyota managers, including John Shook, when they arrived from across the Pacific to start work 25 years ago.)

- NUMMI proved once and for all that lean methods can be sustained indefinitely, over decades. (NUMMI didn't come to end because it ceased being lean. It came to an end because the auto industry changed in ways that no amount of leanness in California could counter.)

- We now have examples of good lean practice in practically every industry, even including government services. *No one who has tried to create a complete lean enterprise with the hands-on participation of top management has failed to achieve dramatic results.* And that is a very powerful statement.

- We are always looking for a crisis as our moment of opportunity, and the world's healthcare systems are all now heading into deep crises as demographics, new technology, and a history of weak process management produce an unsustainable situation. This may be the single most important contribution of lean thinking to society in this generation, and we already have the knowledge to transform healthcare delivery systems. All we need to do is to act together to rapidly deploy our knowledge.

So let's mourn for a moment the passing of NUMMI and the end of the beginning. Then let's all move ahead together to the next set of challenges and opportunities.

April 1, 2010

Lean challenges and opportunities are the subject of the next essay, which was written for the first edition of this book.

Hopeful Hansei: Thoughts on a Decade of Gemba Walks

Hansei: critical self-reflection for the purpose of improvement.

After 10 years of gemba walks, through an enormous variety of human activities on six continents, what have I learned? And what does my learning suggest about the next series of walks on my lean journey? In this final essay, let me engage in a bit of personal hansei—critical self-reflection—about what I have learned, what I have misunderstood and tried to correct, and where I believe I should walk in the years ahead. My hansei cannot be your hansei, of course. But I hope that sharing my process of reflection will be helpful as you assess your own situation.

Let me start with a lesson I kept learning, on walk after walk, year after year: the critical importance of the simple act of walking. Whenever I have found myself bogged down in abstractions or discouraged about my ability to engage constructively with others on the problems at hand, I have rediscovered the power of going to see. Yet I find that the world constantly pulls me in the opposite direction, asking for my opinions in a conference room or lecture hall about things I have not seen. People push for quick solutions even though I have had no chance to look for and understand the root cause of the problem.

Just this past week, in a windowless conference room in a large medical center, I met with a group of doctors engaged in a discussion of their unit's performance. After I was introduced as some type of "lean" expert, they immediately asked me how I would apply lean theory to get better results in a series of processes I had never seen! Surely these doctors didn't make diagnoses without seeing the patient. But they seemed eager to listen to both a diagnosis and a proposed treatment plan from a practitioner who had never been near the bedside.

I'm sure you also face this pressure to leap without looking. So my most fundamental learning is that you and I must always walk and reflect deeply before acting. If we will all simply do this, the world will be a far better place.

I've learned something else about walking. Never walk alone. What is the benefit if only I see the current state and think of a better way to create a future state? Instead, I always need to walk with the people who touch the value stream: their efforts, not mine, are needed to improve it. But again, the world pushes back. It's hard to get everyone together for a task that traditionally has been delegated to staffs or consultants. In addition, the flaws of the value stream in question are often embarrassing for those directly involved. But in the end, I've learned not to compromise. Solo walks rarely produce significant change. So I hope that you keep walking and always proceed as a value-stream team.

Another learning of the past decade has been to expand my focus. In the early years I looked primarily at the steps in whatever value stream I was observing. That is, I looked at the actual work to be done and asked how to remove the waste. I also asked about the support processes getting the right people to the right place in the value stream at the right time with the right knowledge, materials, and equipment. In short, I was primarily concerned with the process itself, its current performance, and its potential for technical improvement. I was approaching the issue like a traditional industrial engineer.

Today I still focus on the process, and I don't regret the time I spent trying to raise process consciousness across the Lean Community. I'm also proud of the investment LEI has made developing process-improvement tools ranging from value-stream maps to methods for seeing extended value streams from end to end. But I now reflect first on the purpose of the process before focusing intently on the process itself. And I then pay special attention to the way people are engaged in its operation and improvement.

By purpose I don't just mean what the process is currently designed to produce. Increasingly, I focus on what problem the customer is trying to solve in his or her life, and I ask whether the existing process, no matter how well run, can effectively address this problem. Indeed, could the value stream be entirely rethought to produce something quite different?

Similarly, I now focus on how the process feels from the standpoint of those operating it and how better performance must be combined with more fulfilling work. There is nothing worse than seeing good people trapped in an unfulfilling process that they lack the power to improve. This is never necessary and should never be tolerated.

Another learning of the past decade is the importance of achieving basic stability before introducing the full panoply of lean techniques. By basic stability I simply mean that every step is capable (able to produce a good result every time) and every step is available (able to operate when it is needed). To achieve this, technical analysis is necessary and work needs to be standardized.

For 20 years I have had a T-shirt on the wall above my desk in my writer's nook. On the front is a line drawing of Taichi Ohno staring down at me with the admonition, "Where there is no standard, there can be no kaizen." Yet somehow I kept thinking smooth flow and steady pull could be created first, with basic stability as an afterthought—or that maybe it would just emerge automatically. In retrospect, it's like believing that a building can be built without first laying the foundation. I now see my error. I only wish I had realized this sooner.

As I noted, I have learned to give the same attention to purpose and people that I give to the process itself. But how are these three aspects of value creation tied together in an effective whole? I now realize that this is the job of management—a critical aspect of lean practice that I should have focused on earlier.

By management I don't mean functional management or the most senior management (the CEO and COO). And this is the heart of the problem. Perhaps "management" is even the wrong word. What I mean is someone taking horizontal responsibility for every important value stream.

This person must assess performance in relation to purpose and identify the problems—including problems for the people involved—that are created by the vertical functions though which the value stream must pass. These conflicts then need to be discussed and reconciled at the top of the organization, as part of strategy deployment. The objective is to counter-balance the vertical authority of the functional managers, by assigning the horizontal (value-stream) responsibility. It is only when both perspectives—horizontal toward the customer and vertical toward the CEO—are balanced, placed in creative tension, and reconciled that a lean enterprise emerges.

Perhaps my greatest regret in looking back is that we have not yet conducted successful experiments with the management methods required to reconcile horizontal and vertical. Thus, as I look forward, I am hoping to observe many experiments by those taking responsibility for value streams. And I am hoping these will be in a wide range of industries (including government and education) in a wide range of circumstances (startups, mature but stable businesses, distressed organizations in need of a rapid turnaround).

I can't conduct these experiments myself—as I noted in the introduction I have no gemba of my own—but I can walk through the experiment sites, ask why, and show respect. And I can help document the results of experiments and share them with the Lean Community. I look forward to this march in the years ahead, a path that will itself require some thoughtful P and D with a lot of C and A.

I'll end my hansei here on a thankful note. Looking back, it is hard to believe that so many people in so many industries in so many countries invited me in as a relative stranger to walk through the core activities of their organizations. I have a reputation for saying what I think, and my thoughts have rarely been completely positive. Yet I have often been invited back, sometimes year after year! This is a real credit to the tolerance and open-mindedness of the Lean Community plus the earnest desire of so many managers and employees across the world to improve. I will always be grateful.

I also want to end on a hopeful note. I have been walking and observing not just during my past decade of essay writing but for more than 30 years. And every advance I have observed on the lean journey has been hard for those who have achieved it. What's more, none of us has made as much progress as we had anticipated or would have liked. But the important thing I am now able to see, by virtue of so many years on the journey, is that things really are getting better despite the ups and downs along the way: It really is harder and harder to buy a bad product. Most companies in most industries really are creating more value with less waste. Velocity and responsiveness to customers is increasing in almost every activity. And consciousness is rising that consumers are not ultimately seeking a greater variety of brilliant but disconnected objects—they just want their problems solved. We are making progress toward a worthy destination!

This hopeful note is especially needed today when the world economy is a mess, some lean exemplars have encountered problems, and a few of us may even be feeling a bit of lean fatigue. Yet I'm confident we will continue to progress as a community as long as we continue four simple practices: Conduct rigorous experiments. Openly share our results. Perform periodic hansei. And take gemba walks together.

GEMBA WALKS IN A NEW DECADE

The 12 additional essays in this section have been written since the publication of *Gemba Walks* in 2011. They cover a number of new topics and also revisit a number of the original topics. To make the connections between old and new, I have provided cross references in the new essays to similar subjects in the original essays. I hope you will find the additional perspectives on many topics to be of value for your own gemba walks.

The Temple of Flow: 100 Years at Highland Park

In April of 1914, at his Highland Park plant on the North Side of Detroit, Henry Ford and his associates brought together the remarkable series of experiments that gave the world "flow" production. As the last step in completing Ford's system, all three production lines were converted to a steady pace, powered by moving chains. The plant employed go/no-go gauges to catch defective parts at the source and assure complete interchangeability, cellularized parts fabrication with operations located in process sequence, a crude pull system for managing the movement of parts toward their point of use on the line, and standardized work at a steady pace. All in a new building designed with continuous flow as its central objective. Most of the individual elements had been previously tried in some form: it was their combination in a complete system that produced Highland Park's remarkable leap in productivity and velocity.

These events of 1914 deserve to be celebrated for their transformation of world industrial practice. And I hope someone at Ford will seize the opportunity on the occasion of the centennial. The Lean Community also should celebrate because what happened at Highland Park was foundational for lean thinking. Henry Ford and his associates were the first truly systematic lean thinkers, with a passion for dramatically increasing value while eliminating waste through careful process analysis from raw materials to finished product. Much of what Toyota achieved later was built on Ford's shoulders, as Taiichi Ohno at Toyota freely acknowledged.

Because of its enormous achievements, for a long time Highland Park existed in my mind's eye as Ford's stately Temple of Flow. This bubble was rudely popped a few years ago when I took a gemba walk and found a sadly dilapidated and largely empty structure. (See the essay, "A Lean Walk Through History" on page 221, and the photo on back cover.) Since my visit I have asked myself: What happened after the great breakthrough of 1914? What can we learn from what happened? And what might happen next at Highland Park?

As Ford's plant was reaching its zenith in the 1920s, Henry was racing to complete his new complex—the Rouge—on the southwest edge of Detroit. While Highland Park was dedicated to a single vehicle, with the idea of maximizing the velocity of product flow from start to finish, the Rouge complex was dedicated to scale. Parts for many types of vehicles, to be assembled all over the world, were cranked out—not in process villages within one plant but in process factories on the massive site. The buildings needed for each category of item—engines, transmissions, bodies, various types of parts—and more massive buildings for transformations of materials—steel mills, foundries, forges—were connected by conveyors under central control. This seemed impressive to visitors, but in practice large buffers of parts were needed at many points to insure steady production. While Ford could claim that the plant started with iron ore on day one and produced a finished vehicle 2.5 days later, this was simply the sum of the time needed for the value-creating steps. Actual start-to-finish time, including waits in buffers, was many times longer and for the vehicles assembled elsewhere—more than 90%—the start to finish time was longer still.

But the Rouge was a compelling idea in an age of industrial concentration and scale economies. If a lot was good, then even more was better, and the Rouge was the most anyone could imagine. When the new facility was completed in 1927 in time for the Model A, Ford also offered a new name—"mass production"—to tout his achievement. The term "flow production" that Ford had coined earlier to describe Highland Park quickly disappeared from use.

(It bears mention that Ford's concept of "mass production" at the Rouge was where Toyota started its thinking about lean production and was the concept our MIT automotive team set out with in our global survey of manufacturing performance. In the 1980s we were simply unaware of the significance of the system created earlier at Highland Park.)

Once the Rouge was in place, Highland Park became an anachronism. Too small for the body shop needed for stamped steel vehicles, seemingly too cramped with its machines crowded tightly together to minimize movement, too focused on a single product.

Highland Park simply didn't scale in an age of scale. So, when Model T production came to an end in 1926, Ford converted Highland Park to high-volume production of certain categories of parts (for shipment to assembly plants around the world) and to low-volume assembly of a few vehicles such as delivery trucks for the Post Office.

Over time, as Ford's original objective of auto ownership for everyone became widespread, workers could drive to new plants far away from the high land costs of the city. Cheap land on the city's edge made it possible to spread out production on one level, making Highland Park look too vertical, with its six floors and gravity slides that moved parts from fabrication in the top of the building to final assembly at the bottom. In just a few years Highland Park had become the picture of the old-fashioned factory.

After 1930, production declined slowly at Highland Park, and with it the population of the tiny (3 square miles) city surrounding the plant, which had grown from 4,000 in 1910 just as the plant opened to a peak of 53,000 in 1930. Decline was checked for a while by the presence of Chrysler's corporate headquarters and engineering center a few blocks away, but Highland Park's descent accelerated after the boom years of World War II when all capacity of any type was needed. By 1973 Ford discontinued manufacturing at Highland Park and in 1974 the property was sold to a developer who tore down a few of the buildings to create a shopping mall. After Chrysler left for the northern suburbs in 1993, to be close to the homes of its managers and engineers, the trend gathered speed and by 2012 Highland Park had a fifth of the population (11,000) of the peak.

Today the buildings on the site are mostly empty except for some document storage for Ford and a garment warehouse. In 2011 the City of Highland Park removed two thirds of its street lamps due to inability to pay the electric bill. Forty percent of the remaining population is living below the poverty level. In 100 years the Temple of Flow transitioned from the most dynamic industrial site in the world in a rapidly expanding city, to an abandoned industrial relic in one of the poorest and most dangerous places in America. Is there any way out of this smoking crater?

I think there is, and for reasons that go far beyond any considerations of urban redevelopment. In recent decades the car industry has progressed from a collection of national industries to a completely globalized activity with a few massive companies selling the same products in many markets. As product technology has converged on unitized steel bodies and every manufacturer strives to sell in every market, the scale requirements for each vehicle "platform" (on which a number of body styles are often based) have risen to a million—or even two million—vehicles per year. In this situation, massive assembly plants —with 250,000 to 500,000 units of capacity—make imminent sense. A facility with the scale of Highland Park has no place.

However, the massive scale requirements of this strategy leave many white spaces in the market where smaller numbers of buyers may want vehicles with very different capabilities. These vehicles can't be produced on the five or six standard platforms of every car maker. Alternative power vehicles, high-end sports cars, specialty trucks, and city cars are examples. The common characteristic of these vehicles is that they are suited for extruded aluminum or fiber-composite body structures with plastic surface panels, which are cost effective at scales of up to about 50,000 units per year.

A recently announced example is the BMW i3, an all-electric vehicle with a carbon fiber cell for the passenger compartment, extruded aluminum structures at both ends for the engine and the storage compartment, and a snap-on plastic skin. BMW plans to build it in a tiny, dedicated factory in Leipzig.

By contrast Tesla and Fisker opted for new motive power vehicles but with conventional metal bodies and chose to build them in abandoned traditional car plants: NUMMI in Fremont, CA, in the case of Tesla, and GM's Wilmington, DE, light truck plant for Fisker's abortive effort to develop a second, high-volume vehicle. With luck, Tesla might generate enough volume to justify a high-scale plant. A better approach for those who follow is to use a new technology body as well, and target lower volumes, building additional modules of production if necessary.

Looking at Highland Park in this new situation, one can see a double opportunity: A producer could use the existing building to fabricate major components on the upper floors and drop them to final assembly on the ground floor, at a modest investment compared with current car industry norms. The building is already there and the state and federal governments would doubtless help with the conversion costs on the hope that something, anything, can grow from the rubble of Highland Park. Using current best practices for production operations, the component and assembly could be remarkably lean with a small work force, perfect first-time quality, and plenty of room for customers to watch their vehicles being built.

The bonus would be that around the corner, in the first building on the site, Ford's original assembly line and one or two component fabrication cells could be recreated and even operated on special occasions to show the advances in our thinking about the organization of work and process capability over the past century. The combined result: an assembly plant, a process museum, and a customer delivery center within the walls of perhaps the most important industrial structure in the history of the world.

The logical company to take on this challenge is, of course, Ford, which is still under family ownership after more than a century. The amount of goodwill Ford would gain from making a commitment to the seemingly hopeless situation of Detroit would surely be comparable to the positive effect on the company's image of refusing the government bailout in 2009. And Ford could also benefit from a spectacular technology-demonstrator vehicle (both the product and its production process) to follow up its recent success in revitalizing its million-unit platforms.

And if Ford is not interested? Enthusiasm for all-electric vehicles in conventional bodies targeting large production volumes has passed. However, a number of teams are now racing to put together the right combination of motive power, body technology, and process technology to serve niche markets at a low capital cost. Perhaps one of them can find a happy home in the Temple of Flow.

Twenty-five Years of 'Lean'

By Jim Womack and John Krafcik, President and CEO, Hyundai Motor America

In June of 1986 we drove down the road from Cambridge, MA, to nearby Framingham, to take a gemba walk at the General Motors Assembly Division plant. This was the beginning of a long series of walks over the next two years, occasionally together, but mostly just John with plant management teams. With these walks, and with a follow-up questionnaire to capture information in a consistent format, we steadily gathered evidence that there was a new and better way to manage manufacturing.

In the fall of 1986 John wrote a paper ("Learning from NUMMI") for the MIT International Motor Vehicle Program's research meeting for its auto company sponsors. In it he compared the quality and productivity of the Framingham plant with Toyota's Takaoka plant in Toyota City and with the General Motors/Toyota joint venture at NUMMI, where John had worked as a quality engineer before joining Jim at MIT. The differences in quality and productivity were quite striking: Takaoka and NUMMI performed at similar levels that were far superior to Framingham.

At the time we had no names for the production systems producing these different results other than "mass production" for GM Framingham and "Toyota" for Takaoka and NUMMI. Nor could we trace the differences in plant performance to differences in management. More work and a large sample were needed.

By the summer of 1987, we had expanded our research to about 40 assembly plants, operated by about 15 companies, in Europe, North America, Latin America, and Asia. It was clear by this point that although the Toyota plants were all high performers, a number of other Japanese-owned plants in Japan and North America and, surprisingly, several Ford-owned plants in North America were also in the "high productivity/high quality" quadrant of our data set.

Our problem at this point was that we needed a name for the production and management system producing this superior performance. As the team leader, Jim asked the MIT graduate students, faculty, and visiting professors on the team to come up with a name. John suggested that we name the system for what it achieved, which was to assemble a "standard car" (of a given size and level of equipment) with less human effort, fewer defects, less plant space, less capital investment (some of the most labor efficient plants were also the least automated), less elapsed time, and in lower volume per product type (on mixed-model lines.) As we looked at the whiteboard where we had written "less," "fewer," "less," "less," or "lower" beside each attribute, John said, "Let's call it 'lean,'" and wrote "lean" on the whiteboard. So there it was. Lean. (For a more detailed account of this event, and subsequent confusion in the use of the term, see "Deconstructing the Tower of Babel" on page 165.)

In the short term we had no public use for the term, sharing it only with sponsors, the world's major car companies. And there was still some discussion inside the project as to whether "lean" was the best term. In particular, Professor Haruo Shimada from Keio University in Tokyo and John Paul MacDuffie (now a professor at the Wharton School at the University of Pennsylvania) wondered if "fragile" might be a better label. They suggested pairing it with "robust" to describe the alternative management approach of firms like GM and Volkswagen that we were proposing to call "mass production".

They believed that the Toyota-inspired production system was fragile not just because the level of inventories was dramatically reduced but because it required strong and continuing engagement of the entire work force by management at all levels. In its absence, performance would dramatically deteriorate and the system might easily regress to the top-down, command-control methods that had been the world norm in the auto industry. They thought the name should warn about this possibility. (They also pointed out that "lean" was already paired with "mean" in popular usage whenever companies pared back and eliminated jobs. Might it be misused to excuse expedient behavior in the future?)

We (Womack and Krafcik) were sympathetic to these considerations but we couldn't imagine selling the term "fragile" to the automotive industry managers we hoped to influence. They loved simplicity—and "lean" was simple if nothing else—and prided themselves on toughness. So we eventually decided that lean it was, with all its potential faults.

By the summer of 1988, with our ever-growing database of nearly 70 plants in 14 countries, we were ready to share our findings and the term lean with the world. John wrote an article for the fall issue of the MIT Sloan Management Review with the title, "The Triumph of the Lean Production System." It appeared in September and the term "lean" was loosed on the world. (You can read and download this article by going to http://www.Lean.org/downloads/MITSloan.pdf.)

A Bit of Hansei

In looking back on this article from the perspective of 25 years we have found five points to note:

First, we remain grateful for the willingness of professionals in auto companies across the world to cooperate on a research project that was certain to make some look much better than others. At the plant management level we found we could almost always expect honest and energetic efforts to answer our questions.

John paid the management teams back for the considerable time they expended gathering data for the survey by giving each plant a briefing on where it stood on all of our performance indicators and why. (The performance of all of the other plants was clearly shown but with no identification.) This practice confirmed our suspicion that most managers want honest feedback on how well they are doing in their jobs but often have no means of getting it. One of the principles of lean management, of course, is to provide accurate feedback to every manager in real time.

Second, we realized how important it was to take gemba walks to see for ourselves what was actually happening and to directly verify every answer to our questionnaire. Doing this invariably gave us ideas for improving the questionnaire. And it also served as a check on incorrect information sometimes supplied by higher levels of management.

Surely the most striking instance was when we were both visiting a plant in Europe and asked where the rework area was. The plant manager stated, "We have no rework area in this plant." And this seemed to be the true upon careful inspection. But there was a problem. Almost every car was rolling off the line with missing parts and visible defects in the finish. There had to be a rework area somewhere and we suspected that finding and counting the labor hours there would correct the plant's unusually high productivity score, which the management attributed to its high level of automation.

So we said, "Is there a rework area somewhere else, perhaps after the vehicles are turned over to the sales organization?" The plant manager stated that this was beyond his knowledge. "I only know about my plant." However, a plant works car soon pulled up and the plant manager motioned for John to get in the back seat. The car disappeared through a mountain pass behind the plant with John as the sole passenger and the driver never saying a word.

When the car reappeared some time later, John reported being taken to a massive rework building belonging to the sales organization with headcount about equal to the assembly plant. John had therefore corrected the plant's productivity score from one of the highest to one of the lowest in our sample.

Our conclusion: Line managers at the plant level are usually proud professionals. But sometimes they are told by higher levels to make the numbers look right. And, in this situation, the only right thing to do is to go and see for yourself. We commend this attitude to managers at every level and have always tried to practice it.

Third, we believe that Professors Shimada and MacDuffie were right about the fragile nature of lean production. Making a "lean leap" is one thing, and may be possible simply by mechanically applying lean tools. But continued high-level performance is critically dependent on continuous engagement of the entire workforce by the management team in a quest for continuous improvement. When this commitment begins to slip and management turns its mind elsewhere—or companies grow so rapidly that they dilute their management culture—bad things are bound to happen.

This was true at NUMMI, which lost its way several times during its 25-year run, requiring a management reboot from Toyota. It was also true at Toyota as it tried to grow too fast in recent years. And, painfully for the story told in "The Triumph of the Lean Production System," it was even more true at Ford, which in the late 1980s seemed to be off to a good start in applying lean principles and then completely lost its way.

This said, we still think that "lean" was the best term we could have used to describe the management system we were discovering. With all its faults—including the difficulty of translation into many of the world languages—lean has been effective in selling our valuable insights to a vast audience.

Fourth, if we got "lean" right, we got "production" wrong. From the very beginning we knew that the lean production system included product development, supplier management, customer support, and general management of the entire enterprise. And this was very clear in the 1990 volume, *The Machine That Changed the World.* But when we said "production system" in 1988 the world heard "factories." So perhaps it would have been better if John had used the title, "The Triumph of the Lean Management System" instead.

Fifth and finally, we find it striking in reviewing "The Triumph of the Lean Production System" how incomplete the characteristics of plant management were. The survey rated facilities on the degree of work standardization, the ratio of direct workers to management support, the level of parts inventories, the amount of in-process buffers, the size of the repair area, and the presence of team systems with team leaders between the front-line workers and the first-level management. These plant practices were then regressed against labor productivity, end-of-the-line quality, and the ability to accommodate a complex product mix.

The real news in the article was the finding of a very high correlation between high productivity, quality, and flexibility and the six lean management practices. What was missing was the presence of policy deployment to set priorities at a high level and cascade them to lower levels, the midlevel management practices of problem solving and improvement through A3 with PDCA, and the front-line management practices of creating and sustaining basic stability to make continuous improvement through kaizen possible. These provide the lean management framework for sustaining lean production.

How could we miss these? It was very simple: Our knowledge of Toyota (lean) management practices was based on what John had learned in two years at NUMMI, with a training stint in Japan at Takaoka, and at that point NUMMI was not overtly practicing policy deployment, midlevel PDCA, or front-line stabilization. These had all been subtly built in the plant's operations by Toyota managers from Japan acting as "shadows" for the American line management. The full complement of lean management practices was only made explicit in later years as the plant's management matured. (The IMVP global surveys of plant performance were continued and improved for many years after John left to pursue a career in the auto industry and Jim left to found the Lean Enterprise Institute. Under the leadership of Professor MacDuffie, these surveys progressively tackled the issues of management and human resource practices as we all continued to learn from Toyota.)

So, 25 years on, we know that the "The Triumph of the Lean Production System" wasn't perfect. But we believe that it was a watershed event in the history of the lean movement and that it helped open a floodgate of new ideas for the world's managers. We continue to see its benefits today and we hope you will enjoy reading the original article in light of what you have learned on your own lean journey.

Work, Management, Leadership

In the essay "Purpose, Process, People" (see page 3), I proposed a countermeasure for what I found to be a frequent but understandable error in the Lean Community. Most lean practitioners sympathize with the people doing the front-line work (which is a fine thing), and so their thinking about how to improve has often started by asking how to "empower" front-line workers. Again, this is fine. But empower the people to do what? Most of the people that I have seen being empowered to do kaizen were never made aware of its larger purpose—how it served the needs of the whole organization. This easily led to improving the wrong things, which is a form of muda.

I often found a second common error that prevented any meaningful improvement. Most improvement teams focused on applying all available lean tools to a given process (value stream), yet failed to identify what was wrong with that value stream from the standpoint of the customer (who was paying everyone's wages). This was another form of muda, the muda of irrelevant kaizen.

Therefore I suggested that anyone thinking about improving a process in an organization should start with the *purpose* of the process from the standpoint of the customer. Then they should ask precisely what type of value it should be creating for the customer and precisely measure the gap between current performance and customer satisfaction. Once the improvement team and the people working the process know and agree on this, they can think effectively about what improvements in the process are needed for it to achieve its purpose. And they can then brainstorm how the people improving and working the process should be engaged in improving and sustaining it. This suggested that the common sequence of "people, process, purpose" ought to be reversed to "purpose, process, people," to achieve better results for the customer, the organization, and the employees working the process. I repeat this mantra—purpose, process, people—every time I take a walk along a value stream.

This approach applies to individual value streams. But today, when I observe the way most organizations think about enterprise-wide lean transformation, I see a similar reversal of the right sequence. I frequently hear that transformation starts when heroic senior leadership tackles the tough problems (often under the banner of a lean program with a kaizen blitz) in order to change people's minds throughout the organization as to what is possible. This is followed by recruiting or creating better managers at every level and then taking on all of the front-line work that needs to be done in a better way by means of pervasive kaizen. This common sequence is "leadership, management, work," with an implicit emphasis on character, courage and resoluteness. It's little wonder that those who view the world this way believe that only heroic top-level leadership can start and sustain a lean transformation. Thus the common excuse I frequently hear that the lack of heroic top-level leadership in an organization makes progress impossible.

This may be true in a few cases but framing the problem this way squanders one of the greatest strengths of the lean movement. Years ago someone at Toyota in Japan told me, "Always start with the work to be done." He meant that when analyzing an organization's problems, I should always observe the way that front-line, value-creating work was actually being done. And only after this rigorous act of observation should I ask a simple question: "What kind of line management is needed to get the work done in the best way, and ensure it is steadily improved?" Ever since then I have been trying to begin by observing the front-line work and the work of front-line management whenever I visit a new organization.

Fortunately questions about what managers do in many cases only need to be asked once for an entire organization, because the management system is very similar across the enterprise. For example, I recently visited a series of stores belonging to a large retailer and quickly confirmed that the managers were not focused on improving the front-line work. Instead they were all busily (and happily) working around individual problems, a good illustration of "management by exception." And they were also occupied with filling out all of the forms and achieving all the metrics devised by top management to make sure they were doing their work correctly. There was no attention to analyzing, stabilizing, and then improving the work, which meant that the managers would always have lots of workarounds to keep them busy and lots of issues to hide from top management.

I was not surprised that this managerial behavior was quite consistent across all the retail operations in this large organization. I actually only needed to visit one store and observe the work and the management of the work to see what needed to change. And I find this to be true in practically every organization I visit. Thus the seemingly massive problem of dealing with a thousand different management problems in a thousand different places in an organization is suddenly, well, manageable. All that's needed is to introduce standard work for managers including standardizing the work of the front-line value creators they supervise and utilizing A3 analysis with PDCA to countermeasure problems and creatively respond to hoshin planning cascaded from top management.

Once I look at the work and how it is actually being done and then look at the work of management—which is to supervise and improve the front-line work—I am ready to ask what type of leadership is needed to transform the management system so that lean managers can work with the front-line troops to stabilize and transform the work. Note that this leadership does not need to solve any problems directly (in fact, it shouldn't) nor does it need to create a fancy "lean" program. Nor does the leader need to strike a heroic pose.

The real work of the lean leader, as I have come to understand it over the years, is transforming the line management system so that the work gets done everywhere in the best possible way with appropriate staff support. And this does not demand heroics. A properly conceived lean approach replaces heroics with one systematic transformation that means that no heroic leaders will be needed in the future.

I do not say that this is easy. Reworking an organization's management system never is. And, this work appears to be less glamorous than our traditional notion of leadership. But it is easier to find a few lean leaders who can change management systems across an enterprise than it is to find a multitude of heroic leaders who will fix every problem in every part of the organization themselves.

So I now have two mantras to suggest as you look at your organization. For transforming individual value streams it is "purpose, process, people." For transforming the entire enterprise it is no longer "leadership, management, work" but instead, "work, management, leadership."

A final thought: If the management system is transformed, managers at every level will automatically think "work, management, leadership" in the future without any need for jolts of heroic leadership. Unemployment for heroes is one form of unemployment that actually creates value.

Starting Up, Growing Up, and Starting Over

Most of the work of LEI and the lean movement has been devoted to transforming "brownfields." We have toiled at old facilities (whether factories or engineering offices or retail stores or hospitals) in old organizations (in practically every industry you can think of) with mature product concepts that have gone a long way down the path of modern management and mass production. The car industry, from which lean thinking emerged, was populated with precisely these types of organizations.

We have tried to introduce lean tools and new management mentalities in a wide range of mature organizations, including methods for developing new products. And we have had considerable success to the benefit of society. Mature enterprises in mature industries account for the vast majority of economic activity, despite the focus of the media and the blogosphere on exciting new concepts.

However, I consider our efforts to date as "rework"—not just for individual products or processes but for whole enterprises. Someone needs to do this work. But it is always hard work because we are effectively asking organizations to start over, to go back to their youth—at a point before they made their first mistakes—and to head down a different path.

It is therefore exhilarating to think instead about startups: new organizations yet to make their first mistakes. I believe that most organizations are born "lean." They start with only a few employees in one room, a clear founder vision, face-to-face communication with no functional silos, and a horizontal flow of value from concept to launch, often across a tiny team. The challenge is to think through the approach to work, the type of management, and the nature of leadership needed to "grow up" these start-up enterprises so they don't head down the cul-de-sac of modern management and mass production.

I'm not the only one to think this. There is now a worldwide "lean startup movement" that is worthy of attention. The canonical text is Eric Ries' *The Lean Startup: How Today's Entrepreneurs Use Continuous*

Innovation to Create Radically Successful Businesses (New York: Crown Business, 2011). I commend it to everyone in the Lean Community, not because I agree with all of it but because I find it very stimulating in rethinking basic lean concepts for new circumstances.

Ries and his collaborators start by suggesting new ways to define (or redefine) value from the perspective of the customer. (This is the first principle of lean thinking as Dan Jones and I explained in Chapter One of *Lean Thinking*.) Getting value right is particularly important to Ries because he comes out of the social media startup world where the value of any product can only be determined by letting potential customers play with it and test it with others in their social networks.

This is a tough challenge, since developing fully refined prototypes for customer tests is expensive and time-consuming in a situation where the very concept of the product may be wrong. That's why as a counter-measure Ries proposes the concept of the "minimum viable product" (MVP), a test product containing only the minimum functionality the customer needs to understand the product concept. This MVP is put in customer hands much earlier than traditional products would be, enabling the provider organization to learn what customers really value, while avoiding the waste of expensive and time-consuming efforts to develop fully elaborated products no one wants.

A second challenge arises once the product is launched: Is the rate of adoption great enough to sustain a viable, growing business? Are customers just responding to the buzz of the moment or are they incorporating the product into their lives? Ries and his collaborators therefore propose new ways to test product success, through cohort analysis of each new tranche of customers attracted to a product as it evolves, and with split tests of new product variants.

Finally, because the organizations Ries works with are mostly venture capital funded and working in highly dynamic markets, these startups face daunting deadlines in proving the value of their products. Their investors expect nine of 10 ventures to fail and are always ready to pull the plug even as the managers deny the reality of their situation. Ries has developed additional methods for "innovation accounting" to judge "the rate of validated learning" so that managers and investors can make more rational decisions about whether the rate of learning about customers is sufficient to stay the course, "pivot" to a new approach to the customer, or abandon ship.

Note that the MVP, cohort analysis, and innovation accounting with validated learning concepts do not apply just to software apps, as many in the Lean Community might think. Different industries with different customer expectations all need different definitions of an MVP, just as they need different ways to determine the success of their initial product, and different ways to decide if their basic course is right. These tasks must be performed in some way and today they are mostly being performed through anecdotal evidence and hunches rather than science.

I believe the Lean Startup movement and the Lean Community have the potential for a productive conversation once startups prove their product concept. This is when they begin to grow up, adding all of the complexity of a mature business, including deep vertical functions with many employees (marketing, engineering, production, purchasing, customer service) and a portfolio of products at different stages of maturity flowing horizontally across these deep functions to reach customers.

Ries does have some advice in the last section of *Lean Startups* for enterprises reaching this point, but to use a favorite phrase of the Lean Startup community for judging performance metrics, is this advice "actionable?" For example, he gives advice on how to begin training managers and engineers about the company's culture, how to develop robust procedures that help employees do a good job consistently but not block their creativity, and how to do problem solving with his version of the "Five Whys" as adapted from Toyota.

But it's all very vague and approximate. It's not a lean management system, which consists of responsible leaders for each product value stream, current-state and future-state maps of each stream, standardized work for every process (developed and continually updated by every work team), and rigorous yet easily understood methods for framing both problems and opportunities by means of A3 analysis that incorporates the Five Whys and PDCA.

These are not trivial additions around the margins of start-up management. They form the core practices of a mature lean organization as it tries to avoid the strangulation of top-down authority while maintaining control of the progress of every product as it flows from concept to customer across deep functions.

Beyond the basic management system, there are important lean enhancements needed in every function as the value proposition for each family of products become clear. In the case of product and process development (and note that these should always occur together) the needed methods are described quite brilliantly in the late Al Ward's book *Lean Product and Process Development* (2007). (Note: This volume will be reissued in 2014 in an expanded version, with the help of Al's longtime student, Professor Durward Sobek.)

When Al's key concepts of the entrepreneurial system designer, the team of responsible experts, set-based concurrent engineering, and truly rigorous cadence, pull and flow are added to the methods Ries describes for startup developers there is a much better chance that an organization will grow to maturity with no need for pushing the reset button.

To test these ideas and determine just how early in the life of a startup they can be applied, we at LEI have been working with a new venture that seeks to reconfigure the entire business eco-system in which it operates and whose value for the customer is derived mainly from this reconfiguration. We have been observing firsthand the challenge of creating an MVP for a molecular product in a molecular environment where "minimal" cannot be not very minimal (although still much more minimal than traditional product engineers would like). This means that early users of the real product need to be partners as well as customers and intense feedback loops need to be built in for rapid response to learning. At the same time we are observing how a lean management system can be installed very early that stabilizes core processes (through standardized work), focuses everyone touching the processes on rapid problem solving (through A3), and yet maintains the ability to "pivot" as learning continues (via a dynamic hoshin process).

An even bigger challenge for an organization growing up is to rapidly create a complete lean enterprise that combines a lean product development process and a lean production process with external partner/suppliers and partner/customers. How can the success of this whole enterprise be evaluated beyond often misleading metrics like sales growth? How can the amount of learning per unit time be measured and how can all this learning be turned to good use?

This said, I wish the Lean Startup movement (not to mention the startups we are studying) every success. And I hope we in the Lean Community can be in close dialogue with the Lean Startup movement in the future. We still have many ideas to share about lean management from the transition point from start up to grow up.

To sum up: Starting up and growing up are two phases necessary for every organization. Lean thinking has traditionally been very strong on the second phase and the Lean Startup community is adding important concepts to strengthen the first phase. If managers get these two phases right they will never need for a third phase, the organizational rework of starting over. This, to cite Ries' phrase from another context, is the land of the "walking dead" where mature organizations often manage to survive but create much less value and much more waste than they should. Surely working together—Lean Startup movement and the Lean Community—we can do much better.

Management in America

Because I have spent half of my working life in the university world and half in the nonprofit research and education world, I'm always hoping for a closer connection between the two. Recently I've found a rudimentary bridge in a paper titled "Management in America," prepared by MIT and Stanford professors in collaboration with the U.S. Bureau of the Census. (Go to CES.Papers.List@census.gov and look for CES 13-01.) I guarantee that the Lean Community will find it thought-provoking. And—given that it's a scholarly economics paper—it's even fun.

On one level I'm encouraged by this paper. It is based on a recent survey of management practices in American manufacturing companies using a questionnaire sent to 47,500 "establishments" (manufacturing facilities). Nothing on this scale has ever been attempted. 37,200 questionnaires were returned, a large fraction for survey research. The analysis of the data shows a wide range of management practices that correlate strongly with differing business performance (productivity, profitability, sales growth) of the facilities being surveyed.

I'm encouraged by this line of research because historically economists (as the authors are) have shown remarkably little interest in how firms actually create value through the internal actions of managers and employees. Instead they have focused on external causes of firm performance that are easier to measure, such as how competitive a firm's industry is, the level of capital investment in production and IT technologies, the training level of employees, and so forth.

Meanwhile, governments (and the politicians leading them) have had even less interest in how firms actually create value, defaulting to ideological explanations of performance. These range from lower taxes and limited regulation (on the right) to government subsidies for R&D to spur new industries (a recent hobby horse on the left).

I'm not counting on economists, bureaucrats at the Census Bureau, or politicians of any persuasion to create better-performing companies. But I think it is good that economists and government researchers are at least starting to ask questions about what goes on inside firms and what managers can do to achieve superior performance. And we can join them in the conversation.

This said, I'm discouraged on a deeper level because of the questions asked in the survey. The authors contrast two models of management, one labeled "structured" and another I will call "traditional." (Oddly, they don't propose a name, even "unstructured.") They find that "structured management practices for performance monitoring, targets, and incentives are tightly linked to better performance" in the form of higher productivity, profitability, and sales growth. (P. 4). This sounds interesting but what, exactly, is structured management?

Let's look at the questionnaire. It has three parts, covering "management practices," "organization," and "background on the establishment." The authors don't report their findings on the importance of organization. (This is promised for a future article.) So I'll focus here on their findings about management.

Under "management practices" the survey asks 16 questions and provides a multiple choice of answers for each. Below I show the polar-opposite answers in parentheses for the 10 questions most relevant to lean thinkers. In each case the "structured choice" is scored as 1 and the "unstructured choice" is scored as 0. (I suggest that as you read through the questions you ask how your organization would score, rating your firm from 0 to 1 and giving fractional scores when your practices lie between the extremes.) The 10 questions are:

1. How many key performance indicators (KPIs) were monitored in this establishment? (None [0] to 10 or more [1].)

2. How frequently were the KPIs reviewed by managers? (Never [0] to hourly [1].)

3. Where were the production display boards showing KPIs located? (Nowhere [0] to all located in one place (e.g., at the end of production line) [1].)

4. How easy was it for this establishment to achieve its production targets? ("With extraordinary effort" [0] to "without much effort" [1].) (Note that this is not a management practice but, possibly, an outcome of management practices. Also note that there is no definition of "effort" or "extraordinary." And, were these in some cases "push" targets leading to overproduction?)

5. When production targets were met, what percent of nonmanagers received performance bonuses? (Zero [0] to 100% [10].)

6. What were managers' performance bonuses based on? (Company performance [0] to individual manager performance [1].)

7. What were nonmanagers' performance bonuses based on? (No bonuses [0] to individual performance [1].)

8. What was the primary way managers were promoted? ("Mainly on factors other than performance and ability (e.g. family connections)" [0] to "solely on performance and ability" [1].)

9. When was an underperforming manager reassigned or dismissed? ("Rarely or never" [0] to "within 6 months" [1].)

And one question that sounds "leanish":

10. What happens at this establishment when a problem (e.g., a quality defect in a product or a machine breaking down) in production arises? ("Nothing" [0] to "we fixed it and took action to make sure that it did not happen again, and had a continuous improvement process to anticipate problems like these in advance" [1].) (Surely "nothing" is a nonsensical answer but the authors apparently think this is what firms do. "Try a quick workaround and move on" would be more sensible as the extreme opposite of "fixed it and took action to make sure it did not happen again.")

The answers to the 16 questions are aggregated to produce a single score with "structured management" [1] at one extreme and what I am calling "traditional management" [0] at the other. (You can calculate your firm's score the same way. You can also obtain the entire questionnaire by going to: bhs.econ.census.gov/bhs/mops/form.html.)

The authors report that firms with scores toward the "1" ("structured") end of the spectrum perform markedly better than firms toward the "0" end of the spectrum. They also report a remarkable "tail" in the distribution of firms that are near "0" with very poor business performance that nevertheless have survived for years, noting that they must be in relatively uncompetitive industries. (Note: If your firm is a using very traditional management practices it's very important to be in an uncompetitive industry full of other poorly performing firms!)

Perhaps of more interest, the authors report that a quarter of the firms surveyed use less than 50% of the "structured" practices. In short, traditional management lives on in an age of increasingly structured management despite the authors' report that structured management has gained significant new adherents in the past five years, as shown by another question in the survey about changes in management practices during this period.

So why am I discouraged after reading through the questions asked in the largest survey of management practices ever conducted? Because the authors' concept of "structured management" is simply modern management. This was pioneered by GM early in the 20th century when finance director Donaldson Brown equipped CEO Alfred Sloan with "objective" measures of manager performance based on clear metrics. It was elaborated by GE through the time of Jack Welch when "make your numbers" became the mantra for career survival. And it has been supplemented in recent years by the ability of firms to collect much more data on performance in real time at much lower cost. (The authors of this paper have written elsewhere on the role of information technology in advancing management practice, so they are fully versed in this latest phase of modern management.)

What is almost entirely missing from the survey are questions about a third approach to management that we call "lean." This is despite (or because of?) the authors' stated belief (on page 5) that structured management is based in significant part on lean management principles described in my, Dan Jones', and Dan Roos' book, *The Machine That Changed the World*. Good grief.

In structured management it appears that higher-level managers set goals and lower level managers and front-line works try to achieve them, receiving an individual bonus if they do and a reprimand or dismissal if they don't. When the objectives and metrics are reviewed more frequently and cover more areas of operations, the firm is even more structured.

So the economists are now inside the "black box," with surveys to see what actually goes on inside firms. *But they are missing the key method of lean management.* This is the intense and "structured" (by means of hoshin, A3 analysis, and kaizen) discussions between higher and lower levels of management about how to set goals (cascading from the top with feedback loops), how to deploy on new initiatives and solve problems, and how to create and sustain the basic stability that permits continuous improvement.

The magic is not in the precise setting of goals or in frequent and intense monitoring of metrics. These are important but are subject to gaming in the absence of a discussion about precisely how the objectives are going to be met. The secret sauce is in the direct interactions between managers at different levels who go to the gemba to see the issues and to reach agreement on the best actions to take after careful discussion of the root causes and evaluation of the possible countermeasures. They can then design experiments to test the most promising countermeasures, to be judged by precise performance metrics. (Note that in contrast to modern management this is not a task for individuals, to be judged by individual performance. It's a team sport with the organization (and the customer) the winner rather than one employee or another.)

So where do we go from here? Let's start by admitting that lean thinkers missed the boat—or the email—on the first round· of the Management and Organizational Practices Survey (MOPS) of the

Annual Survey of Manufacturers (ASM). Shame on us that despite our efforts to interact with the academic community through the Lean Education Academic Network we have not been part of the conversation as economists and management professors get more engaged in the question of what management methods produce the best results.

What's my hope? That future versions of MOPS will include questions that address a third, lean, concept of management. I'll be happy to help the Census Bureau researchers draft the questions capturing this approach if they call and I'm sure many others in the Lean Community would jump at the chance to contribute and to respond to the survey.

The number of firms with high scores for "lean" management practices would surely be small. But my hypothesis is that their performance will far exceed that of modern (structured) management firms, who are far ahead of the traditionally managed firms. This is a hypothesis the Lean Community urgently needs to test and that every manager—traditional, structured, or lean—will benefit from learning the answer.

The Great Stagnation

In the two essays on The Great Recession in the First Edition of *Gemba Walks* (pp. 155, 160), I expressed the hope that the economic collapse of 2008 would not, in retrospect, be widely known as the "lean" recession in which organizations implementing widespread layoffs justified them in the name of lean.

Five years on I think we can safely say that lean was not identified as the villain in the dramatic layoffs in 2008 and 2009. And that is a very good thing. However, what is not a good thing is that lean is not widely seen as a solution to The Great Stagnation that has followed the end of The Great Recession.

Instead, almost all of the public discussion in North America, Europe, and Japan has been about the right macroeconomic policy to end stagnation. Should government spending be increased to spur the consumer economy? Or should it be reduced to restore business confidence and private investment? Should interest rates be maintained at their historic low rates to spur consumption? Or should they be raised, to return to a "normal" economy ready for "normal" growth? At the same time, there has been much speculation in the background about the next wave of innovation, following the internet and the web in the 1990s and social media in the 2000s. What can be the next new thing in the economy that raises all boats? Perhaps nano technology to create a host of heretofore unimaginable products. Or 3D printing of manufactured goods to make conventional factories cranking out volume products obsolete. Or autonomy for many products, beginning with motor vehicles and aircraft, so that no human effort is needed to operate them?

These are serious discussions and—who knows?—the right macroeconomic policy or some economy-changing innovation may be just around the corner. But what about simply doing our everyday work move effectively so that more value can be created with the same effort and resources? This is a simple and surefire way to spur the economy and I see the possibilities for more value creation everywhere.

Just this past week I have walked along the value stream of a major retailer, from suppliers of goods to customers. This enterprise could easily sell the same amount of goods from stores with half the space, a quarter of the total inventory now in the value stream, and half the human effort, while offering shoppers a higher level of service.

The week before I walked from raw materials to customer along a manufacturing, distribution, and retail value stream where roughly the same level of improvement can be achieved. All that's lacking is a realization of the possibilities by the managers of the three firms involved.

And just today I have been reviewing data from a major healthcare provider that I have visited many times over the years. This organization has employed lean methods and lean management to reduce the cost of treating the same number of patients down by nearly 5% per year while costs are rising at 5% or more per year at healthcare providers in the same region competing for the same patients.

So why isn't the public debate on the economy focused on how we can take out waste and create value faster to launch a new economic boom? Why isn't the Lean Community part of the discussion about The Great Stagnation?

I think there are three reasons:

No one in public life seems to have any grasp of process thinking and the broader public has never been educated about its potential. When you think about it, there is no place in our educational curriculum anywhere to teach students the best way to do what they will spend most of their working lives doing: Working in complex processes, usually spanning several organizations, to solve problems with current operations while steadily improving these processes to enable better future performance. So it's not surprising that the public looks instead for magic measures—whether from the head of the Federal Reserve or from heroic entrepreneurs in start-up companies—to spur the economy and create growth industries.

The second reason is that, to the extent public officials and senior managers are aware of lean thinking, they expect it to be adopted by means of government programs and top-level corporate initiatives that offer incentives or punishments for compliance. (Politicians talk about "creating jobs" when they ought to be talking about creating value and C-suites talk about "driving change" from the top when they ought to be talking about engaging workers at every level in improving their work.) What is really needed is millions of managers and front-line value creators changing the way they do their work every day. So from a political and C-suite standpoint, lean doesn't seem to scale.

The third reason, and perhaps the biggest impediment, is that to the extent politicians and the public are aware of lean thinking they equate it with "improving efficiency," which translates in the public mind to "headcount reduction" or "job destruction." (Hence my concern five years ago about lean being blamed for unemployment.) If unemployment is still high and consumer demand is still weak, it seems to follow in popular thinking that what the economy doesn't need is ways to reduce human effort in order to create more value with less.

But this is clearly wrong. Let's take a simple example. Suppose I want a boat (and I very much do as I head toward retirement). But a boat currently costs too much for me to buy because too much human effort and capital are needed to produce it using current (nonlean) methods. So, I'm probably not going to get my boat. And, because other consumers face the same situation, it's unlikely that boat sales are going to increase (except with the incentive of some unsustainable economic stimulation program of the type governments embraced five years ago).

What if a boat builder—let's call this company Lean Boats, Inc.— could employ lean techniques to build my boat with 75% of the previously required labor and capital? And what if Lean Boats, because it operates in a competitive market and wants to grow, passes the savings along to me? I could now buy my boat and I imagine that many other folks in similar economic circumstances could buy one, too. Note that no economic stimulation program, technological breakthrough, or top-down corporate "lean initiative" would be required.

We can't be sure about what economists call the elasticity of demand —the percentage increase in demand accompanying a percentage reduction in price. So we can't know for sure that a 25% reduction in cost and price will lead to a 25% increase in sales. But, holding other economic conditions constant (e.g., interest rates, government stimulus), it's likely to be pretty close. The number of jobs should stay about the same and there would be a substantial gain in labor productivity, which is a good thing because the standard of living can't go up sustainably in any society unless labor productivity increases.

But wait. There is more good news. Many folks were already planning to buy a boat at the higher, nonlean cost and price. And they get lower prices too. That means they have money they were planning to spend for a boat that they can now use to buy something else as well. (How about a couple of water tubes to pull behind the boat and some nice chairs and a table for a new dock?) These purchases will increase employment in the water tube, dock furniture, and dock building industries, even if they do not implement lean methods, and will permit the new workers in those industries to buy more goods as well. A virtuous circle leading toward an expanding economy and one than can support economic stimulus (if it is still needed) without leading to inflation.

What is happening instead? Productivity is barely growing in the developed economies. In the United States, after a brief spike to about 3% in 2010 (as companies increased output with the same number of employees because they hadn't been able to cut employment as fast as sales fell in 2008–09), labor productivity has stagnated at about 0.7% over the past three years. This is far below the long-term of growth in productivity that will be needed to raise the U.S. standard of living.

Now the final piece of the puzzle. Because the economy is stagnant, with high unemployment and practically no productivity growth, the fierce debate continues in Washington and Europe about more or less stimulation and higher or lower interest rates while everyone awaits the next new thing in technology. But no one in high places is talking about lean countermeasures that might actually make a difference.

What can we do in the Lean Community? We can make our case more effectively and lead by example. I'm trying to do the former in my writing, speaking, and discussions with politicians and senior managers.

Perhaps you can do this, too. And I hope you will lead by example by pushing ahead with a lean transformation of your organization. Only our actions will speak to the board audience we need to reach.

Meanwhile, let's stop calling ourselves an efficiency or even an effectiveness initiative. And let's challenge those who call us that and suggest that we threaten jobs. We are a progrowth, antistagnation movement with methods that actually work—the only methods that actually work? We can restart economic growth and create jobs that actually create value, and without any help from the politicians, if we can convince enough managers and front-line value-creators to join us.

Lean Government

About 10 years ago I got a call from the mayor of a major American city who told me he wanted to create the first "lean" city government. What this might mean was unclear to me. I knew nothing about his city and had done no thinking about lean in government at any level. So I went to see him and we had some fun looking at a couple of sample processes: arresting vagrants and processing building permits.

We put a brief effort into taking gemba walks along both value streams, discovering that the best thing to do with vagrants was to create a separate process (a vagrant product family if you will) that was quick, simple, and removed from the arrest process for actual criminals. (This meant the vagrants could be treated more humanely and officers could get back on the streets much more quickly. The important question of whether vagrants should be arrested at all was left for another time.)

By contrast, issuing building permits in this growth-oriented city was straightforward. Rather than asking contractors to come to city hall in the middle of a vast metropolitan area far removed from where buildings were actually being built, it made more sense to create four processing centers in the four quadrants of the city. And instead of sending the permit requests through four different departments, with queues and delays in each department, the countermeasure was to colocate the parts of each department concerned with permits, and pass the applications around a table, pretty much in single-piece flow. It seemed possible to reduce the wait time for a building permit from a month to a day.

So far, so good. But then bureaucracy and politics came into play. The mayor had a limited attention span—I'm being generous—and no one was given responsibility for overseeing the new processes and perfecting the flow of value across different departments. Then, it turned out that resources were needed to do rigorous experiments to test the ideas, and the project had to be put out to public bids—a process that was a nightmare. Ultimately, nothing much could be done or sustained by the earnest line managers without continuing upper-level support and I gave up the effort. It was another interesting gemba walk for me, leading to some great insights on how poorly the existing processes were designed and what might be done to improve things. But nothing was actually initiated or sustained and I moved on to other things.

A few months ago I was asked to spend a day in Australia at the City Melbourne (which is as Manhattan is to New York City, the office-tower center of a vast metropolitan area). This time I was also asked to walk two processes—writing parking tickets (and collecting the money) and planning events (like concerts) in city parks. And it was a totally different world.

In each case a team of representatives from all of the departments and divisions involved had mapped the current process, identified the gap in performance, envisioned a better process, and started a series of PDCA cycles to close the gap. Everything was visual, showing clear responsibility for the performance of each value stream and its improvement across departments. I had the strong sense that the progress the teams were making could be sustained, with standardized work for managers and front-line workers.

The one problem that had arisen was that when a city becomes really, really good at ticketing every vehicle that overstays its parking time by more than five minutes, motorists become really, really good at not overstaying their time. As a result ticket revenues were falling even as other objectives for an improved value stream—better availability of parking spaces and a much better system for resolving disputes about broken meters and traffic officer behavior—were being achieved. This was another example of how every countermeasure designed to improve a value stream creates unintended consequences, which must in turn be countermeasured. It is a normal part of any improvement process.

My Melbourne experience, along with a number of recent calls I've gotten from state and local governments asking about lean thinking and the fact that governments everywhere are facing growing financial pressures at the same time voters expect better performance, have led me to think again about ways that lean principles and methods might be applied to the activities of governments.

Let's start with what governments do. What value do they try to create? I think there are really three streams of work: enacting policies (laws) to regulate behaviors or deliver services; designing the enforcement and delivery mechanisms for these policies; and, operating these mechanisms on a continuing basis.

A simple example: A government (legislative plus executive) enacts environmental rules to address a perceived problem, a state agency writes detailed regulations and designs a mechanism for enforcement (e.g., granting permits), and the agency processes permits and proceeds against individuals and organizations who fail to comply with the rules. This is a vast activity, a substantial part of Gross National Product in every country, and one that seems to grow everywhere. (The Code of Federal Regulations in the United States, which records the detailed provisions of each federal law, now has more than 170,000 pages of text. State and local statutes and regulations contribute many times more.)

The first of these activities—enacting laws—is clearly the most problematic. What a wonderful thing it would be if every public discussion of an issue was in the form of an A3! (If Newt Gingrich could run for president in 2012 on the platform of "Six Sigma for Every Government Activity," perhaps someone in the Lean Community—I'll pass for lack of attitude or aptitude—should be running for president in 2016 on the platform of "A3 for All?") The objective would be to describe what every public issue is about in one sentence, assess whether the problem needs to be addressed (or an opportunity needs to be seized), determine the root cause of the issue, detail the most promising countermeasures to test through PDCA, and identify what evidence will be accepted as to the success of the countermeasures.

Most Americans are familiar with the phrase that "the states are the laboratory of democracy" because of their freedom to try different countermeasures for the same problem. And this even more true of local governments. So there are three levels of government available for doing science. The problem is the will to do so.

The way things actually work is that all political debates start with solutions and work backwards to problems. And we can be sure that every solution is being promoted by someone with an emotional stake in the outcome ("save the planet" by regulating greenhouse gases) or with money to gain (for example, by advocating for mandating a new "green" activity in which they have a large financial stake). And sometimes these can be combined, for example mandating the addition of a minimum amount of ethanol in gasoline before it can be sold to the public, which may save the planet and certainly makes money for corn growers.

To be clear: We in the Lean Community have no standing on whether a government should regulate any activity or provide any service. This is a decision for citizens and their lawmakers. We can only make the humble suggestion that better decisions can be reached if the debate starts with a clear statement of the actual problem, followed by a structured process to identify and test countermeasures. For example, we have no voice in whether governments should license drivers. (Some libertarians probably think they shouldn't; most people think they should.) But if governments are going to license drivers, we can suggest the important questions to ask: What is the best way to design and operate the drivers licensing process? How can we avoid wasting the time of the drivers and government employees while insuring that those who don't have the skills or wisdom to be on the road are not licensed?

Yet when I look at governments at every level today I observe that most issues are not clearly stated, regulatory and service provision processes are not designed using lean principles, and regulations and services are not administered or provided using lean methods. So what can be done?

A3 for the policy-making process may take a while (although I'm always an optimist about the long run, as we demonstrate the power of this method in nongovernmental activities). So I wouldn't wait around expecting progress in that area soon. But the prospect for improving the design of regulations and services is much brighter, as is the prospect for improving the actual conduct of regulation and the delivery of services. But, please, no "lean government" programs to be rolled by elected officials early in their terms, supported by a phalanx of consultants or internal staff teams committed to winning the "war on waste" in short order.

Instead the way ahead is to begin—any place will do—with experiments involving line managers and employee teams (and, yes, the people being regulated or served by the value streams as well). In each experiment make someone responsible for leading the development of an A3 that determines the current performance of a given value stream (for arresting vagrants or issuing building permits or whatever). Post the results – the work, after all, is the public's business and is the business of the employees as well. Determine the gap in performance on whatever dimension is relevant: cost to the taxpayer, cost in wasted time to the person receiving the service, headaches for the government employees (or contractors) performing the work. Identify the most promising countermeasures. Run experiments with the countermeasures. Measure the results. Reflect on what to do next and, in particular, how to sustain positive results.

If any government at any level is willing to try this simple method for improving its value-creating processes, I will be delighted to take a gemba walk and help publicize the results. I'm sure they will be highly positive.

Lean Management for Healthcare

Healthcare started eons ago as a Pop business (that's a Mom and Pop business without Mom, except—later—for the nurse). And it was a "business." (See the discussion about the Hippocratic Oath in John Toussaint and Roger Gerard's *On the Mend*, pp. 102–103.) Doctors in history may have been focused on doing no harm but they were absolutely focused on running successful businesses.

Historically, doctors practiced in small workshops with only a few employees and the senior manager (the doctor) working as both the touch labor at the bottom and the supreme leader at the top, with vast authority due to the laying on of hands. The problem for decades has been that the size of these businesses has grown steadily but the mentality of the management, until recently, has not scaled. Healthcare organizations grew by adding doctors to each "-ology" (hematology, dermatology, gerontology, etc.) and adding -ologies to each hospital and to each primary and specialty care practice until today's vast medical enterprise emerged. Meanwhile the doctors were still the authority figures heading each -ology (and maximizing its performance within the total enterprise) and usually the combined enterprise as well. The interior of these enterprises looked something like the Middle Ages, with many silo castles (the individual practices and -ologies optimizing and defending their points in the overall process), lots of moats with drawbridges for patients to pass over as they trod from diagnosis through treatment, and very little effective management of the enterprise as a whole.

As the management challenges of increasing scale intensified (accompanied by the growing number of elderly patients with complex "co-morbidities" requiring more complex journeys through more complex healthcare systems), one response was to add business-school trained "modern" managers with lots of metrics at all levels. Another was to strengthen staff quality groups, often to form a "lean" team. In my view these seemingly obvious countermeasures often made things worse because they did not address the underlying problems.

Working our way out of this mess has been difficult and has taken far longer than it should but I think we are beginning to make real progress. To cite one notable example, over the past few years, Kim Barnas, president of the ThedaCare Hospitals in Appleton, WI, and her many colleagues have been working hard to create a comprehensive management system suited for today's healthcare enterprises. I've had the benefit of observing their work (which will soon be summarized in their book, "Beyond Heroes: A Lean Management System for Healthcare.") Let me share a bit of what they have done.

First, they did something often unpopular in the healthcare world. Even though they are a nonprofit they decided that they are a "business" and, as such, they needed to be mindful of costs and revenues at every level of the organization. And they needed to do this even as they addressed the usual "True North" goals of any healthcare organization: high-quality outcomes and good experience for patients along with a satisfying work experience for doctors, nurses, techs, managers and all support staff.

Proceeding without taking this step at the front felt more and more like a denial of reality given that all healthcare providers are now experiencing an environment in which insurance companies and governments are steadily pushing done compensation rates. So they call their new management system the Business Performance System, putting "business" first.

The elements of the system are straightforward:

- An annual True North exercise (hoshin) to prioritize their key challenges as an organization and to cascade these few priorities down to every level for action. (This is separate from the familiar annual budget cycle, which is still needed, but in the background rather than the foreground.)

- An A3-based PDSA (Plan-Do-Study-Act) process for attacking problems at every level and seizing opportunities (e.g., achieving vastly lower drug errors than competitors).

- Standard work, documented and continually revised and improved by the line managers and work teams, for all the value-creating and incidental work in the enterprise.

- Standard work for every manager at every level up to and including the president of the hospitals.

  A clear focus on:

- Managing by process, using A3 and PDSA, rather than the traditional method of managing by exception (the firefighting of things gone wrong that occupied most of the time of managers) and managing by metrics set up by senior managers (which occupied the rest of managers' time).

- Managing by using the Five Whys to identify the root cause of problems rather than the One Who to assign blame.

- Managing patient pathways end-to-end within product families of diagnosis and treatment rather optimizing individual points along these journeys. (See the recent LEI publication "Perfecting Patient Journeys" for a method that is consistent with ThedaCare's.)

- Finally, a clear focus on problem solving and improvement by line managers, with technical assistance by a "lean" team, rather than the reverse—which is still the norm in most healthcare organizations.

I believe that ThedaCare's experiments, which everyone there recognizes are far from perfect and in need of continuous improvement, may be a watershed in the great transformation needed in every healthcare organization. They are changing from management as point optimization, with workarounds for problems and pro-forma compliance with metrics, to process optimization of whole value streams by managers coaching their direct reports at each lower level to look a the big picture, clearly identify the current state, assess the performance gap (including the business gap), and conduct continuing experiments to reduce and then eliminate the gap.

I've had the pleasure on my many gemba walks in healthcare of meeting many brilliant doctors who were also wonderful human beings. But I long ago discovered that doctors, if left to their professional instincts and traditional process-free medical educations, will always "practice malprocess" unless they are given a new way of thinking about management and organization. The faster we can do this the better it will be for all of us—doctors, other healthcare professionals, patients, and those of us (ultimately all of us) who will pay for the costs of healthcare.

Move Your Operations Back from China? Consider Leanshoring Instead

What a difference a decade makes. When I prepared the essay "Move Your Operations to China? Do Some Lean Math First" in 2003 (see page 174), there seemed to be something approaching a panic in purchasing organizations of major companies to relocate production from the United States, Europe, and Japan to China. And, as often happens in these situations, the behavior of large, market-leader companies was being mimicked by smaller organizations, including those supplying the large organizations, without much independent analysis.

At that point I had been going to China to look at businesses for 20 years and this whole mindset seemed strange to me. Wasn't it obvious that there were many hidden and indirect costs in obtaining goods from unknown firms or start-up operations located far away? (It took me several pages to list these in my essay.) Above all I disliked the way purchasing could order existing suppliers to move or find new suppliers or offshore work currently being done in-house near customers to new, low-wage facilities far way and do this without anyone else in these big organizations—sales, engineering, operations—having to do anything to improve their own performance. Yet this poor performance had often pushed manufacturing companies to the brink in the first place! Cutting and running therefore seemed like a great way for big companies and their smaller followers to continue to lose competitiveness.

Today the pendulum is starting to swing back. The Chinese economy is slowing, exchange rates are shifting, energy costs are falling in the United States, Chinese wages are rising while wages in North America and Europe are stagnant, and a lot has been learned the actual total cost of offshored items imported for sale in North America, Europe, and Japan. This last factor is another way of saying that much of the offshore "savings" proved to be pretty much imaginary, even without adjusting for the more recent trends, once senior managers looked beyond the accounts of the purchasing organization. That's the place where all of the savings showed up, but none of the extra costs.

There is now a vigorous "reshoring" movement as a consequence of these shifts in fact and perception, although it is far from clear that much has actually been reshored yet. One highly visible example is General Electric's decision to move its home appliance business back to Louisville, KY, from China and Mexico. However, despite GE's high visibility and the long history of other firms following its lead—for example, on modern management, Six Sigma, and being first or second in every industry where a firm chooses to compete—GE alone can't create a trend.

May I suggest that if you are thinking about reshoring (or are still thinking about offshoring), you "leanshore" instead? This approach asks a simple question: What is the leanest way to provide product X for customers in country Y over the period of time (probably a long one) your organization plans to be in this business? By lean I mean the location and production methods requiring the least effort, time, capital investment, and waste of all sorts. In my experience "lean" and "low cost" are not perfect synonyms at every point in time, but over extended periods they are very nearly identical. Creating a truly lean, rapid flow of value from producer to consumer in proximity to the consumer builds valuable capabilities for the future that endure far longer than short-term cost advantages.

Let me cite the example involving GE at Appliance Park in Louisville. (We at LEI know something about this because we have been involved in several experiments connected with this effort.) GE totally outsourced and offshored this business in the 1970s to Mexico and in the 1990s to China. It "hollowed out" the business to the point that appliances inside GE involved only marketing, sales, and advanced engineering activities.

Because appliances are largely air—bulky items without much content inside such as refrigerators, ovens, stoves—transport was always an issue for serving North American customers from the other side of the world. But for a while it appeared that the labor cost savings offset other costs of many types associated with long distance transport of white goods.

Gradually this perception changed. In addition, GE grew concerned that without engineering, production, and supplier management skills coupled tightly to production and logistics, it was increasingly disconnected from important attributes of its business that were critical to long-term success. So a decision was made in 2011 to in-house and re-shore the entire business back to Appliance Park. And in doing this GE has had a chance to totally rethink its business using lean principles.

When GE made its decision many observers questioned the wisdom of this strategy (and the move is strategic). They pointed out that all of the engineering skills and production knowledge once present at Appliance Park was gone. No one knew how to do things in the old way. But this was the very best part! GE could begin anew in what amounted to a startup and apply lean knowledge about the best way to organize and manage production. And it could combine lean production with new approaches to engineering, marketing, sales, and supplier management, all in close proximity on the same site.

Why do I call this "leanshoring" rather than "onshoring" or "reshoring?" Because the move is not primarily about short-term cost savings, although with luck there will be some. It is instead a long-term effort to create a lean enterprise that will provide the maximum value for its customers in a geographic region with the minimum waste and which can continue to create even more value with even less waste over time as its management and technical capabilities continue to improve.

Please understand that I stand by my original essay on doing lean math before moving production to the far side of the world. (My suggestions on how to do the math have been greatly elaborated by the Onshoring Initiative with its Total Cost of Ownership calculator that any company can use. You can go to www.reshorenow.org for details.) With the concept of leanshoring I am now simply adding a time dimension that is beyond the short-term, lowest-cost mentality I was trying to counter. When companies were seemingly moving their operations as far from their customers as possible, I said, "Do lean math first. You may be imaging savings that will never materialize." And now that at least some companies are thinking of moving some operations back closer to their customers, I say, "But do lean math first. You still need to understand long-term total costs across your organization before you do anything." It may be that the lowest long-term cost location is still far from the market of sale. And it is even likely that for some products the long-term, low-cost location is in a lower-wage country on the periphery of the region of sale (e.g., Mexico and Central America for the U.S. and Canadian markets).

I am simply adding the important point that lean organizations should do long-term math, not just math for the moment based on labor, energy, transport, and other factor costs that can change in an instant while truly lean production systems must be built to last over many years.

An important aside here: Toyota was severely criticized during the recent era of the strong yen for failing to move practically all of its operations not needed to serve Japanese customers rapidly out of Japan. But Toyota has taken nearly 70 years to build those operations to their present performance in terms of value and waste. And it has learned the hard way in recent years how difficult—and sometimes impossible—it is to create new production and engineering facilities around the world that can quickly achieve and then sustain the level of performance in Toyota City. Now the yen has weakened, Toyota is headed for record profits, and all of the recent wrong-minded advice is forgotten. But lean managers should not forget: Locate for the long term, not for short-term cost savings.

The great opportunity of the present moment for many firms is to start over with leanshored, greenfield facilities in the right long-term locations and do everything the right way. By contrast, my great fear is that some companies will bring production back to North America or Europe and conduct it in the same mass production, modern management way that got them in trouble in the first place. Think instead of leanshoring as a start-over and start-up opportunity (see "Starting Up, Growing Up, and Starting Over" on page 260), a chance to do everything the right way the second time around.

The Strange Trajectory of Operational Excellence

What was perhaps the world's first "operational excellence" team was formed at Toyota in Toyota City at the end of the 1960s. This was not the quality department. Toyota already had one. And it was not the industrial engineering or manufacturing engineering groups either. These already existed as well. This special operations improvement team was designed by Taiichi Ohno and Kikuo Suzumura to break all of the rules by looking horizontally across existing production processes to speed the flow of value to the customer while eliminating the wastes blocking flow. Its key instrument was the five-day kaizen designed to grasp the situation, define the problem, get to the root cause, consider the available countermeasures, test one, and record the results with a bit of thought about next steps, all within the space of one week.

The method was developed specifically to spread Toyota Production System practices very quickly to Toyota's group of suppliers in Toyota City, who were stuck in the world of mass production. The results were almost invariably spectacular. Not only was waste eliminated and flow accelerated, but a whole generation of managers had their brains recalibrated as to what rate of improvement was possible.

Without the Operations Management Consulting Division, as it came to be known, Toyota's rate of improvement across its extended enterprise would have been much slower and it would have had a much harder time dealing with the sharp recession following the 1973 oil shock, when most other Japanese firms were knocked backwards. Toyota however surged ahead. (This was the event that confirmed in the minds of most observers that there was something superior about Toyota's operational methods.)

My own learning about lean thinking was greatly aided by watching graduates of the initial OMCD offensive in Toyota City as they set out as independent consultants across the world at the beginning of the 1990s. I too experienced the miracle of the five-day kaizen as a participant. It seemed almost to good to be true. Very nearly instant improvement with dramatically better performance!

Unfortunately, in the long light of history it is apparent that the miracle of five-day kaizen was mostly was too good to be true. The common pattern outside of Toyota, where OMCD made repeated visits to every supplier for years to sustain improvements, was a leap in performance in the area being improved, followed by a fairly rapid regression to the original level of performance once the improvement team moved on. And the reasons soon became clear: Not enough knowledge was transferred to line management, the employees on the front lines were not truly engaged, and the new process did not fit with the existing metrics for judging management success.

As time has moved on and lean concepts found wide acceptance along with those flowing from the quality movement and merging with lean (Six Sigma in particular) the labels changed. But most large organizations have now converged on the practice of creating a unified process improvement group. They label this the lean team or continuous improvement group or Six Sigma or Lean Six Sigma or Lean Sigma, and, increasingly, simply "operational excellence," with the understanding that its activities extend to all operational and transactional activities in the organization.

During my gemba walks I have recently observed the work of a number of these teams and even attended several of their annual reviews with senior management. It has been quite puzzling.

From a technical standpoint I see highly proficient people with a deep understanding of lean concepts such as A3, PDCA, hoshin planning, and standardized work for front-line value creators and managers. But the projects the teams are working on seem to have little relation to the most important problems facing their organizations. And even when the projects are focused on critical issues, sustainable results are hard to find. Why is this happening?

I think there are three basic reasons:

Operational excellence teams are supposed to solve problems rather than improve managers. That means analyzing the problem, designing an intervention, conducting the experiments, and tallying the results (often in the form of cost savings for the company), often with little interaction with line managers who seem to be happy to outsource problems. By contrast, coaching line managers to solve problems by teaching them A3 analysis (a staff Sanderson in dialogue with a line Porter for those familiar with John Shook's *Managing to Learn*) is not part of the Op Ex team's work. So when the Op Ex team moves on to the next problem the old problem tends to remerge pretty quickly. Neither management methods nor sufficient technical knowledge has been transferred.

Operational excellence teams try to avoid trouble with their higher-level bosses. They do this by sticking to problems that don't cross organizational boundaries. Yet most important problems do cross organizational boundaries and are important problems precisely because the managers and workers on both sides of the boundary can't see the full dimensions of the problem. The managers therefore engage in point optimization, often at the expense of those on the other side. The Op Ex team is in the best position to see the whole problem but in a poor position organizationally to tackle it.

Finally, *Op Ex teams are not consulted while a new value stream is being designed.* The manufacturing and industrial engineers are involved along with IT. But who is looking at the process from end-to-end to make sure that lean performance will occur from Job 1? Usually no one. In the absence of this poka-yoke, Op Ex teams are relegated to fixing problems after the fact, once operational issues surface, through kaizen as rework.

So what can be done?

Operational excellence teams can be given a management development mandate by an organization's senior leadership, to coach line managers in how to do the work of improvement that is normally reserved for the Op Ex team. (And, unlike classroom management development programs organized by the HR Department, this is learning by doing in which the Op Ex coach asks a line manager to select an issue and then coaches the line-manager through the problem identification and countermeasure process, not once but a number of times.) This is not the sort of short-term-with-instant results work that improvement teams are normally asked to perform. It requires an entirely different scoreboard for judging results. But it can be a critical element in introducing and sustaining lean management practices in every organization.

Equally important, operational excellence teams in an organization can be given the responsibility for thinking horizontally about the performance of each value stream as it flows across complex, vertical organizations. In most organizations today I still find that this thinking doesn't happen with any rigor and is not sustained over time as conditions change. Shouldn't there a person in Op Ex taking responsibility for the performance of every major value stream (and, in particular, every cross-functional value stream) by continually updating the current state, identifying the problems, prioritizing countermeasures, and recording improvement results as the line managers touching the stream at many points conduct the actual improvement activities? No change in the organization is needed for this to work except that the Op Ex group should report to the COO, who has (or should have) the job of thinking about operational performance across the enterprise. Then when the Op Ex person taking responsibility for the performance of a value stream encounters problems with one or more of the heads of the functions and departments the problem can be escalated as necessary to the COO for resolution.

Finally, the Op Ex person who is going to be responsible for the performance of a new value stream should be one of the key team members designing the value stream so that it starts life as a lean stream, ready for improvement of course, but from a very high level at Job 1.

Having an Op Ex team is a great idea and the widespread adoption of this concept is a big step forward. The problem is that most teams are being asked to do the wrong things in the wrong way. Fortunately, there are simple countermeasures for addressing these problems if senior managers in large organizations will simply try and perfect them through PDCA. Perhaps the next step for your Op Ex team is to develop an A3 on the topic: Is the performance of our Op Ex team adequate for addressing our organization's problems?

Bringing Respect for People to the World's Sweatshops

I've been gemba walking in what I call sweatshops for a long time, beginning in China in the early 1980s. By a sweatshop I don't just mean a factory that employs (if that is the word) underage workers, requires long hours with wages arbitrarily adjusted by management through bonus systems, has no rules for discipline other than more management arbitrariness, and lacks the most rudimentary safety precautions such as adequate fire doors that are never locked. I also mean factories that squander their workers' labor by making no effort to improve productivity (except urging workers to work harder to get a bonus), that pay no attention to ergonomics, and that—above all—show no respect to the people who are actually creating the value by asking them to help improve the work.

The world mostly focuses on the former attributes of sweatshops because they are visible and periodically lead to horrific incidents like the recent factory fires in Bangladesh. But I think the latter attributes are equally bad because they often lead to the former. Poor work design with low productivity, fatiguing working conditions that guarantee mistakes and rework, and a lack of involvement of the workforce in improving the work almost guarantee that managers will squeeze wages and raise bonus targets to make money in the face of low productivity.

In recent years protests from Western advocacy groups have shone a light on the bad practices of sweatshop contractors used by multinational producers of consumer goods, garments in particular. And surely some good will come of this. But I fear that the box-checking, "compliance" focus of these efforts will simply drive bad practices further underground as contractors see a business need to employ bad practices to make money in low-productivity businesses in highly competitive markets.

I was therefore delighted some years ago when Nike approached some of our LEI faculty members and asked how lean principles could be applied to their contractors. Their idea was simple: Help contractors deploy lean practices to improve the way work is done in their 700 contractor factories around the world that employ a million workers. This would substantially improve productivity and lower costs so that Nike could demand that its contractors treat workers fairly and provide safe buildings. And Nike could do this while maintaining its competitive position against OEMs that don't do any of the right things with their contractors. You might think of this as "benevolent selfishness"—Nike's bottom-line objective was and is to protect its bottom line and its image through this concept, which it calls "sustainability"—but I will take it if it works to make work better for millions of people.

Recently I have been working with one of Nike's contractors in Central America as a way to support an NGO in a very poor country. I'm able to report that the first thing Nike did in offering this contractor a Nike contract was to require that the contractor use no subcontractors (which increased wage costs) and do all of the work in one building with good sight lines. This eliminates one of the most common causes of worker abuse in which contractors operate nice facilities—that are frequently audited by the OEM—which simply box and ship the work of subcontractors running the actual sweatshops somewhere nearby. Transparency is one small but critical step.

This Nike contractor has taken the lead in organizing an annual lean conference in this country, with the proceeds going to the NGO to help keep kids in school and to make the schools worthy of keeping their students. I have been donating my time to make the conference possible and also provide a bit of free advice to the contractor and the NGO.

This work has given me a chance to see on the gemba what Nike and its contractors are doing to employ lean principles. I am impressed even though the journey will be very long. But my objective here is not to praise Nike. It is to ask a simple question: Doesn't every OEM have an obligation to respect the work of its contractor workers by demanding that their labor be used productively through application of lean principles? (Achieving this goal can be another opportunity for OEM Op Ex teams to make their work more relevant by following in the footsteps of the original Toyota Op Ex team in the 1960s, as mentioned in the previous essay, "The Strange Trajectory of Operational Excellence.") And doesn't every worker in contractor enterprises have a right to have their work designed so they can do it safely with high productivity? Note that if done correctly these measures cost the OEMs practically nothing. They get paid back with competitive product pricing from more productive, safe factories that show respect for their workers. And the OEMs can advertise this fact to their customers. (Why Nike doesn't advertise its virtuous work is a bit of a mystery—its Nike Operating System activities are practically a secret—but that's Nike's business, not mine.)

So I'm hopeful that a few innovators like Nike, as pushed along by advocacy groups, can gradually reduce the number of sweatshops in the world. But what can we in the Lean Community do to help more directly and speed up the demise of the sweatshop? How about creating a "Lean Corps" comprised of those of us who have been on the journey a long time, who have made most of the money we need to retire or at least to cut back on our work hours, and who don't want to stop doing the lean work that always makes us feel better? (Note that Taiichi Ohno was forced to retire from Toyota when he was 65 but immediately began advising any company who would listen on implementing the Toyota Production System and continued doing this for years, and that Shigeo Shingo was doing kaizen in a factory in his 80s when he felt ill, was taken to the hospital, and died. My guess is that kaizen helps keep oldsters alive and there is certainly a long tradition of "geriatric kaizen" in the lean movement that we can take inspiration from.)

How could you do this? One good way is to volunteer your services to one of the 17 affiliate organizations in the Lean Global Network to work with small companies in poor places that can't afford expensive advice. Another is to find a worthy NGO operating in some poor country and offer to help run a lean conference for local firms if they will contribute the proceeds to the NGO. This is what I have been doing and it has put a spring in my step. And I have recently asked a friend with deep lean experience to coach a group of small, local companies (including the Nike contractor) on their lean transformation for a reduced and shared fee. If you would like to learn more or just to discuss your situation please write to me at jwomack@lean.org.

I feel I have been given a special opportunity to live at a time when lean thinking makes so many good things possible. I hope you feel that way too and that you will give serious thought about ways to pay back this gift by sharing your knowledge with the sweatshops of the world. From conversations with many managers in these enterprises I'm convinced that most want to do better. They just don't know how and can't afford to ask some expensive consultant. That's where the Lean Corps might play a critical role.

Whatever Happened to Toyota and What Happens Next to Lean?

When we launched the First Edition of *Gemba Walks* in 2011, Toyota was in the midst of a remarkable series of crises: The global market had collapsed and mix in product demand had shifted from larger, higher-margin products as the world plowed through the Great Recession. The massive product recalls followed and then the earthquake and tsunami in Japan that dramatically reduced Toyota's production capacity. On top of these setbacks, the strong yen dramatically increased Toyota's costs in export markets and then the geopolitical challenge in China for all Japanese consumer-products firms slashed Toyota sales in the world's largest market.

Today the crises have passed and Toyota has survived with a record amount of cash on hand and approaching record profitability. This is a major achievement. How many large companies have ever encountered so many major problems in such quick succession? And how many would survive if they did? Amazingly, Toyota has now regained the number one position in global motor vehicle sales and all appears to be right with the world.

However be aware that Toyota may soon find a more comfortable spot as number two or three in sales behind GM and Volkswagen. This is consistent with the modesty Toyota had always shown before adopting the goal of being number one at the end of the 1990s and is likely to be more profitable as well. As in auto racing, it is easier and less risky in the auto industry to draft the leaders than to lead (except during the last lap —but Toyota is on an endless journey!) And it is likely to be more profitable as well. The company in second place that doesn't care about first place doesn't need to throw incentives on its products at the end of reporting periods in order to win the sales championship and can level its production instead, resulting in higher revenue and lower production cost per vehicle.

This said, it wouldn't hurt if Toyota offered some truly innovative products. (For example, is there really any there there for its long-running fuel cell project?) It has been 16 years since the launch of the Prius and hybrid technology is now offered by a majority of its competitors. What's more, its core products are widely perceived to be competent but bland when many customers want excitement. But this is a quibble. The crisis is over. Toyota has gotten back to basics and is doing fine (as I predicted in the essay, "A Large Enough Wave Sinks All Boats" on page 160).

The important point of these events for the Lean Community is that when our lean poster child went flying off the road into the high grass in 2009—in a truly spectacular multiyear spin-out—it made no difference for the lean movement.

I was holding my breath at first, fearing the worst. But I soon discovered that most folks now know enough about lean thinking to realize that there is an important difference between lean as a set of ideas and practices (that were to a significant extent pioneered by Toyota) and the degree to which Toyota successfully applies these ideas and practices on any given day. In short, the world doesn't think that Toyota's tribulations reflect badly on the ideas themselves. (Something similar happened with Henry Ford in the 1930s when the company lost its way and was passed by General Motors. The world still acknowledged Ford's achievements and copied his best practices, while trying to avoid his mistakes.)

What does all of this mean? That we in the lean movement are now free to fashion our own fate, regardless of what happens to Toyota in the future! So where are we going, now that we are on our own? Let me offer five suggestions for your consideration:

Let's complete the transition to lean management. I focused on this need in the essay "Hopeful Hansei" (on page 238), and I think we are making steady progress but we are still just at the beginning.

Let's complete the lean enterprise across the functions. "Lean Production" was always meant as a complete system of enterprise: Product and process development, fulfillment from order to delivery (including what is often called "production" but adding information management and logistics), supplier management, and customer support. (See "Twenty-five Years of 'Lean'" on page 250, for further thoughts on this point.)

But in many ways we have gotten stuck in production. At the point when lean concepts began to spread rapidly in factories they might have been applied in the other functional areas as well. But the movement spread instead along the path of least resistance. (See "The Strange Trajectory of Operational Excellence" on page 289.) With help of operational excellence teams first created for factory conversions, lean ideas were deployed in every operational and transactional process within manufacturing and then in operational activities in every type of industry from insurance to retail to healthcare.

Today this work continues across the world and it will continue for a long time. But it would be easier if the other elements in the lean enterprise were more developed and our progress there has been much less impressive. As far back as the publication of *The Machine That Changed the World* in 1990 we knew about the potential for leaning all the elements of an enterprise, even if we did not know the precise methods to use. And in the years since our knowledge about lean methods for every aspect of the enterprise has steadily deepened. Yet most product development organizations today are little changed from the 1980s. Supplier management is still about squeezing margins rather than eliminating waste. And the customer is still pretty much alone in trying to turn brilliant products, usually a combination of goods and services, into actual solutions to life's problems. Our problem today is not a lack of knowing what to do but a lack of focus on doing it. We need to get to work as a community and to share our experiences.

Let's complete the lean enterprise from end to end. Dan Jones and I presented a simple method for seeing the whole value stream from end to end for a product family in *Lean Thinking* in 1996. And we refined the method in *Seeing the Whole Value Stream* in 2002 (Second Edition 2011). Yet this past week I walked a value stream from raw material to customer in a major company where it would easily be possible to eliminate three-quarters of the time, space, and human effort involved. And the firms and its supplier sharing this stream were completely amazed. They had still not learned to see. This is an area where operational excellence teams can play a particularly important and productive role if they will expand their scope and redefine their mission.

Let's complete the diffusion of lean thinking to every sector. On some days I think I've seen it all—manufacturing, retail, healthcare, financial services, customer services, military operations. And then I realize that I am only now getting acquainted with lean in government and that lean for education still lies ahead, two sectors that account for a substantial fraction of the economy. Until we have proof-of-concept examples of lean thinking in every area of life we haven't done our job.

Let's apply lean to social problems. There is today a nice combination of social problems needing lean thinking and lean thinkers at an age when they have the time and resources to do something for society. (At LEI, for example, we have been applying lean concepts to soup kitchens and meals on wheels for the elderly as a pro bono contribution to the community.) All we need is a way to connect the resources with the need and to share experience.

There. That should be enough to keep us busy! The lean movement has successfully started up and is now starting to grow up in activities of all sorts in all sorts of industries. But the rework of starting over in many areas of the economy where the practices of the age of mass production and modern management still hold sway is massive. This means that the journey has just begun and we will all need each other for a long time to share experience and give each other courage. So let's keep gemba walking together and sharing what we learn.

INDEX

Lean Enterprise Institute

Lean Enterprise Institute Inc. was founded in 1997 by Jim Womack as a nonprofit research, education, publishing, and conference company with a mission to advance lean thinking around the world. LEI teaches courses, holds management seminars, writes and publishes books and workbooks, and organizes public and private conferences. LEI uses surplus revenues from these activities to conduct research projects and support other lean initiatives such as the Lean Education Academic Network, the Lean Global Network, and the Healthcare Value Network. For more information visit *www.lean.org*